PLAY IT RIGHT

PLAY IT RIGHT

THE REMARKABLE STORY OF A GAMBLER WHO BEAT THE ODDS ON WALL STREET

KAMAL GUPTA

Copyright © Kamal Gupta, 2022

Published by ECW Press
665 Gerrard Street East
Toronto, Ontario, Canada M4M 1Y2
416-694-3348 / info@ecwpress.com

All rights reserved. No part of this publication may be reproduced, stored in a retrieval system, or transmitted in any form by any process — electronic, mechanical, photocopying, recording, or otherwise — without the prior written permission of the copyright owners and ECW Press. The scanning, uploading, and distribution of this book via the internet or via any other means without the permission of the publisher is illegal and punishable by law. Please purchase only authorized electronic editions, and do not participate in or encourage electronic piracy of copyrighted materials. Your support of the author's rights is appreciated.

Editor for the Press: Jennifer Smith
Copy Editor: Jen Knoch
Cover design: Dorian Danielsen

LIBRARY AND ARCHIVES CANADA CATALOGUING IN PUBLICATION

Title: Play it right : the remarkable story of a gambler who beat the odds on Wall Street / Kamal Gupta.

Names: Gupta, Kamal (Investor), author.

Identifiers: Canadiana (print) 20210388021 | Canadiana (ebook) 20210388072

ISBN 978-1-77041-660-4 (hardcover)
ISBN 978-1-77305-964-8 (ePub)
ISBN 978-1-77305-965-5 (PDF)
ISBN 978-1-77305-966-2 (Kindle)

Subjects: LCSH: Gupta, Kamal (Investor) | LCSH: Capitalists and financiers—United States—Biography. | LCSH: Wall Street (New York, N.Y.) | LCGFT: Autobiographies.

Classification: LCC HG172.G87 A3 2022 | DDC 332.6092—dc23

This book is also available as a Global Certified Accessible™ (GCA) ebook. ECW Press's ebooks are screen reader friendly and are built to meet the needs of those who are unable to read standard print due to blindness, low vision, dyslexia, or a physical disability.

Purchase the print edition and receive the eBook free. For details, go to ecwpress.com/eBook.

PRINTED AND BOUND IN CANADA   PRINTING: FRIESENS   5 4 3 2 1

MIX
Paper from
responsible sources
FSC
www.fsc.org   FSC® C016245

This book is a memoir and consists of my recollections of an important time in my life. Some names and characteristics of individuals portrayed have been changed, events have been compressed, and dialogue has been recreated.

For Kathleen, Jay, and Deven

Any game worth playing is worth playing right.

CONTENTS

CHAPTER 1

Eighteen Seconds

"Eighteen seconds on the clock!" someone shouted. "Go!"

I didn't know it then, but the entire course of my future hinged on those eighteen seconds.

A crowd of traders hovered around me. One removed a single card from a well-shuffled poker deck, and while keeping it hidden, handed me the remaining fifty-one cards. I had eighteen seconds to comb through the deck and identify the missing card. As Bud Fox had said in the movie *Wall Street*, life indeed came down to a few moments.

This missing card trial-by-fire was the culmination of a day's worth of grilling about my gambling prowess during a lengthy job interview at Lehman Brothers. I had presented myself as a professional blackjack player and the investment bank's bond traders were intent on putting that claim to the test.

All day long, the masters of finance had cross-examined me about every aspect of the game that they could think of.

Why are six decks worse for the player than two? Why do you split two eights against a dealer ten? How did you size your bets to account for the fluctuating probabilities? If the odds were in your favor, would you bet your entire bankroll on one hand? How many times were you kicked out of a casino? What was your annualized return on investment?

1

The Lehman traders fancied themselves great gamblers and they tried over and over to trip me up. Despite their best attempts to befuddle me, I sailed through the interviews. I knew more about blackjack than all my interrogators combined, and I made sure to let them know that. Interestingly, my swagger didn't turn anyone off. They almost seemed to approve of my brash attitude.

All that remained was this grand finale, a live demonstration of my card-counting abilities.

Under normal circumstances, it would have been simple for me to figure out the missing card in eighteen seconds. I had been successfully counting cards in Reno and Las Vegas for the past two years. Being under the spotlight on a Wall Street trading floor, however, was a very different kind of pressure.

In a casino, my senses were constantly under assault. I had to keep track of the count amidst the jangle of slot machines, the screams of the gamblers who had finally won one, as well as the lounge singer belting out the oldies. At the same time, cocktail waitresses were tapping me on the shoulder every few minutes for refills. Then there were the pit bosses. They watched every player like a hawk as it was their responsibility to guard the casino's bankroll against cheats and card counters. It had taken months of practice for me to be able to count cards amongst all the distractions in a casino. In contrast, this was my first time doing it on a Wall Street trading floor.

A crowd had gathered to watch me perform this parlor trick. This made me especially uncomfortable. Blackjack had been a solitary pursuit for me, not a spectator sport. I had toiled away in obscurity, trying to separate the casinos from some of their cash, and wasn't looking forward to the public shaming that would follow if I got this wrong.

For the Lehman bosses, that was precisely the point. They wanted me to count a deck in their presence to make sure that I wasn't all talk. The audience had been assembled to test my ability to perform under pressure, a skill they considered vital for a trader.

Even more than the trading floor atmosphere and the crowd's scrutiny, I was concerned that I had just one shot at this exercise. No card counter is perfect and errors are inevitable during long hours of play. In a casino, one mistake wasn't fatal and every shuffle gave me a fresh start. Not so at Lehman.

Here, a momentary lapse in concentration or a slight miscalculation would not only make me a laughingstock but also destroy my job prospects.

Despite my misgivings, I was keenly aware that any sign of apprehension on my part would be perceived as a show of weakness. Even though I had spent only a short time on the trading floor, it was apparent that testosterone ruled the day. I had no choice but to bite the bullet and submit to this public test. If I failed and fell flat on my face, then so be it.

I picked up the deck and gave a nod to the timekeeper to start the clock.

He did, and I flew through the cards in a controlled frenzy. Like I had done countless times before, I scanned them in groups of two or three. It would have been impossible to count fifty-one cards individually in such a short time. I had only a fraction of a second to eyeball each bunch and determine its count.

After what seemed like ages, I reached the end of the deck and shouted, "Done!"

The timekeeper stopped the clock with two seconds to go.

The trader with the mystery card crossed his arms and glared at me, "Okay, hotshot, what's the card?"

"It's a nine," I replied calmly, even though my heart was racing.

With great flourish, he flipped the card over for all to see.

It was the nine of clubs!

I breathed a quiet sigh of relief while maintaining a nonchalant attitude. *Of course it's a nine, what else could it be?* The crowd murmured its approval and dispersed. I slumped into a chair.

A tall, bespectacled man, wearing a gray suit and a strangely benevolent smile, put the cards back in their case and motioned me to follow him. This was Michael Gelband, and he guided me to a small office off the trading floor, closed the door, and handed me a thin envelope.

"Open it," he said.

Inside was a one-page letter addressed to me. It began, *We are pleased to offer you a position as a junior trader at Lehman Brothers . . .* and ended with his signature.

I sat there in disbelief, clutching the letter, reading that line over and over again. Against the advice of my family and friends, I had given up on a career in computers and devoted two years of my life to blackjack. It had been a struggle, but I had beaten the casinos and grown my bankroll to thirty-two times its original size. And now, I had thrown a Hail Mary to the biggest casino of them all, Wall Street, and scored a job offer on the spot.

I had made the journey from San Francisco to New York for this interview on a whim, figuring that I was wasting my frequent-flyer ticket on a foolish pursuit. Lehman had insisted that I pay for my own flights because "you don't seem serious about this business," an obvious fact that was hard for me to argue against. After an initial reluctance, I had decided to take a chance and used my airline miles for the trip. The gamble had paid off more handsomely than I could ever have imagined.

Now that I had an actual job offer, I wasn't quite sure what to do with it. Michael expected a yes right there and then. However, sitting in that office, I wasn't prepared to uproot myself from a city that I adored and relocate to one that terrified me.

I cleared my throat and said, "I need to think about it. I'll let you know in two weeks."

Michael looked flummoxed, the smile evaporating. "Two weeks? Are you out of your mind? Do you have any idea what we're offering you? Look around, half the people on this trading floor get paid more than most CEOs. Do you know how hard it is to get your foot in this door? There is a long line of Ivy League graduates standing outside that would kill for this opportunity."

I didn't know and I almost didn't believe any of it. Never in my wildest dreams did I expect to land a Wall Street job so quickly. An initial rush of euphoria was quickly followed by a growing sense of dread. What had I gotten myself into?

I refused to budge and insisted that I needed time to make such a big decision. In the end, Michael relented and gave me the two weeks that I had asked for. The next day, I flew back to San Francisco to ponder the biggest gamble of my life.

Without knowing the first thing about finance, was I willing to take a chance on Wall Street?

CHAPTER 2

A Gambler at Heart

S hortly after arriving in America, I had promised myself three things:

I will never work on Wall Street.
I will never live in New York City.
I will never marry a non-Indian.

From afar, Wall Street of the eighties appeared to be a den of thieves, populated by the likes of Michael Milken, Ivan Boesky, and Gordon Gekko. Even if they weren't all crooks, it was inconceivable that someday I would run with the "greed is good" crowd. To me, greed was the root of evil.

Likewise, I considered New York City in the eighties to be a dark, dirty, and depressing place where criminals ran wild. On my first visit to the city, as I stepped out of the Port Authority bus terminal, I found myself accosted by a furtive young man.

"Want some hash? Want some cocaine?"

That brief encounter, and one look down the sleaze of 42nd Street, took care of any desire that I might have had to live in Manhattan.

As far as marrying a non-Indian went, even the thought was unimaginable. Without exception, every wedding that I had witnessed in India had been an arranged union and couples were within the same caste, if not the same subcaste. Once the two families had deemed each other compatible, the boy and the girl were allowed one or two meetings in which to make up their minds. Given that upbringing, the idea that I would not only fall in love with but also marry an American woman was just as terrifying as the thought of living in New York City and working on Wall Street.

I realized that accepting the Lehman job offer would mean breaking my first two vows, but I felt that I had broken them the moment that I had mailed my résumé. I also knew that I couldn't walk away from this once-in-a-lifetime opportunity because, deep down, I have always been a gambler at heart.

After a week of deliberations, I called Michael back and accepted the job offer. I decided to give New York, Wall Street, and finance a two-year try. After that, I would head straight back to San Francisco, to a life of traveling the world playing blackjack.

Two years earlier, the choice of giving up on a career in computers and playing blackjack had been an easy one. I had found life in the computer industry to be dull and soul crushing. At both of my jobs, Honeywell in Minneapolis and Oracle in the Bay Area, it had been a struggle to get out of bed and make my way to the office for another pointless day of writing software. I had managed to keep up the facade for almost four years, but it was bound to crumble sooner or later. I had found blackjack just in time.

It was during a weekend trip to Lake Tahoe that I first came across the game that would change my life. After a long day of skiing at the aptly named Heavenly Mountain, a friend and I crossed Stateline Avenue to have dinner at Harrah's Casino in Nevada. I had been in a casino twice before — once in Atlantic City and once in Las Vegas during a meandering three-thousand-mile road trip from Minneapolis to San Francisco — but had no interest in playing games where the odds were so clearly stacked against the player. From the chandeliers down to the carpets, everything in a casino was paid for by the losses of its customers. I found it astonishing that casinos boldly advertised their slot machines as *ninety percent payout!* Didn't the poor souls putting their hard-earned money into the one-armed bandits realize that meant for every dollar that went into the machine, only ninety cents came out?

On our way out of Harrah's, my friend stopped by a blackjack table to try his luck. As I watched him play, I found myself getting fascinated with the simplicity of the game: get as close to twenty-one as possible without going over. I played for a short while as well. A few minutes later, down fifty bucks, I realized that I was out of my depth and walked away.

The following Monday morning, while at work in Oracle's shiny new headquarters, I happened to casually mention blackjack to my boss, a gentle giant of a man called Hamid. The next few words out of his mouth altered the course of my life.

"You know, Kamal, blackjack can be beaten," Hamid said.

"Beaten? How?" I asked him.

"By keeping track of the cards, you can gain an edge over the house," he replied.

I couldn't believe it. A game where the player had an advantage over the casino? That was impossible.

"No way!" I exclaimed.

"I'm serious. Go read this book," Hamid said as he jotted the information on a piece of paper and handed it to me.

The book was *Million Dollar Blackjack* by Ken Uston.

I pulled out the yellow pages and called every bookstore in the area, eventually locating a copy at the Palo Alto Bookshop, a twenty-minute drive away. I dragged my friend Lalit — we had started on the same day at Oracle and he lived around the corner from me in San Francisco — out of his office saying, "We're going to Palo Alto for lunch." Lalit, whose first name I would adopt as my own in many casinos, shrugged and said okay.

We made a quick stop at the bookstore, where I purchased the yellow paperback for $14.95 — easily the best fifteen dollars that I have ever spent in my life.

I spent days poring over the book, trying to understand every aspect of the game. My first order of business was to make sure that the math involved was correct, and that the player could indeed gain an advantage over the house.

The house has an edge in blackjack for the simple reason that the player acts first. If a player goes over twenty-one and busts, he immediately loses the bet even if the dealer also busts afterwards.

A blackjack dealer is not allowed to make any decisions. Casino rules force him to keep taking cards up until he reaches seventeen or until he goes over twenty-one. Simply by acting last, the casino gains almost an eight percent advantage over a player who plays in the same manner. A handful of rules that benefit the player — splitting of pairs, doubling down on the first two cards, and a three-to-two payout for a blackjack — whittle the casino edge down to under one percent, but only if a player sticks to a simple method known as "basic strategy." As the name implies, basic strategy is easy to follow and casinos will even allow a player to look at a cheat sheet in the middle of a hand. Despite that, the vast majority of gamblers choose to rely on gut instinct instead, thereby surrendering a substantially greater advantage to the house.

A player at the blackjack table is not bound by the same rules as a dealer. Instead, he can play his hand however he wishes. He is free to stand on an eight or take a card on a twenty. While both of these moves would be foolish, that freedom of action is one of the keys to beating the house.

After every hand, the dealer scoops up the cards and puts them into a discard pile, where they sit until the next shuffle. By keeping track of the cards as they come out of the shoe, a player can determine whether the odds for the next hand are in his favor or in the casino's.

A shoe rich in aces and high cards gives a player an edge due to the increased likelihood of getting a blackjack and the higher probability of both sides busting. Even though the dealer is equally likely to get a black-jack, the three-to-two payoff makes the situation greatly advantageous for the player. Moreover, when there is a preponderance of high cards in the shoe, a player can choose to stand on sixteen whereas the dealer must take a card. Consequently, when a card counter sees a larger number of low cards being dealt, he increases his bets and lowers them when the opposite occurs. The odds can fluctuate dramatically from one hand to the next, especially near the end of the shoe, and the card counter varies his bets accordingly.

Blackjack is a fast game where a hand is frequently over in less than thirty seconds. It would be impossible, and frankly unnecessary, to keep track of every card in such a short time. Card counting solves the problem by dividing them into three groups: high, low, and medium.

The most commonly used card counting system — the Hi-Lo Count — assigns a +1 denomination to low cards and −1 to high cards (medium cards have a zero value). By keeping a running count of the cards as they are dealt, a player can determine the composition of those remaining in the shoe. A net count of +5 implies that five more low cards have left the deck than high ones, thereby leaving the deck rich in high cards and tilting the odds in the player's favor.

Although it sounds fairly straightforward in principle, card counting is extremely difficult in practice. The numerous distractions inside a casino make it challenging for the aspiring card counter who has to count not only his own cards, but those of every other player as well. In parallel, he has to determine the odds, place his bets, and play his hand in accordance with the state of the deck. Throw in the added stress of a fluctuating bankroll and the card counter's task becomes next to impossible. And when casinos encounter that rare blackjack player who manages to overcome the numerous obstacles, they reward him by throwing him out.

By the time I reached the end of *Million Dollar Blackjack*, I was greatly troubled by the casinos' behavior. Ken Uston had not only been barred from several establishments, he had also been arrested and beaten for having the audacity to use his brain while playing the game. It became obvious to me that the gambling houses of Nevada were not in the business of offering a fair game to their customers. They were only interested in catering to those who could easily be parted with their money.

That only made blackjack more enticing for me. The game was the perfect combination of the three things that I cared deeply about: numbers, taking calculated risks, and fighting against unfairness. I decided to follow in Uston's footsteps and teach the casinos a lesson. I would have sought him out had he not died three years earlier.

I announced my decision to the world.

Almost without exception, my pronouncement was met with laughter and ridicule.

To most people, my obsession was indicative of a dark addiction, and they were convinced that it would lead to my ruin. Some went so far as to say that I was destined to go broke and throw myself off a bridge. They refused to believe that I was motivated by the mathematics of the game or a sense of fairness.

My conservative parents in India were the most distressed of all. Their worst nightmare had come true. Their beloved son had gone to America and was now on his way to becoming a degenerate gambler. Adding to their shame and making matters much worse, he was dating a divorcée from Hong Kong who had a seven-year-old son. That relationship, however, was destined to fail. Mae-Lin despised gambling, mainly because her father had worked in an underground casino when she was a child. It also didn't help that we had very different priorities in life.

"I want to make a million dollars," she said one day.

"Why?"

"I want to be rich," she replied, probably wondering why I was asking such a stupid question.

"I get paid seventy thousand dollars a year," I said. "I'm already rich."

"You have no ambition," she scoffed.

Ironically, a little over two years later, long after we had broken up, I would end up on Wall Street, where seven-figure paychecks were routine.

The negative reactions did little to dissuade me from my objective. I had decided to become a professional blackjack player and that was that. I retreated to my apartment in San Francisco's Haight-Ashbury district and started practicing in every spare moment.

Right from the start, I had chosen to master one of the most difficult counting systems, the Uston Advanced Point Count (APC). The card values in APC range from +3 to −3, instead of the standard +1, 0, or −1 in simpler systems. Complicating the task even further, the APC requires a side count of aces. The added effort was made worthwhile by the greater advantage it offered over the house. My choice of counting system also proved instrumental in landing me a Wall Street job. I was able to identify the exact number of the card at Lehman because nines have a unique value in the APC, as do fives, tens, and aces.

Uston had determined that a professional blackjack player should be able to count a deck of cards in under twenty-five seconds. When my first attempt took several minutes, I knew that I was in for the long haul. It took two months of practicing for up to six hours a day for me to get to Uston's target. I didn't stop at twenty-five seconds, though, and kept going until I was able to count a deck in as little as fourteen seconds.

But counting a deck quickly wasn't enough to beat the house. I also had to figure out how to play each hand according to the state of the shoe, and how to vary my bets to exploit its shifting probabilities. To that end, I draped a sheet over my coffee table and turned it into a blackjack table, using nickels, dimes, and quarters as chips. For hours on end, I played against this pretend house and kept detailed records. Over the next few months, I worked harder at this than I had at anything else in my life, a fact that would be lost on everyone around me when they tried to play blackjack themselves. After practicing for several months at home, and winning more often than not, I flew to Reno to teach Goliath a lesson. Instead, I fell flat on my face, just like I had done on my first run down a ski slope.

Blackjack inside Bally's Casino was a very different game from the one that I had been playing in the solitude of my apartment. The cards and the rules were the same, but the atmosphere threw me off-balance. Every time the waitress tapped me on the shoulder, I forgot the count as I placed my order for a Campari and tonic. The same thing happened whenever the pit boss asked for my player's card, a slot player squealed in delight, or the table changed dealers. The biggest distractions by far were the other players at my table. Between telling me how to play my hand, howling in agony or screaming in joy at the turn of a card, talking about their lives and asking me about mine, or taking interminably long to play their hand, they seemed determined to break my concentration. And they succeeded.

The first time I tried counting cards in a casino, it was such a disaster that I seriously considered giving up blackjack altogether. Perhaps it had been a mistake to spend all that time practicing in the peace and quiet of my apartment. The loss of money was painful, but it was the loss of confidence that really hurt. I was racked with self-doubt.

The odds were in my favor, how could I lose four hands in a row? Was my count wrong? Did I play the hand right? Was the dealer cheating? Does card counting even work?

There was only one way forward. I would play for the lowest stakes possible until I had doubled my bankroll, no matter how long it took. That would give me the time to build up my confidence as well as avoid needing to inject more funds into my bankroll. Having put down the marker, I made numerous trips to Reno, grinding out small profits. The smaller stakes had a calming effect on me and I was able to get accustomed to counting cards in the loud casino atmosphere. I also went back to practicing four to six hours a day while in San Francisco. It took many months and several hundred hours of play but I managed to double my bankroll.

That feat alone wasn't enough to convince me of my skill. A back-of-the-envelope calculation showed that there was a ten percent probability that I had simply gotten lucky over the past few months. However, if I could double it again, the luck factor would drop to under one percent and I could be certain that I had beaten the casinos with skill.

A few months later, having quadrupled my original bankroll, I was convinced.

That's when I got thrown out of a casino.

CHAPTER 3

Life of a Blackjack Player

"**S**ir, please step away from the table."

I was annoyed by the sudden interruption. The count was high and I had just made my largest bet. I saw the dealer's hand stop midstream with the next card half out of the shoe. The action on my table came to a standstill as I turned around to see who was responsible for the stoppage. There was a tall, distinguished-looking man standing behind me wearing a dark suit and eyeglasses. The sixty-year-old gent had a serious look on his face and was flanked by two equally stern-looking security guards. He had to be a casino bigwig.

"Can I finish this hand?" I asked.

"No," he said brusquely and signaled the dealer to deal me out. The dealer did as he was told and pushed my bet back.

"What's going on?" I asked the gentleman.

"You're not welcome at Bally's anymore," he said.

It had finally happened. I was getting barred! The other players on my table stared at us with their mouths open. It had to be their first time witnessing an event like this as well.

"Why?" I asked him.

"You know why. Now take your chips and go," he said curtly.

The one saving grace about getting barred was that Bally's did not confiscate my chips. Even though my mind was reeling, I gathered myself together, picked up my chips, and walked away from the table. I had been acutely aware that casinos barred card counters, but somehow I never thought that it would happen to me. I took a final look around at the casino that had served as my home base for the past year and headed for the cashier's cage. The lady behind the thick metal bars laid my chips out neatly for the benefit of the cameras and, as she counted out the hundred-dollar bills, I spied my executioner entering the room from behind her.

"Who's that?" I asked, pointing at the suit.

"That's Bill, the shift manager," she replied.

On an impulse, I asked her if I could speak to him. The request was unusual but she complied. Bill looked at me and lifted his index finger as if to say, "Just a minute."

He met me outside the cage.

"What happened there?" I asked him.

For someone who had just thrown me out of his establishment, Bill was surprisingly friendly.

"Look, Mr. Gupta, we've been watching you for months. You're just too good. We can't afford to let you play."

I knew there was no point denying that I was counting cards. Bill wasn't stupid. Instead, I asked him one burning question.

"How did you catch me?"

"We have a card counter who comes in during my shift. He flagged you three months ago," Bill said.

A turncoat had turned me in! I was shocked to discover that a card counter had used his skill to betray a fellow player. Sitting inside the casino's surveillance room, this traitor had trained the eye-in-the-sky onto my table and counted the shoe along with me. If he was any good, he would have found me out in a few hours. Why had it taken him so long? Perhaps working for the casino was the only way for him to profit from card counting.

I felt a range of emotions wash over me. Strangely enough, the first feeling was pride. Bally's admission of defeat had validated a year's worth of effort, even more than the increase in my bankroll had. Vanity, however, was replaced by horror when I realized that all my hard work would go to waste if I couldn't play. The past year had been a great struggle but I had survived the ups and downs to emerge victorious. I had managed to gain control over my emotions, weathered countless losing streaks, and learned the value of staying disciplined. Not to mention overcoming the nearly universal disdain that I had suffered for having chosen the path of a professional gambler. After having gone through so much, not being able to play was unimaginable.

Back home in San Francisco, I pondered my next move. Bally's was just one casino and I would recover as long as the problem didn't spread to other establishments. To prevent a repeat occurrence, I came up with a series of countermeasures and put them into practice, one by one.

I started playing under fake names, a separate one for each casino. Unfortunately, it was Kamal Gupta who had been thrown out of Bally's. The next time, however, it would be either Ananth Reddy, Nikhil Sharma, or Lalit Verma who would get the boot. In the early 1990s, casinos made you a player's card with whatever name you gave them. (The only place I used my real name was at the Golden Nugget, where I had to use official ID to take out a substantial line of credit, which I would then use to bankroll my play at other establishments.)

Next, since most aspiring card counters are mathematicians or computer scientists, I needed an entirely new persona, one that was as far removed from computers as possible. I took on the identity of a successful, globe-trotting plastics import-export businessman and dressed for the part by wearing the tackiest of clothes — a black-and-gold dinner jacket along with the gaudiest ties I could find and brightly colored suede shoes. The globe-trotting part was easy. On my trips to India, I sent the pit bosses postcards from London, Zurich, Delhi, and Singapore. The deception worked so well that several dealers asked me for a job in my nonexistent company. I told them, "Sorry, we're not hiring right now."

Third, I abandoned my quiet demeanor and turned myself into a maniacal gambler, putting on great displays of emotion. Thousands of hours of practice had made it possible for me to count cards with just a glance and I used the extra time to act like a buffoon. By being loud and obnoxious, I had hoped to distract the casino management from my play. I also ordered drink after drink and pretended to be tipsy when I was stone-cold sober. I took my Campari and tonics to the men's room, far away from the prying eyes of the pit bosses, and watered them down. When I walked back to the table, the drink in my hand retained its color, but hardly any alcohol.

Finally, if all else failed and the pit bosses picked me out as a card counter, I had to make them believe that I was a money-losing one, and that it was worth their while to let me play.

I lowered my bet variation from eight-to-one to four-to-one, which sharply reduced my profits. However, I felt that being able to play the game for a long time to come was far more important than how much money I could win in the short term. I had even taken the liberty of calling the Horseshoe Casino in downtown Las Vegas, anonymously of course, and asking the shift manager what bet variation they would tolerate from card counters. To my great surprise, he answered, "We allow somewhere between three- and four-to-one." Casino management believed that as long as a card counter played every hand and his high bet was no more than four times his lowest, blackjack couldn't be beaten. They were either not aware of the Uston APC or didn't believe that it could be mastered. A careful analysis revealed that, even with the reduced betting ratio, I would retain an edge over the casino, albeit a smaller one.

In what had to be the strangest maneuver of all, I started stealing my own chips. Pit bosses are required to track every player's wins and losses, especially at the higher-limit tables. Every few minutes, I palmed a chip and squirreled it away into my pocket, making my stack appear artificially small. Consequently, whenever the dealer colored me up (exchanged my lower denomination chips for higher denomination ones) — ostensibly to make it easier for me to carry them as I walked around, but in reality to allow the pit boss to keep track of my profit or loss — it appeared that I had either won less money than I had, or I had lost more. I would cash the stolen chips in small increments throughout the day. Sometimes, I would even bring them back to San Francisco and use them on my next trip to Las Vegas.

Every time I walked up to a blackjack table, I felt that I was on a stage, performing the role of an out-of-control plastics importer from India who loved to gamble. The show had just one purpose: to prevent me from getting barred from a casino.

As blackjack took over every aspect of my life, I left Oracle for Ingres, a small software company across the Bay Bridge, where my new boss would have an even greater influence over my game than my old boss. Hamid had given me my start in blackjack, but it was Vinh who turned me into a professional.

By sheer chance, Vinh turned out to be a gambling fanatic. As a refugee and one of the Vietnamese boat people, he had been chased by pirates on the high seas and held in a concentration camp in Thailand before joining his sister in America. Once here, he had gained an education and became a software engineer. His faith in his good fortune was reinforced when, two years earlier, the Nimitz Freeway had collapsed right in front of him in the 1989 Loma Prieta earthquake.

"What did you do then?" I asked him.

"I turned my car around and went home," he said, displaying no emotion about his narrow escape.

Vinh and I made numerous trips to Reno and Las Vegas. We made an odd couple, and not just because of our looks. I moved slowly and deliberately, partly because of the arthritis that I had been suffering from since age fifteen, while he rushed through the casino like a whirlwind. Our gambling styles were also polar opposites: I was careful and conservative while Vinh's play could only be described as wild and carefree.

On one of our trips to Reno, Vinh lost his patience with me.

"Why are you still playing on a ten-dollar table?" he demanded angrily.

I tried to explain the mathematical relationship between the size of my bets and my bankroll, but Vinh wasn't interested.

"You need to play with green chips," he said, cutting me off. Vinh wanted me to move up to a twenty-five-dollar-minimum table.

"I'm not ready," I said.

"Yes, you are. I've watched you for long enough."

"But Vinh, with splits and double-down, I could have three hundred dollars or more riding on one hand," I objected. "I might lose thousands of dollars in an hour. It's too much risk. I don't think I can handle it."

That did it for him. He had had enough of my being a chicken.

"Maybe you can't, but I can. You'll play with my money and we'll split the profits fifty-fifty," he said forcefully, ending the discussion.

It was an incredible offer, one that I couldn't refuse. Vinh was willing to bankroll me and assume all of the losses for only half of the profits. After handing me a large stack of green and black chips, Vinh walked off to play baccarat. It was a staggering display of confidence on his part. Not only was he placing his trust in my abilities as a card counter, he had also placed a large chunk of his bankroll at my disposal, without any supervision.

I was surprised to discover that, while playing with Vinh's money, I felt more nervous than when I played with my own. I couldn't bear the thought of disappointing him and played extra carefully as a result. Over the course of the next few days, however, I managed to accomplish two objectives. I earned us a tidy profit and, more importantly, I realized that I could handle the stress of playing for higher stakes. I also discovered that I didn't like playing with someone else's money and would refuse all such offers in the future. Vinh was exempt from this rule, and I played on his behalf whenever he asked me to.

Vinh's influence over my blackjack career extended far beyond simply making me play for higher stakes. My friendship with him, coupled with a minor miracle that I had pulled off at work, allowed me to devote an entire year to blackjack while still being employed.

My job at Ingres required me to measure the speed of the company's software and figure out ways to make it run faster. The task was similar to taking a car that had been built by someone else and tuning it for the racetrack. Sometime during 1991, I discovered that the latest release of the software ran considerably slower than the prior version. Vinh took my concerns to the software developers, who were not pleased to hear them. Who the hell was I to say that their design was flawed? I stuck to my guns and so did Vinh, turning the matter into a political football between two warring factions of the company. The other side kept insisting that the fault lay in my driving, and not with their car. In a final attempt to get us to back down, they threw down the gauntlet.

"Fine, if you think it's our software then tell us which part of the code is to blame for the sluggish performance."

I was incredulous. They had to know that this was an absurd demand.

"The software consists of a million lines of code. How on Earth do you expect me to find the source of the problem?" I protested.

The villains smiled smugly. They knew as well as I did that the task was practically impossible. I was surprised that Vinh didn't push back. Instead, my boss took me aside and said glumly, "Just give it your best shot, Kamal."

I hated everything about the situation. I hated how the builders of the software had refused to take responsibility for its performance. I hated being forced to look for a needle in someone else's haystack. Most of all, I hated computers. Despite my anger, I threw myself into the wild goose chase. Miraculously, and by pure luck, one week later I had identified the exact lines of code that were responsible for the slowdown.

We arranged for a showdown with the opposition. The three software developers and their boss sat on one side of the table while Vinh and I sat on the other. Without saying a word, I pushed forward the sheets of paper containing the results of my detective work.

The developers might have been our enemy but they weren't stupid. Seeing the proof in black and white, they capitulated and agreed to fix their code. The meeting concluded with an unqualified victory for my boss.

"I don't know how to thank you, Kamal," Vinh said, once we were alone.

"Cash will do nicely," I replied jokingly.

It wasn't in Vinh's power to make Ingres give me cash. However, he had the power to give me something far more valuable. Time. From that point on, I was untouchable inside the company. I took full advantage of my newfound status and spent all my time on blackjack. For days on end, I wouldn't show up at work and on the days that I did, it would be for at most a couple of hours. Amazingly, this situation persisted for an entire year. In those twelve months, I went from being a low-stakes gambler to an almost-professional one.

My co-workers weren't thrilled with the arrangement, but there was little they could do about it. My blackjack obsession was well known inside Ingres as was my friendship with Vinh, both at work and at the casinos. Moreover, everyone around me wanted to learn how to count cards and needed my help.

With Vinh's continued encouragement, I slowly increased my bets even further, all the while taking care not to get thrown out of the casinos. It didn't always work out that way and I suffered a few more bans, one of which occurred at the Sands Casino in Las Vegas.

On that day, I was gambling as Lalit Verma. The pit boss, who had never seen me before, came up to the table and introduced himself.

"Hi, I'm James Woods," he said, which made me smile. He also looked like the famous Hollywood actor.

"Hello, I'm Lalit Verma," I said.

"Where are you staying, Mr. Verma?"

"At the Golden Nugget," I replied truthfully for a change.

"Here's my card. Next time you are in town, give us a call. We'd love for you to stay with us."

"Sure thing," I said, pocketing his card. My average bet at the time was over a hundred dollars and Mr. Woods wanted to retain as much of my action as possible. However, whenever I was in Las Vegas, I always stayed at the Golden Nugget and under my real name. Casinos don't grant you a credit line worth tens of thousands of dollars without verifying your identity or your bank information. Using the Golden Nugget credit line, I was able to play at any Las Vegas establishment without having to bring large amounts of cash from San Francisco. I not only ate, drank, and stayed at the casinos for free, I also used their own money to beat them.

After handing me his card, the pit boss left me alone. I played undisturbed for the next hour and was getting ready to take a break when Mr. Woods returned.

"Mr. Verma," he said.

I failed to react as Verma wasn't my name. So he said it again, a bit louder this time. I finally realized that he was talking to me.

"Hi!" I said.

"I was just wondering, Mr. Verma, are there any other games that you like to play?"

I should have smelled a rat but I didn't and persisted with my standard bullshit. "Oh yeah, I like baccarat and poker," I replied, which was a complete fabrication.

"That's good," Mr. Woods said.

"What do you mean?"

"Because, Mr. Verma, the next time you come into this casino, you won't be allowed to play blackjack," he said calmly.

I was heartbroken. Not again! I put on the most innocent face that I could muster. "Why is that?"

That made Mr. Woods angry.

"Don't play games with me! You know what you're doing, and we know what you're doing. Now get out!" he shouted.

Arguing with the pit boss was futile. I picked up my chips, cashed them under the watchful eye of Mr. Woods and his goons, and left his establishment. Four years later, I watched with some satisfaction as the Sands came down in a controlled demolition.

I considered it a minor miracle that in two years, I was barred only four times and never beaten up. The only place that came close to threatening violence was the Clarion in Reno, probably because the casino's management felt betrayed at my hands. For over a year, the pit bosses had believed this wild and crazy Indian to be their friend, but he turned out to be no better than a dirty card counter. I would have been angry too if I were in their shoes.

With every trip to Nevada, blackjack became more and more like a job for me. I set up a strict office-like routine, playing seven to eight hours throughout the day but never more than one hour at a stretch. Card counting was exhausting, mentally as well as physically. To prevent errors from creeping in, I took a ten-minute break every hour. When the time was up, I would get up from the table regardless of whether I was winning or losing. I would, however, stay till the end of the shoe if the count happened to be in my favor.

I went to bed early to avoid the late-night rush, waking up at five o'clock in the morning to take advantage of the quietest part of the day. I would take a shower and walk down to the casino floor feeling as fresh as rain, but looking disheveled and exhausted. Dealers and pit bosses assumed that I had been gambling all night and gave me a wide berth. I played for a couple of hours in the morning, followed by breakfast, and then gambled a little more before noon. After lunch — always at the newly opened California Pizza Kitchen — I made it a point to spend some time at the Golden

Nugget pool, under vented pipes that sprayed a cool mist on the guests. A little more blackjack followed by dinner and, if the casino wasn't too crowded, a short session before bed.

I finally felt at ease inside a casino and it showed in my performance at the tables. My bankroll grew steadily and I started using cash for all my expenses in San Francisco. My landlord became convinced that I was a drug dealer when I offered to pay my rent in hundred-dollar bills.

At around this time, I began to notice a marked shift in people's attitudes towards me, and towards gambling. I found it amazing that the same folks who had made fun of me a year earlier now wanted to play blackjack themselves.

Needless to say, it did not go well.

CHAPTER 4

Everyone Wants to Play Blackjack

Experience has taught me that although the world hates a gambler, it loves a winner. Since most gamblers lose money, this contradiction rarely gets tested. In my case, however, the transformation of my friends' and acquaintances' contempt into admiration was unmistakable, especially when it came to women. Those that had found me loathsome a year earlier all of a sudden saw me as glamorous.

"I don't even wanna gamble, KG. I just want to stand behind you, wear a long, flowing dress, and smoke a cigarette through a skinny holder, watching you play," said Lalit's girlfriend one day over lunch, much to his consternation. We never did play out her roaring-twenties fantasy.

My success in gambling would even attract a piano-playing ballet dancer from Mumbai who would go on to act in Bollywood movies. My relationship with a French-Canadian co-worker from Montreal had ended not too long before. Looking back, I am surprised that it lasted for as long as it did. I had never touched a cigarette in my life, and France — her parents had named her after the home country — chain-smoked Export "A"s.

But back in the summer of 1992, everyone around me wanted to play blackjack. I had unwittingly created even more fodder for the casinos by giving the impression that blackjack could be beaten easily. These novices hadn't seen the hard work that I had put in nor the long hours when I had toiled away for months on end. Some even believed that a weekend of reading would be enough.

My friend Ajay was to learn this lesson the hard way. A lanky computer scientist with a head for numbers, he became convinced of his skill after practicing for just one week. A confident Ajay drove to Reno, where an early winning streak made him even more fearless. This was easy! He decided to play for higher stakes, a blunder that would haunt him for years.

Ajay had mistaken luck for skill and he wasn't ready, either psychologically or financially, to deal with the increased volatility of a higher-limit table. The inevitable reversal of fortune exposed not only his woefully inadequate bankroll, but also his fragile mental state. In no time he had lost his entire stash along with all of his confidence.

A shell-shocked Ajay staggered out of the casino and got into his car, a daunting two-hundred-mile drive ahead of him. As he made his way down the busy Reno strip, replaying the events of the afternoon over and over in his head, he failed to pay attention to the traffic.

Ajay was jolted back to reality when he discovered that he had rear-ended a police car that was stopped at a red light right in front of him. A visibly angry officer jumped out of his cruiser, gun in hand, and yanked a horrified Ajay out of his car. The officer bent him over the hood and handcuffed him, believing that my friend must have been drunk or high to drive in such a reckless manner. The poor guy's shame was compounded by the large number of onlookers pointing and laughing at the idiot who had rammed into a police car in broad daylight.

Tears welled up in his eyes as a distraught Ajay told the cop about how he had lost an ungodly amount of money. The Reno police were no stranger to victims of uncontrolled gambling, and the officer realized that he was telling the truth.

"What happened next?" I asked, trying hard not to laugh.

"I must have looked really pathetic. He felt sorry for me and let me go," he replied.

"How did you drive home after that?"

"Very slowly," he said, shaking his head.

"I told you, man, you need to practice more."

"Fuck that!" he shouted. "I'm done with this stupid game. Card counting doesn't work and I'm never going to play blackjack again."

Ajay stayed true to his word and never entered a casino again. As painful as the experience had been for him, I believed that it could have been much worse. During my time in Reno and Las Vegas, I had met many sad souls who had lost everything to gambling — cars, houses, wives, families, as well as their sense of self-worth. There is no place to hide in a casino. You can pretend all you want, but when your money is gone you are no longer welcome at the table.

Another individual who should never have been allowed anywhere near a casino was my Oracle officemate, Rich. We had shared a small cubicle for about six months when, one afternoon, I overheard him talking about the game of eight-ball on the phone.

"You play pool?" I asked, after he had hung up.

"Yeah, I've played all my life," Rich replied.

"We should play sometime," I suggested.

Rich burst out laughing. He found the idea of an Indian playing the quintessentially American game to be hilarious. Apparently, he had never heard of snooker.

"Yeah, right. I bet you don't even know the rules."

Now I was offended. I had spent years playing billiards in college and took great pride in my pool skills.

"You never know, Rich. I might beat you," I warned him.

I didn't know that he was capable of laughing as hard as he did just then.

"If I don't kick your ass on the pool table, Gupta, I'll take off all my clothes and run buck naked across the bar," he declared.

I found his bravado astonishing and his offer of a one-sided bet downright foolish. That should have been my first clue that Rich's gambling abilities would leave something to be desired.

"You're on," I said.

That evening he drove me to his neighborhood bar, where I told every waitress what the stakes were. This led to them all rooting for me to win. My opponent was a handsome guy and they wanted to see him strip.

Rich won the toss and broke the rack with a powerful shot but, unfortunately for him, nothing went in.

"Let's see what you can do, Gupta," he said, turning the table over to me.

Over the next few minutes, Rich's jaw hit the floor as I ran the table. Pocketing the eight ball with a flourish, I said, "Time to take your clothes off!"

"What the fuck was that?" said Rich, looking like someone who had just realized that they had been hustled.

"I tried to warn you," I said.

"You're such a loudmouth — how come you never mentioned that you could play?"

"It never came up. Just be glad that we weren't playing for money."

Much to the disappointment of the waitstaff, Rich refused to fulfill the terms of our bet. I didn't care one way or another, I was only there to play the game and had no desire to see him in his birthday suit.

Despite his shellacking that evening, Rich and I stayed friends and I attended his wedding a few months later. I was gambling heavily at the time and Rich would listen to my escapades with great interest and with a sense of longing.

"Man, I wish that I could come on a trip with you," he said wistfully.

"What's stopping you?" I asked him.

"Susan," he replied, with a grimace.

When I asked his new wife about it, she didn't mince her words: "No way in hell!"

I didn't understand why she was so violently opposed to his going to a casino. Rich was a grown man, and a responsible one at that. What could possibly go wrong? A lot, as it turned out.

Rich pleaded with Susan for two months, wearing her down.

"Fine, you can go to Tahoe for the day, but only if Kamal goes with you."

I would have preferred a longer trip but, seeing how excited Rich was, I gave in. Susan also insisted that I pick him up as well as bring him home. That too should've been a warning sign, but I missed it.

The following Saturday morning, Rich and I drove up Interstate 80 to the Sierra Nevada mountains. He talked excitedly, like a kid on his way to a candy shop. I, on the other hand, felt no excitement whatsoever. The thrill of gambling had long worn off for me. I was headed to Lake Tahoe to do a job.

A little after noon, we reached Harrah's, the place where I had first encountered blackjack. I got right down to business and Rich played next to me. I ordered Campari and tonics and took them to the men's room to dilute them, as I usually did. Rich also had a few drinks, undiluted. We were having a great time and everything was under control. I was beginning to wonder why Susan had made such a fuss.

After an early dinner, I told him that our time in Tahoe was coming to an end.

"We'll leave in an hour, okay?"

"No problem, bud," a happily buzzed Rich said.

A few minutes later, when he picked up his chips and went to a table across the casino, I didn't think anything of it. I was busy counting cards and time was running short. A little over an hour later, I went to look for him.

In the time that I had left him alone, Rich had undergone a startling transformation. He was not only drunk out of his mind, but he was also gambling like a man possessed. Believing that an intoxicated gambler was their best customer, the house had plied him with one double scotch after another. As long as he had chips, the spigot was open. Rich had blown through all his cash and had made a few trips to the cash machine conveniently located nearby. The ATM didn't care how drunk Rich was, as long as he typed the correct pin number.

I needed to get him away from the table as fast as possible, but his belligerence made it impossible.

"Leave me alone!" he shouted.

"Rich, we have to go," I pleaded.

"Faack off, I gotta win my money back first."

It wasn't easy but I dragged him away from the table and cashed out his few remaining chips. He tried to fight me off but, in his drunken state, I had the upper hand in our slow-motion boxing match. I propped him up and half-dragged him out to the parking lot.

"Get a room, you two!" I heard a woman shout in the distance.

It must have appeared to the two young women lounging outside Harrah's that Rich and I were locked in an embrace. Even if that were true, the remark was uncalled for. However, I had my hands full and ignored them. So they said it again.

"Faggots!"

This time Rich heard them loud and clear.

"What the faack are they saying, Gupta?" he slurred.

"Nothing, let's go," I said, pulling him towards my car.

"Dude, they called us faggots," he said, sounding both drunk and offended at the same time.

"Who cares?" I said, trying desperately to bundle him into my Acura.

"I do! We gotta go back!"

"What? Why?"

"We gotta kick their asses," said Rich, to my great shock.

"Are you out of your mind? We'll get thrown in jail."

"That's okay. I've been there."

"Whaaat? You were arrested? Here? In Lake Tahoe?"

"Just once," he said, making my head reel.

I was stuck in my worst nightmare, saddled with an out-of-control, drunk gambler who wanted to beat up two women in a casino parking lot. And he had an arrest record to boot. Susan was right. This man should never have been allowed to gamble.

I strapped him into my car and drove away from Harrah's as fast as I could. Rich, however, was relentless about wanting to settle the score with the two women.

"Turn this car around, Gupta. We gotta go back and kick their asses," he must have said at least a hundred times.

Rich finally fell asleep and I drove the last seventy miles in silence, which gave me time to think about what had transpired. Everything made sense now. Susan had insisted on my presence because she knew that, if left to his own devices, Rich wouldn't have found his way back home. He would likely have passed out on the sidewalk or, worse, spent another night in lockup. I wished that she had warned me so that I could have kept a closer eye on him.

It was nearly one in the morning when I handed Rich off to his bleary-eyed wife and went home, muttering, "Never again."

CHAPTER 5

"You should work on Wall Street."

B y late summer of 1992, I had become highly confident in my abilities as a blackjack player. My bankroll had grown to almost thirty times its original size, undoubtedly due to my card-counting skills. I had kept a detailed record of my play and calculated that I had gained an edge of almost one percent over the house. That slender advantage was enough for me to make a living from the game. And that's what I had intended to do for the rest of my life.

This, however, was not to be. Life intervened and I ended up on Wall Street less than six months later. A fish out of water once again, I found myself gasping for breath in the world of high finance, a place that I had never imagined I'd be.

Wall Street and blackjack both appeared in my life by accident, but under very different circumstances. When I found blackjack, I was restless, desperately searching for something, anything, that would distract me from the tedium of the computer industry. In contrast, when I found Wall Street, I was at peace with myself and my chosen vocation. Gambling and high finance did share a common trait though. The probability of success in each case was small.

I decided that the month of August in 1992 would be a dry run for the rest of my life; two weeks of blackjack and two weeks of R&R. I started by gambling for a week in Las Vegas, and then flew to Delaware to visit my older brother for a few days. Ami had earned a PhD in chemical engineering from Princeton University and was working for DuPont in Seaford, a bucolic town of 6,000. As I sat on his front porch, staring at the corn stalks across the street, I made a spur-of-the-moment decision to go to New York City.

I had been to New York before and had found the city to be gritty and gloomy. Still, I didn't know when I would be on the East Coast again and thought it would be a good idea to look up some friends in Manhattan. A convoluted mix of bus and train travel brought me to their Upper West Side apartment. On my first evening in the big city, they took me to the now-defunct, but then-trendy nightclub Le Bar Bat. On that night, the throngs of people in that gothic chamber all seemed to work in finance. They spoke in a language that was foreign to me — equities, fixed income, bulls and bears, long or short, and something called the sell side — so I kept my mouth shut. Finally, one of them turned to me and asked, "What do you do?"

"I'm a professional gambler," I replied.

It was the very first time that I had referred to myself as such, and I was surprised by how easily the words rolled off my tongue. After two years of hard work, I felt that I had earned the privilege. Moreover, what else could I have called myself?

The words *professional gambler* stopped everyone in their tracks and the group looked at me with a mixture of incredulity and fascination.

"Seriously?"

Over the next two hours, I recounted the story of my past two years. I told them about counting cards, about my use of aliases and my made-up identity as a plastics importer, as well as the tactics I had used to evade detection. I also described how several casinos had barred me.

"They can throw you out just like that?" someone asked.

"Sadly yes," I said and told them that the Nevada courts had reaffirmed a casino's right to deny service to anyone, and for any reason.

The group stood transfixed as I continued with my stories. I told them about the seventy-five-year-old Vietnamese lady who had once screamed at me, "You are an idiot! Go and play somewhere else. This table is only for professionals." All because I had chosen to stand on a sixteen and the next card turned out to be a five, giving the dealer a twenty-one.

"Were you ever cheated in a casino?" someone asked.

"To the contrary, a dealer once cheated in my favor," I replied.

"What?"

It had happened during the graveyard shift at the Riviera. As soon as I sat down at the empty table, George the dealer whispered, "I'm going to make you rich." I laughed it off, as every dealer pretends to be on the players' side in order to earn more tips. George, however, had meant exactly what he had said. On the very next hand, as I waved my hand indicating that I wanted to stand, he mumbled under his breath, "Better take a card." I went along with his advice and was stunned to see him deliver the exact card that I needed to win the hand. George then started calling out cards from the shoe before they were turned face up, seven of clubs, ace of diamonds, jack of spades. It was quite a show and I was mesmerized by his skill. After watching him for a few minutes, I made an excuse and left the table. It was one thing to get barred as a card counter, it was entirely another to get thrown in jail for defrauding a casino. No one would have believed that we weren't in cahoots. At any rate, my idea of beating the house did not involve cheating.

As the evening at Le Bar Bat drew to a close, one of the members of the group said to me, "You should work on Wall Street."

"And do what?" I asked.

"Trade," he said.

I had no idea what the guy was talking about. I thought that trade was something that happened between countries. Before I could say anything else, he reached into his backpack, pulled out a book, and thrust it in my hand. It was *Liar's Poker* by Michael Lewis.

Later that week, on the five-hour America West flight from D.C. to Las Vegas, I started reading the book. I found Lewis's account of the financial industry only mildly interesting until I reached page 125. Then I was riveted. The story of Howie Rubin was eerily similar to mine. Howie had been bored with his humdrum existence as a chemical engineer and, after seeing a *60 Minutes* segment on blackjack (featuring Ken Uston I believe), had become a successful card counter. There was one big difference, though. Howie's path to Wall Street was made possible by an MBA from Harvard University, something I had no interest in pursuing. Despite that, by the time I landed in Vegas, an outlandish idea had started to take hold in my brain.

For the next week, I forgot all about Wall Street and concentrated on playing blackjack. Once I was back home in San Francisco, however, I couldn't get *Liar's Poker* out of my head. Even though I had vowed never to work on Wall Street, it seemed like a natural progression to go from the biggest casinos of Nevada to the largest casino in the world. Also, I felt that I had conquered blackjack and that a new challenge wouldn't be the worst thing.

It was in a Haight Street pizzeria, with a group of friends, that I first said out loud what I had been thinking for days: "I'm going to work on Wall Street."

My friend Tom roared with laughter and literally fell off his chair, so off-balance that all 250 pounds of his six-foot-three frame was sent crashing to the floor. We had been colleagues in the computer industry, and he had been similarly amused when I had said, "To hell with computers, I'm going to become a professional blackjack player." Beating the casinos was one thing, but Wall Street? Surely that was an impossible dream for an Indian immigrant who didn't know the first thing about business.

Tom wasn't alone in his reaction. My idea of working on Wall Street was met with universal skepticism, just as my plans of becoming a professional blackjack player had been. Once again, I stuck to my guns and put together a résumé highlighting my gambling expertise, placing my computer background at the bottom of the page. I sent my résumé to a few investment banks, two of which agreed to interview me.

The first of those was Merrill Lynch, where a trading manager concluded the hour-long interview by saying, "I have no idea how to evaluate you."

The next day, I walked into Lehman Brothers.

The rest, as they say, is history.

CHAPTER 6
From Haight Street to Wall Street

O n my first day of work, standing in the lobby of the World Financial Center, I was nervous. In what seemed like a flash, I had been transported from Haight-Ashbury, the birthplace of the hippie movement in the sixties, to its very antithesis in downtown Manhattan. The idea of living in New York City terrified me, as did the thought of working on Wall Street. And yet, here I was, waiting for an elevator to take me up to the Lehman trading floor, a sinking feeling taking hold in the pit of my stomach. Had I made a terrible mistake?

It would be years before I realized that playing blackjack had been the perfect training for a career in high finance. On my first day, though, I didn't know anything about the business of Wall Street. While I fully expected to be exposed as an ignoramus, I was still surprised by how swiftly it happened. I didn't even make it past the one-hour mark.

The trading floor was abuzz by the time I strolled in at eight in the morning, a full hour before I had ever shown up at work in the computer industry. "We start at seven," Gelband said curtly and turned me over to Donnie, a balding thirty-something member of the Lehman back office. I felt like kicking myself. The one thing that I knew about Wall Street was that the stock market opened at nine thirty in the morning and closed at four in the afternoon. How was I supposed to know that the bond market's hours were from eight a.m. to five p.m.? Or that Lehman held a meeting every morning at seven, partly to set the agenda for the day and partly to make sure that everyone showed up bright and early.

Over time, I was surprised to discover that investment banks had adopted the upstairs-downstairs culture of a British manor house and divided the trading floor into front and back offices. The front office aristocracy was composed of the investment banks' traders and salespeople. Responsible for producing the lion's share of the firm's profits, they were treated with extreme deference by the lesser beings around them. The back office, on the other hand, was occupied by the support staff whose sole function was to keep the front office running smoothly. The cooks and maids of Wall Street, they checked out every trade, reconciled every line item, and produced the nightly profit-and-loss reports. If not for their efforts, the edifice would have collapsed long ago.

This class structure was on display at all times. Members of the front office were loud and obnoxious whereas the occupants of the back office were quiet and docile, just like Donnie.

He led me on a tour of the trading floor, listing each area — government bonds, corporates, mortgages, emerging markets, high yield, repo. Despite not having the faintest idea what any of those words meant, I nodded along. At the end of our little excursion, Donnie sat me down and made a simple statement. Or so he thought.

"Bond prices are quoted as a percentage, ninety-eight and sixteen, for example."

I knew that he had meant ninety-eight percent, but had no idea what the second number was. Unaware that I was about to make a complete fool of myself, I asked, "What's this sixteen?"

"Sixteen ticks," Donnie said matter-of-factly, as if it were the most obvious thing in the world.

I racked my brain but was unable to come up with an explanation for that phrase. This being a Wall Street trading floor, I was reasonably certain that he wasn't talking about insects. Was it the ticking of a clock?

"Ticks? What's that?" I asked him gingerly.

"A thirty second," he said, a furrow appearing between his brows. Surely I knew what a tick was.

I didn't, and Donnie had only made matters worse. The ticking of a clock followed by thirty seconds. He had to be talking about units of time. It made no sense whatsoever.

Even though it made me sound like a fool, I couldn't help asking, "What does time have to do with bond prices?"

"What the hell are you talking about?" he blurted, now giving me his undivided attention.

Words stumbled from my mouth. "You said ticks, as in tick-tock. Then you said thirty second, as in thirty seconds on the clock."

Donnie looked dumbfounded. "Wow, you really don't know anything!"

At this point there was no denying what we both knew was true. Donnie let out an audible sigh and spoke slowly, as if I were a child.

"It's not thirty seconds of time. It's a *thirty-second*, as in one divided by thirty-two. So ninety-eight and sixteen is ninety-eight percent plus sixteen divided by thirty-two, or 98.5 percent."

"Why not just say ninety-eight and a half then? Why complicate it with ticks?" I asked.

"Look, man, I don't make the rules. I just work here," he snapped.

Donnie had worked at Lehman for years and had seen many traders come and go, including several young and inexperienced ones, but he had never encountered one who showed up without knowing what a tick was. The look on his face left no doubt as to what he was thinking: *How on Earth did this idiot get into this business?* One hour into my Wall Street career, I felt the same way.

Donnie's annoyance was likely rooted in the fact that this idiot had been hired into Lehman's front office, something that most back-office personnel would have given their left arm for. Salespeople and traders hogged all the glory on Wall Street, along with most of its riches. It wasn't unusual for the pay of a seasoned member of the front office to be ten times higher than that of his back-office counterpart. Unfortunately for Donnie, migration between the front and back office was extremely rare.

As the hours passed, the day didn't get any easier for me. My ticks gaffe made its way around the trading floor, further increasing my embarrassment. The bravado that I had displayed during my interview had deserted me, replaced instead by a timidity that I hadn't experienced in a very long time. I shuffled aimlessly about, trying not to look hopelessly lost.

"Sit.here," someone said, putting me out of my misery. I looked at my desk and immediately noticed two things. One, it was at the very end of the row; and two, it was next to a hulk who went by the name of Gavin.

A Wall Street trading floor is a vast open space, devoid of partitions, composed of rows upon rows of desks where traders sit cheek by jowl and back to back. Every aisle is a self-contained business with the head of the trading desk sitting in the middle, surrounded by his deputies who have their own lieutenants next to them. Consequently, power in a row radiates outwards from the center, diminishing rapidly with every seat. It made sense that, being the new guy, I was placed furthest from the center of the action. Much like Abhimanyu's struggle against the chakravyuh in the Indian epic *Mahabharata*, every Wall Street trader strives to make it to the center of the row. Also, like Abhimanyu, once you reached it, there was no way back. You survived there for as long as you could, until the inevitable fall.

My new neighbor greeted me with a series of loud belches and farts, making it clear that a trading floor was no place for social niceties. Although his seat was only one removed from that of the least important person on the trading floor, Gavin was a full-fledged trader who walked about with the swagger of a silverback. No sooner had I sat down in my uncomfortable chair than he turned to me and delivered a vital lesson.

"The first thing that you need to understand about this business, Kamal, is that it is ruled by two words," he said.

I was surprised to hear that Gavin was able to distill Wall Street into just two words. Since I didn't have the foggiest idea what he was talking about, I said, "What are those?"

"Fear and greed!" he exclaimed triumphantly, looking as if he had handed me the keys to the kingdom.

I was flabbergasted. Fear and greed? That was the gist of Wall Street? What an awful existence, I thought.

I would soon discover that Gavin was right. Virtually every action of a Wall Street trader was driven by his greed (traders are overwhelmingly male) for an ever-larger bonus. Since those bonuses could easily stretch into millions of dollars, the fear of losing them was an equally powerful motivator. Of course I had seen plenty of greed in the casinos of Nevada, but I would soon realize that was nothing compared to the toxic environment on Wall Street. Life on the trading floor boiled down to 364 days of fear and greed punctuated by one day of ecstasy or of great disappointment.

A bonus was the furthest thing from my mind that morning. The way that things were going, I wasn't sure if I would last the month, let alone an entire year. My immediate objective was far more primal: just make it through the day.

Seeing that I was wholly unfamiliar with the business, Gavin decided to continue with my education.

"Do you know what we make here?" he asked.

I didn't realize that he had posed the question rhetorically. "Stocks? Bonds?" I replied, trying to sound somewhat intelligent.

"No, you dummy. We make money!" a visibly amused Gavin chortled.

"As in printing presses?" As soon as those words came out of my mouth, I knew that I had made another mistake.

Gavin guffawed and made a few more bodily noises as he rocked back and forth in his chair.

"I didn't say that we *create* money. What I said was that we *make* money."

I didn't understand the distinction but I didn't dare ask for clarification. I couldn't take the chance of another ticks-type fiasco and make an even greater fool of myself. I nodded as if I understood, and Gavin went back to work, making no attempt to explain himself.

That phrase, we make money, stuck in my mind. Over the next few weeks, as I tried to acclimatize myself to the trading floor environment, I searched for its meaning. It didn't take long to find the answer.

What Gavin had meant to say was that investment banks don't produce anything. These pillars of high finance engage in a range of activities with the sole purpose of making a profit. Some of those activities are visible to the public, such as Initial Public Offerings, commonly known as IPOs. However, a significant amount of an investment bank's business is conducted out of the public eye, such as advising corporations on mergers and acquisitions as well as the daily buying and selling of financial instruments, also known as trading. All of these activities have one thing in common: they don't produce anything other than money.

Mercifully, my first day's ordeal ended at six o'clock in the evening. By every measure, my start at Lehman had been an abysmal one. My bet, swapping blackjack and San Francisco for Wall Street and New York, was starting to look like a losing one. However, at the end of that exhausting day there was one small saving grace. I was meeting a friend of a friend for dinner.

I hailed a taxi and headed up to the Bank Cafe in midtown Manhattan, unaware that I was about to come face to face with the woman who would make me break my third vow.

CHAPTER 7

The Bank Cafe

A chance encounter with blackjack in Lake Tahoe had brought me to Wall Street and, similarly, a blind date in Minneapolis led me to my future wife in New York City.

One of my colleagues at Honeywell was acquainted with a young Indian woman. So he did the obvious thing and set me up with her. That's how I met Aarti, an effervescent young woman who had recently moved to the Twin Cities after graduating from Drake University in Des Moines, Iowa. I was amused to learn that this daughter of Indian immigrants had grown up in Peoria, the Illinois city that had become a metaphor for mainstream America.

Aarti and I got along fabulously but there wasn't any romantic spark between us. Nevertheless, we became good friends and stayed in touch even after I had moved to California. When my flight from New York to San Francisco had a stopover in Minneapolis, I called Aarti from an airport payphone and told her about the job offer from Lehman.

"In New York, you'll have to meet my college roommate Kathleen!" she said, giving me her friend's phone number. At the time, I didn't give it much thought. I wasn't sure that I was even going to accept the Lehman job, let alone move to Manhattan.

Two months later, I landed in New York and called Aarti's friend. We made plans to have dinner the evening of my first day at Lehman.

"How will I recognize you?" I asked her on the phone.

"I'll be wearing a long purple coat," she said.

Before I could say anything, she added, "And I have a lot of hair."

I found her reply a little strange but I didn't pry any further. As it turned out, her description of herself was spot on. Just those two pieces of information would have been enough for me to pick her out of a crowd. Upon entering the restaurant, the first thing I noticed was the back of a long purple coat with a mass of dark curly hair above it.

We secured a table by the window on busy Third Avenue and ordered dinner. Even though it was our first meeting, the conversation flowed remarkably easily. She talked about growing up in Newburgh, sixty miles up the Hudson River from New York City, in a large Italian-American family. I told her about my childhood in India and about coming to America for graduate school. She did raise an eyebrow when I mentioned playing blackjack and how it had brought me to Wall Street.

"Today was your first day at Lehman?" she asked.

"Yeah, I flew in from India two days ago," I said. I had spent two months wrapping up my affairs in San Francisco and visiting family in Delhi, much to Gelband's dismay.

"Wow! Good luck," she said.

"I'm going to need it," I replied, meaning every word of it.

"By the way, what's wrong with your neck?"

Her question caught me by surprise. The Bank Cafe waiter, mistakenly thinking that we were already a couple, had seated us next to each other at a square table. She had noticed that I found it hard to turn my neck and that I had angled my chair to make it easier to face her.

I sighed and said, "It's a long story."

"What is it?" she prodded.

I paused for a moment, then decided to tell her something that I rarely discussed with friends, still less with someone I had just met.

I told her about how when I was fifteen, a persistent pain appeared in my left knee. Initially, no one thought much of it. Not me, not my parents, and not the general practitioner who lived across the street from our house.

Everyone had assumed that I must have banged my knee somehow, or hurt it while playing cricket with my friends after school. A month later, when the pain was no better, my parents hauled me in front of several specialists, each performing a battery of tests that failed to explain my symptoms. The pain grew more intense and spread to the other knee as well as both my ankles. I started to walk with a limp, much to the consternation of my parents. The specialists came up with a variety of reasons for my condition.

There is extra fluid in his knee; we'll need to drain it. That doctor had no answer for why my ankles also hurt.

We should do a biopsy, suggested another, causing me to panic. Did he suspect cancer? No, he said, but he still wanted to do a biopsy. I refused.

Send him for physical therapy. This made sense and I underwent therapy for a month, having my joints layered with hot dripping wax and subjecting myself to electrical stimulation. The pain didn't get any better, but the center for physical therapy helped put matters into perspective. The sign at the door said, "I cried that I had no shoes, until I met a man with no feet."

"Interesting," Kathleen said.

"Why?"

"I'll tell you later. Now go on with your story."

I continued telling her how my parents, at their wits' end after a year of running around to a series of doctors, took me to Delhi's top orthopedist. On the evening of my appointment, we walked past an impressive row of cars parked in the driveway, climbed a flight of stairs, and sat down in a small waiting room.

When it was my turn to see the doctor, I was confronted with a stern-looking man. Despite his impressive reputation, he looked no different than the twenty other specialists I had seen.

The orthopedist sat expressionless as my parents went through the events of the past year. They described how the pain had started in my left knee before spreading to the other joints.

The doctor examined me perfunctorily. He bent my knee this way and that.

"Ouch!" I exclaimed.

He showed no reaction to my discomfort, which I found troubling. I would soon discover why.

Three minutes later, his exam finished, he pointed at the door and said, "You wait outside."

Once I was out of earshot, the doctor turned to my parents.

"How is Kamal doing in school?" he asked.

"Huh? What does that have to do with his pain?"

"There's nothing wrong with him. He's faking it," the doctor said.

"Why would he do that?" my parents asked him.

"To cover for his poor performance at school."

My mom and dad burst out laughing and walked out of his office.

I was floored when I heard about his diagnosis. This genius, Delhi's top orthopedic specialist, could not have gotten it more wrong. I had my share of problems at school, but my grades were nothing short of exemplary.

Kathleen, too, found this part funny and asked if I ever found out what was wrong with me.

"I did, and in the most remarkable fashion," I said.

I told her about how my condition was finally diagnosed four years later, when I was in my second year of college at the Indian Institute of Technology (IIT) in Delhi. My high school friend Dheerendra had gained admission to India's top medical school, the All India Institute of Medical Sciences (AIIMS). One morning, he took me to see one of his professors, who managed to do in ten seconds what so many doctors had failed to do in four years.

"I can tell what's wrong with you by the way you are walking," Dr. Malviya said as soon as he laid eyes upon me.

Yeah right, I thought. To say the least, I was highly skeptical of the professor's claim that he had diagnosed me from my limp.

"What's wrong with me?" I asked, playing along.

"You have ankylosing spondylitis arthritis. You'll have joint pain for the rest of your life but take this pill. It'll make you feel better."

Dr. Malviya was right. As I researched the disease, I discovered that the pain would spread to every joint in my body, and that my vertebrae would eventually fuse together. My spine would become rigid and inflexible, hence the other name for the disease, bamboo spine. No wonder every other specialist had missed it. Not many fifteen-year-olds suffer from arthritis.

I ended the narrative there, thinking I had said too much. I didn't tell Kathleen about how the prognosis had been a scary proposition for my eighteen-year-old self or about the medication that Dr. Malviya had prescribed, Indocin. While effective in controlling the pain, Indocin was not without side effects. Large doses destroyed the lining of my stomach and caused intense pain in my abdomen, especially during the night. Dealing with constant pain was debilitating, both physically and mentally. Despite that, I rarely mentioned my disease to anyone. It was difficult for people to understand how I could play tennis one day and yet find it difficult to get out of bed the next morning. Sometimes I walked briskly and at other times, with a limp. The day-to-day inconsistency made most people reach the same conclusion that the orthopedist in Delhi had. I must be faking it.

Kathleen, on the other hand, understood perfectly what I had been going through. After completing an undergraduate degree in biology at Drake University, she had earned a master's in physical therapy from Columbia University. For the past five years, she had been working at the Mount Sinai Medical Center on the Upper East Side of Manhattan, treating patients who were recovering from all sorts of injuries.

We stayed at the Bank Cafe for hours, talking about everything under the sun. After dinner, as I watched her walk away into the cold Manhattan night, I knew that I was smitten with the Italian-American physical therapist. I flagged a yellow taxi to take me downtown, unaware that she and I were destined to be married, two years later.

CHAPTER 8
Angel Food Cake

Fuck off and leave me alone, you insect!

I had heard that line, or something close to it, repeatedly during my first few months at Lehman Brothers. Having been exposed early on as a know-nothing, I was assigned only the most menial of tasks — making copies, faxing documents, and answering phones. My most important mission, however, was fetching food for the masters of the universe. I was a glorified waiter.

The experience, already humiliating, was made worse by the verbal abuse from my superiors. I put up with the daily degradation because I knew that the only way I would learn anything was by watching the traders at work. It was a far cry from my carefree life in San Francisco and from the bright lights of the Nevada casinos, but I bit my tongue and played by the rules of Mordor.

I found even the ten-minute walk from my company-paid apartment to the office to be excruciating, and not just because of my joint pain. A cold and bitter January wind rose up from the Hudson River and whipped across my face as I trudged up South End Avenue, feeling utterly miserable. I had lived in the Midwest where temperatures fell much lower, but there was something about that lashing wind in the concrete canyons of

Manhattan that made it feel much colder. It didn't help that I was headed for twelve straight hours of ill treatment at the hands of Lehman's traders, who never missed an opportunity to remind me just how worthless my existence was.

Fuck off and leave me alone, you insect!

All I was trying to do was to get the senior trader to bless the sheet of paper in my hand before I faxed it to a client. But he couldn't be bothered. When I persisted, he jumped out of his seat and shouted, "Fuck you, Kamal!" The sight of this five-foot-five-inch bully yelling obscenities at me was a reminder of just how far I had fallen. In Las Vegas, I had mastered the game of blackjack, and in New York, I didn't even know what the name of the game was. In San Francisco, I had managed to earn the respect of even my detractors, but on Wall Street, I was barely worthy of contempt. I longed to return to my previous life, but I had promised myself that I would give Wall Street two years, and this was a promise that I was determined to keep.

There was just one silver lining in this dark cloud. After staying friends for a couple of months, Kathleen and I had started dating. I introduced her to south Indian food at the newly opened Madras Mahal restaurant on Lexington Avenue and was relieved to see that she was able to handle idlis, dosas, sambar, and vadas without trouble. To my great surprise, she even enjoyed the restaurant's fiery tomato rasam. I tried to impress her with my Italian cooking but failed — the pasta was undercooked and the garlic bread was burnt. She laughed it off and suggested that we go out for pizza instead.

My personal life was on the upswing but my work life remained as bleak as ever. Week after week, the abuse on the trading floor continued unabated. It was only a matter of time before this treatment took its toll and I retaliated. As it turned out, my first act of defiance was triggered by an order for dessert, a slice of angel food cake.

The incident had an innocuous start. I was on my way to the third-floor cafeteria to pick up a late lunch when my months-long training compelled me to ask my boss if I could get anything for him. There would be hell to pay if I didn't.

"Fred, do you want something from the cafeteria?" I asked, desperately hoping that he would say no.

Most traders would devour anything that was placed in front of them, but not Fred. He was particular about his food. If a single strawberry in his bowl had a blemish, he was liable to explode. Every morning, as I picked up breakfast for the desk, I took great care to assemble a plate of fruit that would pass Fred's inspection. Not always successful, I steeled myself for an outburst whenever I delivered food to his desk.

"Hmmm. I've had my lunch, but I could use a piece of angel food cake," said Fred, rubbing his belly.

I smiled inside. I couldn't imagine a more perfect dessert for someone with Fred's sensibilities. A pristine white slice of angel food cake with no adornments and no complications. I took his order and headed for the elevator bank. I had barely made it to the end of the aisle when I heard him shout.

"Hey, Goopta!"

I stopped and turned around, "Yes, Fred?"

"Do you even know what angel food cake is?" he said loudly, a sly smile betraying his agenda.

"Of course," I snapped and stomped off the trading floor.

I was annoyed because I knew why Fred had asked me that question. I was a foreigner. He seemed to have forgotten that all the desserts in the cafeteria were labeled and that I could read.

Fred had made a habit of picking on the foreign-born members of the trading floor, but only the junior ones. He once christened a freshly minted finance PhD from Sweden as Olof, after the assassinated former prime minister. When the rookie protested, Fred barked at him, "Shut the fuck up and get out of my face, Olof!" Then there was Li, an immigrant from China who had the misfortune of having placed first in a nationwide examination. Every time Li made a mistake or asked a question, a relatively frequent occurrence for the newcomer, Fred made sure to put him down with "I thought you were the smartest man in China, Li. How come you're so dumb?"

As I rode the elevator down to the cafeteria, I decided that Fred's presumption couldn't go unpunished. If he believed me to be an ignorant immigrant, I would act like one, if only for a short while.

I picked up a slice of Fred's cherished confection and placed it on my tray, hiding it behind my plate. I then scoured the dessert shelf for an antidote to angel food cake. I found the perfect foil, a slice of chocolate and coconut mud pie — two layers of chocolate cake, separated by caramel sauce, flecked with pieces of coconut, and covered in dark frosting. Not satisfied with the way it looked, I shook the clamshell until the dessert collapsed into a gooey, brown mess. No one in their right mind would mistake it for angel food cake.

Positioning my masterpiece at the front of the tray, I went back to the ninth floor, making my way past rows of trading desks until I reached Fred's. I found him hunched over, deeply engrossed in a phone conversation. After quietly placing the Frankenstein pastry next to him, I scurried back to my desk and waited for the volcano to erupt.

I didn't have to wait long.

"What the fuck is this?" screamed Fred, looking at the clamshell in horror.

"Angel food cake," I replied.

"Are you fucking kidding me?" His shouting made a few people look up from their desks.

"Are you sure that's not it?" I said, with a straight face.

"Of course I'm sure, you moron!"

"How's that possible? The shelf said angel food cake," I said.

"You asshole! I even asked you if you knew what angel food cake was. And you were so short with me."

"Are you absolutely certain that's not angel food cake?" I prodded him further.

Fred had had enough. He looked like a madman, foaming at the mouth. Not only had he been deprived of his afternoon snack, he was also forced to contend with a jackass who kept insisting that this hideous brown mess was angel food cake.

"I'll fucking show you how sure I am!" In one motion, he lifted the dessert high over his head, took a deep breath, and slammed it full force into the garbage. Many in the audience were startled by the intensity of his reaction. It was only dessert after all.

I retrieved the slice of angel food cake from my tray and held it up for all to see.

"Well then, Fred, perhaps this is?" I said.

"What the . . . ?"

"Here's what you asked for. I don't know why you're getting so upset," I said, setting the light, fluffy white cake on his desk. To drive in the final nail, I put a fork on top.

Fred's eyes were like two daggers aimed at my heart. He had been played for a fool and he knew it. To my great surprise, he ate the cake, but not before delivering a parting shot.

"I'm going to get you for this."

His first try came a few weeks later. Late one afternoon, I received a phone call from someone claiming to be from Lehman's legal department.

"Mr. Gupta, we've discovered a serious problem with your immigration status. You need to come up to the fifteenth floor right now and bring all your papers with you."

I almost burst out laughing. Despite his best attempt to disguise it, I had recognized the voice as that of a salesman who sat two aisles over. I asked the "lawyer" to hold on, gently placed the phone on my desk, and walked over to find Fred and the salesman huddled together.

"Harassing a foreigner over immigration! Is that the best you can do?"

"Damn it!"

CHAPTER 9

A Kitchen-Sink Deal

"Goopta, you are not going to get food anymore," Fred announced one morning as I returned from the cafeteria. Just like that, my three-month stint as a Wall Street waiter came to an end.

It wasn't that Fred had had a sudden change of heart or developed some newfound affection for me. His decision was based on simple economics. I had proven to be a quick learner and he had decided that my time was better spent structuring deals. To make sure that his food supply continued uninterrupted, Fred passed the task on to another fresh arrival and asked him to take my order as well. In an instant, I went from being a waiter to being waited upon.

Under Fred's supervision, I set about tackling my first real job on Wall Street, structuring what were known as collateralized mortgage obligation (CMO) deals. A CMO deal chops mortgage cash flows into several pieces, with the aim of selling them for a higher aggregate amount. The idea is similar to a grocery store quartering a watermelon and selling each piece for more than one-fourth of the price of the whole fruit. Unlike a watermelon, however, the slicing in many CMOs is not visible to the naked eye and clients don't always know what they are buying.

This was my first time seeing how the sausage gets made on Wall Street and it wasn't a pretty sight. Fred was a master at creating deals that concealed the true nature of their bonds and pawning them off to unsuspecting clients. I learned about aptly named techniques such as barbelling and whip bonds that were just as dangerous (for investors) as they sounded. It didn't take long to figure out that the more obscure the structure of a deal, the more profitable it was for the investment bank. It would take a year or two for investors to discover that they were proud owners of a lemon, and not a watermelon — time enough for the dealmakers to blame the clients' losses on ever-changing market conditions.

In a particularly egregious case, long after I had left Lehman, a structurer took these tricks to their logical conclusion. He created a deal that was so devious and so misleading that it verged on fraud. For a client not to lose his shirt in that deal, a pencil would have had to stand on its pointed end while an 8.0 earthquake rumbled underneath. In what was an extremely rare occurrence, this illicit enterprise saw the light of day and Lehman was not only forced to buy the bonds back from angry customers but also to fire the structurer. All of his managers, however, escaped unscathed.

Unfortunately, when it came to structuring deals where clients were assured of losing money, my hands weren't clean either.

In the fall of 1993, barely nine months into my Wall Street career, I was given the sole responsibility of structuring a $225-million deal that was fittingly called a kitchen sink. Unlike a regular CMO deal, which was backed by the simplest of mortgage bonds, this deal contained some of the most complex mortgage derivatives known to man. Traders had used this structure as a repository for the garbage that had been sitting on their books, gathering dust — hence the name kitchen-sink deal. When I was finished structuring it, the deal's arbitrage — a fancy term for its potential profit — took my breath away.

In a regular CMO deal, we were lucky to earn a profit of half a percent. In contrast, this kitchen-sink deal of mine stood to earn almost ten percent, or over twenty million dollars! As I looked at the numbers, I could scarcely believe my eyes. The deal had transformed Lehman's garbage into gold.

This alchemy would not have been possible without the complicity of the credit rating agencies. The rating agencies are charged with providing an independent assessment of a deal's creditworthiness and the likelihood of its default. They are a critical factor in the success of any deal because their ratings determine the interest rate paid to the bondholders. The highest rating, AAA, is reserved for the safest of bonds, thereby allowing them to pay a low interest rate to investors. On the other end of the spectrum are the high-risk D-rated bonds which carry a significantly higher interest rate.

To make the kitchen-sink bonds appear attractive to investors, I needed a AAA rating from two reputable rating agencies. The task, which appeared daunting at first, turned out to be considerably easier than I had expected. The agencies were far more interested in pocketing their fees than protecting the interests of the bondholders. The fees were miniscule — around one percent of the kitchen-sink deal's expected profit — and Lehman was only too happy to pay them. In return, the agencies shared their models for determining the deal's cash flows, allowing me to tailor the structure to their requirements. The process felt akin to taking a test where the instructor had not only handed me the questions beforehand, but also helped me formulate the answers.

Even though I had been on Wall Street for less than a year, I was keenly aware that the agencies had been unduly lax in their analysis and that they had made it too easy for me to game their models. Had they set the bar higher, our profits would have been lower, but the bondholders would have been better protected. It is not difficult, in hindsight, to draw a straight line from my kitchen-sink deal to the rating agencies' role in causing the financial crisis, fifteen years later.

When I shared my thoughts with people around me, the message that came back was brief and to the point: "Shut the fuck up!"

It was made clear to me that my job was not to ask questions but to structure the deal for maximum profit and obtain the AAA rating. So that's what I did, fine-tuning the kitchen-sink deal's structure until I had achieved those twin objectives. Armed with a shiny AAA rating, Lehman quickly sold the kitchen-sink bonds to customers in the Far East.

The deal was considered a personal triumph for me. Even Fred paid me a back-handed compliment, saying, "Good thing you didn't fuck this up."

While I felt an element of pride in a job well done, the job itself felt like highway robbery. Ripping off naïve customers was hardly something to be proud of. Over the past several months, I had made my peace with the various deals that I had structured. The kitchen-sink deal, however, made me lose sleep. A standard CMO deal at least gave investors some chance at success, which was not the case here. As I watched Lehman book the deal's outsized profits, all I could think about was the sign above the casino slot machines, *ninety percent payout*. At the very minimum, the clients who had bought my bonds would lose ten percent of their investment. In reality, they ended up losing far more than that.

As was the case with most CMO deals, the kitchen-sink deal performed admirably for the first few months, lulling its owners into a false sense of comfort. When the Federal Reserve started raising interest rates in 1994, however, the bottom fell out of it. Rising interest rates stripped the deal of its veneer and revealed its true colors. It soon became apparent that the kitchen-sink deal would not generate enough cash flow to pay its bond-holders in full. This in turn led to a precipitous fall in the price of its bonds, causing investors to suffer losses of upwards of fifty million dollars.

All we needed now was a good excuse.

In December 1994, southern California's Orange County filed for the largest municipal bankruptcy in U.S. history, the result of risky investment strategies employed by the county's treasurer, Robert Citron. The subsequent liquidation of Orange County's holdings roiled markets, providing Lehman with the perfect cover for the catastrophic losses suffered by the owners of the kitchen-sink deal.

"It was Orange County. There was nothing we could do."

A few years later, Merrill Lynch paid $437 million to settle claims that it provided Orange County with reckless investment advice. It was only then that I understood why my kitchen-sink deal had been exclusively marketed overseas, far away from the reach of U.S. regulators.

CHAPTER 10

"Hey, Goopta! Wanna give me a blow job?"

"**H**ey, Goopta! Wanna give me a blow job?" Fred hollered for the whole world to hear on a slow Friday afternoon.

Here we go again, I thought, feeling completely deflated.

I had suffered many indignities during my first year and a half on Wall Street, but nothing came close to the anti-gay slurs that my boss routinely doled out. The simple fact that I had lived in San Francisco was reason enough for him to unleash a torrent of verbal abuse against me.

"You must be gay! Why else would you live there?"

"What kind of guys do you like?"

"Are you a pitcher or a catcher?"

It was the first time in my life that I had encountered such harassment, and under normal conditions, I would have fought back. However, my first few months at Lehman were challenging enough, and by the time I got my bearings, it was too late. Fred had already gotten into the nasty habit of pelting me with insults.

After a year of this treatment, I was fed up with Fred and I was fed up with structuring CMOs. In the spring of 1994, I told the powers that be that I no longer wanted to be a structurer and that I wished to become a trader. They nodded in agreement and then immediately forgot about my request. To be a bond trader at Lehman Brothers, and especially in mortgages, was considered to be the pinnacle of Wall Street. So of course I wanted to be one, they must have thought. But then, so did everyone else at the firm. In my case, though, it wasn't the glory of being a trader that I was after; I was simply looking for an escape from my current situation. My superiors' refusal to move me from the structuring desk caused me to become increasingly frustrated, thereby laying the groundwork for my rebellion.

Upon hearing, "Hey, Goopta!" I looked up from my desk to see my tormentor leaning back in his chair, a toothpick dangling from his lips and the usual self-satisfied smirk playing across his weather-beaten face. It was a slow afternoon and Fred was bored. What better way to pass the time than to humiliate a junior employee? Especially one that he owed for making a fool of him over a piece of angel food cake.

Fred was obviously kidding about the blow job, but that didn't make his actions any less degrading. In today's environment no one would dare say anything like that. Dismissal would be instantaneous. But in 1994, Wall Street was a very different place. Not only was there no punishment for the offensive remark, there was even a smattering of giggles around the trading floor. I had hoped that the harassment would cease once I became a productive member of the firm, but that hope was starting to fade. His vulgarity on that day was the last straw. I decided that I had to fight back.

I stood up from my desk, turned around slowly, and faced him.

"You know what, Fred? I do."

The people sitting around us were stunned. They had heard this type of chatter from Fred before and no one had given it a second thought. My saying *I do*, however, had a dramatic effect. Several people looked up from their desks, some stood up, and a handful sidled over to our aisle, hoping for a confrontation between a junior employee and a seasoned professional. There was no better entertainment during work hours.

I walked over to Fred's desk and said loudly for all to hear, "Yes, Fred, I'd like to give you a blow job."

He burst out laughing. "Yeah, right!"

"I'm serious. You asked me for one, everyone heard it. Let's go," I said. The lack of emotion in my voice surprised me, given the rage I felt inside.

Even though the last thing Fred had expected was for me to reply with a yes, he wasn't about to let an underling show him up. So he raised the stakes even higher, expecting that I would back down.

"I meant that you give me a blow job right here, right now!"

"Sure, that works," I replied calmly.

He pushed his chair back from the desk and commanded, "Get down on your knees!"

Revolting though it was, I complied with the demand and knelt on the floor. It says something about the culture of an industry that not one person in the audience intervened. They were all more interested in the show that was unfolding before them.

It slowly dawned on Fred that there was a fatal flaw in his plan. For me to fulfil his demand, he would need to first undress, and in front of onlookers. A few of the bystanders were female and I couldn't help wondering about the abuse they must have endured.

It was humiliating to kneel in front of his chair, but I knew that I had Fred cornered. I couldn't imagine a homophobe like him taking his pants off. While a Wall Street trading floor was a pretty crazy place during the nineties, I had never seen anyone disrobe. In the highly unlikely event that Fred were to do so, I would simply get up and walk away. Both of us would get fired but, for me, the risk was worth it. I'd had enough.

He made another half-hearted attempt to get me to fall back, "All these people are witnesses. You agree to give me a blow job, here and now!"

"Absolutely," I said, again in a quiet voice.

The chatter in the crowd started to go up in volume. By now, it had become clear to everyone that I had boxed Fred into a no-win situation. To drive that point home, I put my hands on his waist, grabbed his belt, and pulled. "C'mon, Fred, take these pants off. I really want to give you a blow job." I knew that I was putting my career at serious risk by taking such an aggressive step, but I was past the point of caring. One way or another, I wasn't going to put up with this kind of behavior anymore.

"Wha-what are you doing?!" Fred stammered.

"I'm trying to give you what you asked for," I replied, somehow still managing to sound unruffled.

The belt was tight around his waist and Fred was holding on to it for dear life. The audience loved the spectacle; it's not often that you see someone trying to forcibly remove their boss's pants in front of a crowd.

Having failed in my attempts to take his trousers off, I took a different tack, one that would bring this game to a swift end. I put my right index and middle fingers on his left knee and started walking them up. It was now evident to everyone watching that I was hell-bent upon teaching Fred a lesson.

I didn't choose to play this game; it had been forced upon me. Fred had used his power to belittle me, just to alleviate his boredom on a slow day. His demeaning conduct had gone on for far too long. I was simply taking his game to its conclusion, no matter the consequences. If I got fired then so be it. It's not like my Lehman job was anything to write home about.

For a brief moment, I imagined that our roles were reversed. What would I have done in Fred's situation? I have found that, in any conflict, it is a good tactic to try to see the situation from your opponent's point of view. The added perspective allows you to stay one step ahead of your adversary, making it easier to outmaneuver them. And sometimes, when you put yourself in the other person's shoes, you might even realize that they are right and you are wrong. Had it been me sitting in Fred's chair, I would be certain that the guy walking his fingers up my leg was bluffing. I would sit still and see how far he would go. He would have to stop.

As my fingers began their slow march upwards, I started to get nervous. Knowing that I would only go so far, I took my time with each step, prolonging the game of chicken.

I needn't have worried. My fingers had barely covered any distance when Fred jackknifed out of his chair, and ran screaming down the aisle, "Get this crazy bastard away from me!"

I wasn't prepared to let him off the hook just yet. I got up from the floor and chased after him, shouting, "C'mon, Fred, don't you want that blow job?"

Not being in the best of shape, my oppressor ran out of breath quickly.

"What the hell do you want from me?" he wheezed, as I caught up with him.

"I don't want you to talk to me like that ever again!" I screamed at him, my anger finally bubbling to the surface.

"Okay fine. I won't," Fred mumbled.

"I want you to swear in front of everyone!"

"I swear," he muttered, looking downright pitiful.

"That's all I want," I said and walked back to my desk, trembling. The show was over. The public had gotten their money's worth. Fred must have hated it but he never called me names again.

It may be hard to believe but, a decade and a half later, Fred and I almost became friends. After losing his job during the 2008 financial crisis, he turned to me for help with finding work at a hedge fund. I could only marvel at the reversal of fortune and assisted him the best I could.

Not long after that Friday-afternoon incident, the managers at Lehman granted my wish to become a bond trader. A mere nineteen months had passed since Donnie had taught me what a tick was, and I was ecstatic. My euphoria, however, would soon turn to dismay. The bonds that I had been asked to trade were none other than the bane of my existence: CMOs.

CHAPTER 11

A Broken Branch

After two years at Lehman Brothers, I desperately needed a break, partly to preserve my sanity and partly to decide if I should continue. Having served out the time that I had promised myself, I walked away from Wall Street, not knowing if I would return.

I could have looked past the abuse that I had suffered at the hands of the Freds of the world, but I couldn't turn a blind eye to my role in the kitchen-sink deal. Losses suffered by the investors in that deal made me realize that, for the first time in my life, I had been a party to perpetrating unfairness instead of fighting against it.

I had always had a deep aversion to injustice, especially when committed by those in positions of authority. My life before Wall Street had been governed by two guiding principles: taking calculated risks and a refusal to tolerate unfairness. Had the casinos not treated Uston in such an unfair manner, I doubt I would have been as motivated to play blackjack. Although it had started gradually, and at a young age, my hostility towards those who abused their power had solidified into a bedrock principle by the time I was in my twenties.

The first time I found myself in trouble with the law, I was no more than twelve or thirteen years old. My crime? Breaking a branch in the schoolyard.

It happened during lunch when I was in the seventh grade at Springdales Public School in New Delhi. As with all the K–12 private schools in India, Springdales was open to the public, but only those who could afford its high tuition. The school's monthly fee, 120 rupees, or fifteen dollars, was a princely sum for my parents, but they scraped it together somehow. Their motto — *we save money wherever we can, but not on education or on food* — is one of the few I have adopted.

The founder of Springdales, Rajni Kumar, was born Nancie Jones in England. She had decamped to India with her fiancé, Yudishter Kumar, changed her name to Rajni, and started a school in her living room. That small school had grown and was now housed in an imposing, gray four-story building. Mrs. Kumar, as she was called by everyone, ruled the school with an iron fist, using the phys ed teacher as her enforcer. Economical with words, he'd administer a tight slap to the back of your head to let you know your hair was too long. Having been on the receiving end of a few of those smacks, I braced myself whenever he passed behind me during the morning assembly.

With temperatures approaching a hundred degrees, April in Delhi was hot. A ring of large gulmohar trees along the outer perimeter of the school provided much-needed shade during lunch. During one of those breaks, I found a low-hanging branch irresistible and threw myself at it. I had swung from it for only a few seconds when I felt the branch give way with a slow-motion craaaack. I quickly let go, but it was too late. The sad-looking branch, about as long as me, lay slain at my feet. As I pondered what to do with it, a loud bell announced that lunch was over. I picked up the branch, tossed it over the wall into an empty field, and went back to class.

Fifteen minutes later, an announcement came over the intercom.

"Kamal Gupta to the principal's office!"

It was the first time I had heard my name on the school-wide public address system and my chest puffed out with pride. Word had finally reached Mrs. Kumar about my excellent academic performance and she was no doubt going to give me a pat on the back. I practically ran down the two flights of stairs to her office on the second floor.

I knocked on her door.

"Enter," said the principal, in a loud booming voice.

"Are you Kamal?" Mrs. Kumar said. She didn't know me by sight as I was somewhat new to the school. Most of the hundred-or-so kids in my grade had entered the school in kindergarten and thus were well known to her. I, on the other hand, had started at the school only the year before, the result of my father's job transfer from a remote corner of India to Delhi.

The principal was unknown to me as well. It was the first time that I had seen her up close and the resemblance to India's prime minister was striking. Mrs. Kumar looked like a Caucasian version of Indira Gandhi, who was in the midst of ruling India with an iron fist herself.

"Yes, I'm Kamal," I said cheerfully.

"Did you break a branch at lunch?" she asked.

"I did," I replied without any hesitation. It was only then that I noticed the angry look on her face.

"Why did you do it?" she asked me, her voice rising.

"I didn't mean to. I was just fooling around and it snapped."

And then I made the mistake of uttering the four words that she did not want to hear.

"It's no big deal." I shrugged.

"You don't get to decide what is a big deal and what is not! You don't run this school, I do!" Mrs. Kumar shouted. At this point, I wasn't sure what had made her more upset, the broken branch or my flippant attitude towards the whole affair.

"Go to the library and sit on the floor by the front desk," Mrs. Kumar commanded me.

"For how long, ma'am?"

"The whole day!" she snapped.

Now I was worried. This was a serious punishment and one that I felt was not commensurate with my infraction. The library was located in the center of the building and the front desk was clearly visible from the hallway. Hundreds of students would pass by in the next three hours. They would see me sitting cross-legged on the floor, without a book in my hand, and assume the worst. Had I gotten in a fight, stolen something, or done something equally bad? Certainly no one would think my crime was as trivial as breaking a branch. Mrs. Kumar could have allowed me to sit on a chair and read, but it was clear she was after some form of public humiliation.

Before I went to the library, I sought more clarification from the raging principal. I couldn't imagine that missing one afternoon's worth of classes would be the end of my punishment. What about the next day?

"Ma'am, am I being suspended from school?" I asked.

That all but sealed my fate. If she wasn't going to suspend me before, she was certainly going to do so now.

"Yes, you are!" Mrs. Kumar shouted.

"For how many days, ma'am?"

That pushed her over the edge. I was only trying to understand the fine print of my punishment, but Mrs. Kumar saw my questions as continued proof of my insolence.

"Shut up and get out!"

I stopped talking and went to the library.

It was a humiliating afternoon. I felt the scornful eyes of hundreds upon me. The librarian felt sorry for me, but Mrs. Kumar's strict instructions forbade him from handing me a book or letting me sit on a chair. That afternoon felt as if it lasted a lifetime. As it wore on, I found myself getting angrier and angrier.

By the time I reached home that evening, Mrs. Kumar had had a peon deliver a note to my house.

Come see me tomorrow, it said.

When I described my offense, my parents laughed it off.

"Don't worry about it. I'll go see her tomorrow," my father said.

The next morning, he accompanied me to school. Since I was under a suspension, I waited outside the front gate while my father went inside to meet the iron lady. He came out fifteen minutes later and said, "Everything is fine. Go back to class."

I was nonplussed. The principal had clearly told me that I was to be suspended. What had changed?

What had changed was that Mrs. Kumar had asked her secretary to pull out my report card. No doubt she was looking for additional proof of my being a bad seed, hoping to use that information during the meeting with my parents. Instead, she discovered that not only had I never been in trouble before, but I was also ranked at the top of my class. She would look pretty foolish saying "Your son is an excellent student, but he broke a branch. So we have to punish him with a week's suspension."

Instead, Mrs. Kumar did what people in positions of power often do when they realize that they have made a mistake. She brushed the whole matter under the rug and told my father that everything was fine.

Everything wasn't fine. Not as far as I was concerned. It was all so terribly unfair. Why did something so insignificant even percolate up to the principal's office? The branch was small and its removal posed no danger to the health of the massive tree. I understood that my unrepentant attitude had contributed to my punishment, but it should never have come to that in the first place. And the public shaming was too much for this thirteen-year-old to bear.

"I'm not going," I said.

"Huh?"

"This school doesn't deserve me. I want to go somewhere else."

It took my father fifteen minutes to talk sense into me, and to explain how difficult it was to get admitted to a good school in Delhi. Instead of being allowed to leave Springdales, I was left with a simmering resentment that periodically bubbled to the surface.

After the branch incident, I became extra suspicious of the school's management. It didn't help that, at times, I felt that the establishment went the extra mile to tilt the playing field against me, thereby destroying whatever little faith I had left.

One such event, which occurred a few years later, involved a math test. Although it had always been my favorite subject, I was the math teacher's least favorite student. She had once thrown me out of class for having the temerity to propose a "better" solution to a problem than the one she had written on the blackboard.

"You clearly know more than me, so you don't need to come to my class," she had said sarcastically, leaving me confused. I truly believed that my solution was more elegant and if I couldn't say so in math class, where could I? Nevertheless, neither one of us had anything to gain from a prolonged confrontation. So we called a truce. I agreed to keep my mouth shut and she allowed me back in her class. The suspension of hostilities lasted until the finals.

The test was particularly difficult and left many of my classmates close to tears. I managed to get a ninety-six, but the next best score was only seventy-eight, earned by a student who was one of Mrs. Kumar's favorites. Class rank was determined by the cumulative score across all subjects, and I was counting on the eighteen-point advantage to maintain my first position overall.

Unfortunately, the math teacher had other ideas. She made an announcement that left me stunned and angry.

"The test was very difficult. We'll assume that the score was out of eighty instead of one hundred, and scale it up."

She was giving every student an artificial twenty-five-percent boost, turning my classmate's seventy-eight into a ninety-eight. I had never seen anything like this done before at Springdales. Nor would it be done again during my time at the school.

I was about to protest, but before I could say anything, she quickly added, "Kamal, you'll get a hundred." Incredibly, she thought that this would satisfy me.

Not only did it not satisfy me, it left me deeply unhappy. My eighteen-point advantage in math had been reduced to two. As far as I was concerned, if everyone else was getting their score grossed up by twenty-five percent, so should I.

Later that day, I marched into her office and laid out my demands.

"The fair thing to do is to make my score 120."

"Kamal, don't be ridiculous. The score cannot be above 100," she replied.

"Ma'am, if everyone is getting a twenty-five-percent increase, then so should I. The school owes me another twenty points. Otherwise it's not fair."

"Kamal, you should learn to be more magnanimous," she said.

As a sixteen-year-old, I had never heard the word *magnanimous* before, and had no idea what it meant. Rather than ask her for an explanation, I pointed out that this was the first time that any teacher at Springdales had done anything like this. The previous year, despite the highest score in his class being a lowly seventy, the physics teacher had left the marks untouched. Also, I found it especially unfair that this "curving" was being done only in math and not in any other subject.

The math teacher was starting to get frustrated with me, and not for the first time either.

"Well, Kamal, what do you propose we do about it?"

She had posed the question rhetorically, but I had come prepared with an answer.

"My score in English is less than eighty. Why don't we add the twenty points there? That way we won't breach a hundred anywhere."

The math teacher was incredulous.

"Are you insane? We can't take points from math and add them to English."

"In that case, ma'am, why don't we just leave things the way they were?" I said quietly. "I'm fine with that."

My attempt at a negotiation failed. No matter how hard I tried, the math teacher refused to budge. A part of me wondered if it was a conspiracy. Perhaps the school wanted to give a boost to the number-two student to knock me off my perch. No matter their motive, I found the situation deeply unjust. I felt strongly that the math teacher, having set the test herself, should accept responsibility for the results.

Despite the school's best efforts to rig the game, I managed to retain the top rank that year. My math teacher, however, couldn't resist taking a parting shot on my annual report card. Instead of complimenting me on the 100, she wrote something along the lines of "Kamal's attitude to his environment needs to change. He needs to develop a fuller personality." Far from being magnanimous herself, she had chosen to take a cheap shot in a forum where I couldn't fight back.

By the time I had reached the eleventh grade, I was firmly on the outs with the school. A series of skirmishes, starting with the broken branch, had led to my feeling like an outcast. Most teachers, even the ones I got along with, kept their distance from me as did many of my classmates. It was an early lesson in how expensive it can be to go against the establishment. I couldn't wait to get away from Springdales School.

A way out presented itself at the end of the year in the form of one of the hardest tests in all of India, the Joint Entrance Examination (JEE). The JEE was the sole requirement for entering one of the five elite engineering institutions in the country, the Indian Institutes of Technology (IIT). Most students taking the JEE in 1980 had completed twelfth grade; but that year, due to changes in India's educational system, students could choose to take the test after eleventh grade. The IITs didn't care if you had graduated from high school. If you did well on their test, they took you in. The odds, however, were steep. With tens of thousands vying for 1,250 spots, the admission rate was around two percent. In contrast, Harvard University had an acceptance rate of almost twenty percent that year.

Most students spent two years studying for the JEE, but I had been more focused on maintaining my class rank and had chosen to wait until after my finals. That left me with only three weeks to prepare. A cottage industry of coaching classes had sprung up to help students get ready for the test. After tallying my score on a sample test, a coaching center had even offered me tuition-free instruction. I turned them down. I had no desire to see my face plastered on billboards (as one of their success stories) if I managed to get through. The only concession I made was to borrow notes from a friend who had been diligently attending prep classes for the past year. The material was massive, and I quickly realized that the time I had left myself would not be nearly enough.

The two-day JEE consisted of four three-hour sections — English, physics, chemistry, and math. The English section required only a passing score, which wasn't a problem. Math was also not an issue, as it had always come easily to me. I was on shakier ground in chemistry and spent a great deal of time studying it. By the time I got around to the final two physics sections — electricity and magnetism, and sound and light — I realized that I was going to run out of time.

Knowing this, I took the biggest gamble of my young life and decided to skip electricity and magnetism altogether. While risky, the strategy wasn't as crazy as it appeared. The JEE tests were large and unwieldy, with most students being unable to finish. Rather than letting the physics test dictate which questions would go unanswered, I decided beforehand that it would be the ones on electricity and magnetism.

My classmate Sanjiv, who lived down the street from my house in the middle-class neighborhood of New Rajendra Nagar and whose notes I had borrowed, was floored.

"You're not going to study electricity and magnetism at all?"

"That's right," I replied.

"What if there are a lot of questions on those topics?"

"That's a risk that I'm going to have to take," I said.

I didn't have the heart to tell him that, to a smaller extent, I had deployed the same strategy in math and chemistry. I had focused on my strengths and ignored the areas where I was weak. Sanjiv, on the other hand, had diligently studied everything under the sun. The idea of skipping entire sections had never occurred to him, or to anyone else that I knew. For me, there was no other alternative. The problems in the JEE were known to be exceedingly tricky and required a deep understanding of the subject matter. I was much better off knowing part of the material really well than skimming the surface of every topic.

My bet paid off. The physics test that year was heavily weighted in favor of sound and light. There were only a handful of questions on electricity and magnetism, all of which I left untouched.

The following day, I ran into several twelfth graders at my high school who were discussing the test. I was surprised to hear that their solutions to many of the problems were substantially different from mine. When I offered my two cents' worth, they became annoyed. How dare this eleventh grader tell them that they were wrong? After a while, I gave up and stopped arguing.

One month later, the JEE results were posted on a bulletin board inside the IIT Delhi campus. My father sent an assistant to look them up. It took him a while, but he found my name and rank.

Kamal Gupta 109

Not only had I gotten in, but my rank would allow me to attend IIT Delhi and choose my field of study. Most importantly, I could bypass twelfth grade altogether and escape from Springdales. Two twelfth graders from my school were also admitted but with ranks considerably lower than mine. Sanjiv did not make it, either that year or the next.

My approach to the JEE — taking a calculated risk while spurning conventional wisdom — would become a recurrent theme in my life. In addition to allowing me to enter IIT one year early, it would also enable me to complete a master's degree in record time. If not for my penchant for placing bets when the odds favored me, I would not have become a professional blackjack player. Nor would I have ended up on Wall Street, where, at least for the moment, I was in the middle of a losing streak.

CHAPTER 12

IIT Delhi

───────

I was filled with anxiety when I first arrived at the sprawling IIT campus in south Delhi. Most of my classmates had completed twelfth grade and graduated from high school, giving them a one-year advantage over me. On my first day of class, one even bragged that he had already completed two years of college math, which made him three years ahead of me. It turned out to be an idle boast but, at the time, it made me feel even more uneasy.

One of the most astonishing things about the IITs was their low fees. Full tuition at India's top engineering school cost only fifty dollars a year, an amount that even my parents could afford. Room and board were an extra twenty dollars a month, but having earned a scholarship at the end of my tenth grade, I had that covered. In contrast, Harvard's tuition in 1980 was $6,500 a year.

Despite charging meager fees, IIT Delhi not only provided a world-class education, it also had world-class facilities. International Computers Limited, a British computer manufacturer, had donated a state-of-the-art computer system and Prince Charles delivered a speech at its inauguration. More than two decades earlier, in 1959, his father, Prince Philip, had laid the foundation stone of the institute.

After my fitful start, I settled in for the long haul. The school atmosphere was intensely competitive with most students having finished at the top of their class. I managed to hold my own, earned a decent GPA, and even made a friend.

Jaspal, a tall and athletic member of the Sikh community possessing a quiet disposition and a dry sense of humor, became my closest friend. Every morning, in the hallway outside our rooms, I helped him fold a twelve-foot-by-three-foot cloth that he would then tie into a tight turban around his head. His faith prohibited him from cutting any of his hair, and every so often, I watched with great amusement how he kept his moustache in line: he chewed the ends off. Although he had entered college with a scraggly beard, he left with a full flowing one.

The two of us soon discovered billiards and snooker. The billiards room at IIT Delhi consisted of three tables, each twelve feet long and six feet wide. This was my first opportunity to play the games that had long been the preserve of the upper classes in India. I liked that when it's your turn in billiards, your opponent must sit on the sidelines and wait for you to miss. The game comes down to you, a five-foot-long cue, and the physics of balls rolling and colliding on the green felt.

With every passing month, we found ourselves spending more and more time in the billiards room. By the time we graduated, Jaspal excelled at English billiards, played with just three balls, whereas I preferred the chaos of snooker's twenty-two multicolored balls. At the time, neither one of us realized that we had gained a skill that would prove immensely useful in America.

Right next to the billiards room, surrounded by a high stone wall, was the campus swimming pool. The shimmering water provided an escape from Delhi's intense heat and I couldn't wait to jump in. But I had never been in a swimming pool before and, more importantly, I didn't know how to swim. At Springdales there was a swim club, but it met at a municipal pool a few miles away and I had never participated.

When a fellow classmate, who happened to be a member of the IIT swim team, offered to be my instructor, I jumped at the opportunity. I imagined that, in no time, I would be gliding effortlessly through the water, just like Mark Spitz.

Reality turned out to be something else entirely. When it came down to it, I couldn't even tread water. Worse still, I couldn't figure out how to float on my back. Without those basic skills, there was no hope of my learning to swim. My tutor tried everything, but failed. After a few frustrating weeks, he gave up, saying, "You'll never learn how to swim."

That was all the encouragement I needed. I didn't care how, but I was going to learn. I went to the pool daily and tried to mimic the actions of freestyle and breaststroke swimmers. I soon realized that I would never be able to learn to swim that way, let alone coordinate my breathing. Instead, I set a narrow objective for myself: just learn to float on my back. What seemed simple in theory — my nose would stay out of the water for easy breathing — proved difficult in practice. My stomach buckled and I would go under, causing water to go up my nostrils. It was an uncomfortable sensation, but I kept at it and, after several weeks of trying, I got it. Once I was able to float, learning backstroke was easy. I only had to swing my arms like the oars of a rowboat. I was filled with pride when I finally managed to swim to the deep end and back.

World-class facilities notwithstanding, the food at IIT was decidedly third rate. The dining hall where we gathered for all our meals was fittingly called the mess. Disinterested cooks served mushy, flavorless vegetables with bulletproof naans that were meant for playing frisbee, not eating. Thankfully, there was a small open-air café in the center of the campus that served halfway decent aloo parathas. It stayed open late into the night and we would often sit around and watch jumbo 747s fly low over our heads as they landed at the nearby Delhi airport. Years later, inside one of those jumbo 747s on my way back from America, I would make it a point to pick out the IIT landmarks from the air.

As it had been at Springdales School, the defining event of my IIT years was also a conflict. This time, though, my dispute was not with the establishment, but with my fellow classmates. Still, it was rooted in an injustice, a wrong that I felt compelled to right.

The clash had its origins in a midterm test where the professor, after handing out the questions, had left the examination hall. While this was not the first time that the class had been left unsupervised, it was the first time that I observed outright cheating. I saw one student pass his answer sheet to another, who then passed it on to yet another. When the answer sheet made its way back to the source, I was shocked to see that it was one of the smartest students in my class. He had quickly solved the problems and handed the solutions over, guaranteeing his co-conspirators a perfect score.

When I noticed the same thing happen during the next test, I decided to confront the head of the hydra.

"Why are you letting these guys copy from you?" I asked him in the hallway.

"Fuck off."

He couldn't deny what he had done. I had seen it with my own eyes, not once but twice. His hostility was understandable: no one likes to be confronted about their wrongdoing. It was his motives that I didn't understand. He was brilliant and guaranteed to get an A himself, so why was he doing this?

The answer to that question lay with the rest of the group. They were the so-called cool kids of the class, to the extent that there were any cool kids at an IIT. The place was a nerd haven. The smart guy's willingness to boost their score made him an integral part of the pack.

The cool kids were alarmed to learn of my attempt to kill their golden goose.

"This is none of your business," they said, accosting me.

"Of course it's my business," I replied. "You guys are cheating in my class, right in front of me, and affecting my grades." The competition at IIT was fierce. With only a limited number of As given out in every class, there was a distinct possibility that the gang's activities would hurt my GPA or someone else's.

"Fuck off!"

The fuck off was just bluster, further proof they had no arguments to support their position.

The impact of the cheating became clear when the semester grades were posted. There was an A next to my name but Jaspal, who should have earned an A, only received a B. Several undeserving members of the gang received As when they probably should have gotten Cs.

During the semester break, as I thought about this further, I was greatly bothered by the unfairness of it all. When their antics continued into the next semester, once right under the nose of a professor who had dozed off, I'd had enough.

I confronted the gang once again. "You need to stop this nonsense. I'm warning you!"

They burst out laughing. "What can you do?"

"You'll see," I said quietly.

My efforts to rally the other forty-or-so students in the class failed. No one wanted to get involved. It was an early lesson in just how far people are willing to go to avoid conflict and to fight for what is right. Regardless, I was determined to put an end to this wrongdoing.

After thinking long and hard about the problem, I went to see the professor.

"There's rampant cheating on your tests," I said.

"Really?" The professor had no idea about what was going on.

"Yes," I said, "I've seen it with my own eyes."

"Who is it?" he asked.

"I'm not going to give you any names."

"Well then, what do you propose I do about it?"

"There's a simple way to prevent it," I said. I had come prepared with a solution, as always.

"What do you suggest?"

"Make everyone sit alphabetically during the exam," I said.

The cheating was made possible by the professor's allowing everyone to choose their own seats. The group would arrive early and sit in a formation with the smart guy in the center. Dispersing the gang throughout the room would make it impossible for them to pass answer sheets around.

At the start of the next test, the professor made an announcement.

"Everyone, take your seats according to your ID numbers."

He had done exactly what I had asked. Our ID numbers were alphabetically assigned. The cool kids looked mortified. I suspected that some of them hadn't even bothered to study for the test.

Over the next several days, the gang trained their anger upon me. Their threats of retaliation were intimidating, but ultimately proved hollow. I found it astonishing that some of the smartest young men in India were demanding that they be allowed to cheat on tests, as if it were a civil right. It didn't help that I had proudly owned up to what I had done.

"I told you I was going to do something about it. Just be glad I didn't rat you out."

A few days later, someone did rat them out. It wasn't me, but everyone assumed that it was. My defense — the problem is solved, why would I rat you out now? — fell on deaf ears. After a while, I stopped fighting the accusation and accepted my fate as an outcast. I had never been all that popular to begin with and this episode all but turned me into a pariah. Not one of my classmates came to my defense. Barely twenty years of age, I was convinced that the world was an unfair place and that fighting against that unfairness carried a price.

That price, however, is one that I have been prepared to pay throughout my life. For me, the price of not fighting against it is even higher.

CHAPTER 13
The 1984 Riots

Without a doubt, the most shocking events that I have ever witnessed in my life occurred during my final year at IIT Delhi. The mind-boggling scenes of violence and destruction left an indelible mark on my psyche and shattered whatever little faith I had left in authority.

On the morning of October 31, 1984, Mrs. Indira Gandhi, the prime minister of India, was shot by her two Sikh bodyguards at her central Delhi compound. Her death led to two days of savagery against India's Sikh community that left thousands dead and tens of thousands homeless.

Although she had enjoyed widespread support among India's electorate, Mrs. Gandhi had autocratic tendencies. In 1975, she had declared a state of "emergency" that allowed her to rule by decree. Making full use of her newfound powers, she had curbed civil liberties, censored the press, postponed elections, and imprisoned her political opponents. A program of population control went horribly wrong and led to countless forced sterilizations, especially among the poor.

Mrs. Gandhi allowed free and fair elections in 1977, only to suffer a humiliating defeat. The opposition parties, despite winning almost two-thirds of the seats in the Indian Parliament, made a mess of their time in office, allowing Mrs. Gandhi to sweep back into power three years later. She was prime minister once again.

During the early eighties, there was a demand for greater autonomy in the Sikh-majority state of Punjab in northern India, with some even seeking the creation of a new Sikh nation. In June 1984, Mrs. Gandhi ordered the Indian army to launch a full-scale attack on the Golden Temple in the city of Amritsar, supposedly to flush out the militants who had taken refuge in the complex. The resulting damage to their holiest site caused great distress in the Sikh community and led to Mrs. Gandhi's assassination.

It was around noon on Sunday, October 31, when we first heard that something was amiss. India's state-controlled radio and television had announced that Mrs. Gandhi had been taken to AIIMS, Delhi's premiere hospital. There was no mention of an assassination attempt.

AIIMS was located three miles from IIT Delhi and I had visited Dheerendra there frequently. He was in his penultimate year of medical school, and I much preferred the food in his dorms to my own.

I made a spur-of-the-moment decision to go to the hospital and see for myself what was going on. AIIMS was only a fifteen-minute drive away, and I had my parents' car with me. Although they had made it clear that the antiquated Ambassador automobile was meant strictly for campus use, I figured that the circumstances warranted an exception. When my class-mates heard that I was driving to AIIMS, cries of "me too" rang out and seven or eight of us squeezed into that small car.

I drove extra carefully, first taking Outer Ring Road from the IIT campus and then turning left onto south Delhi's major artery, Aurobindo Marg. The streets were calm, and everything appeared to be in order. As we got closer to AIIMS, however, we saw that a large crowd had gathered. The masses were chanting "Indira-mata." Indira, our mother.

I parked the car a safe distance away and headed to the hospital on foot. My classmates were uneasy but followed me regardless. The heavy security at the front gate made passage impossible, but I knew of several back entrances to the hospital. One of those smaller gates had been left unguarded, and we used it to slip in unnoticed. Entering the main hospital was out of the question. Fifty to a hundred armed guards stood outside. I did manage to get the attention of a nurse who was rushing past us. The small gold cross dangling outside her white uniform and her accent made it clear that, like many nurses in Delhi's hospitals, she was from Goa. When I asked her what was going on, she paused for a second.

"It's bad, very bad," she said.

"Mrs. Gandhi?" I asked her.

"Yes."

"You saw her?"

"Yes," she said for the last time and ran off.

It was around twelve-thirty p.m. and Mrs. Gandhi had been at the hospital for three hours. Even though the official time of her death was recorded as two-twenty p.m., there was little doubt in my mind about what the nurse had implied. We would find out later that thirty-three bullets had been fired at Mrs. Gandhi. Thirty bullets had found their mark and twenty-three of those had passed right through her body. It was unlikely that she had even made it to the hospital alive.

We left the hospital and headed for my car. The crowd outside had grown twice as large and four times as loud. *Indira-mata! Indira-mata! Indira-mata!* Perhaps they had sensed what was soon to become public knowledge. The mood in the car was somber as I drove back. No one said a word.

That evening, after India's state-run TV had announced her death, there were reports of sporadic acts of violence across the city, but things appeared to be under control.

The next day, Delhi descended into madness.

November 1 was a Monday, but our classes had been canceled. We sat glued to the small television in the hostel's common room when we heard loud noises from the street just outside the campus. Our hostel was situated at the edge of the IIT campus with only a modest wall separating it from the main thoroughfare, the Outer Ring Road.

The scene outside was straight out of a horror movie. A crowd, about a hundred strong, had positioned themselves in the middle of the road and had stopped all traffic. They were hunting for Sikhs. Sikh men were easily identified by their turban and beard, and the mob set upon each and every one. They dragged the men, young and old alike, from the buses and yanked off their turbans. The emotional pain of losing a symbol of their faith was soon replaced by intense physical suffering as the beatings commenced. The crowd showed no mercy to any Sikh.

We called the police many times, but no one came. A band of cops finally showed up in their trademark blue jeep, surveyed the scene for a couple of minutes, and deemed everything to be in order. The crowd had momentarily gone quiet only to start up again as soon as the cops had left.

We couldn't watch this in silence, and while geeks are generally a timid lot, a group of us rushed to the street and grabbed as many Sikh men as we could and brought them inside our hostel to safety. For some reason, perhaps because of the revered position that IIT held in the city, the crowd didn't dare follow us inside. Their fight wasn't with us and, moreover, there were half a million Sikhs in Delhi. Plenty more for them to hunt.

The carnage continued all day. After the first killing of a Sikh man in East Delhi that morning, thousands more would be slaughtered over the next forty-eight hours. An uncle of mine was on his way to Delhi when a swarm of villagers stopped his train, pulled Sikh men from its carriages, and lynched them right in front of his eyes. The crowd's preferred method was to place a used tire around the frightened man's neck and set it on fire. Cheap, effective, and utterly terrifying.

The group of Sikhs sheltering inside our hostel were scared out of their minds. With tears streaming down their face, many asked us to cut off their hair so they couldn't be marked so easily. Some of my hostel mates used blunt paper scissors to accomplish the task. A few of the Sikhs ventured outside and went home — I have no idea what became of them — but several stayed the night.

Then there was Jaspal, my best friend. Not particularly talkative under the best of circumstances, he had gone completely silent. He had tried to reach his family all day with no success and was terribly worried about their safety.

It wouldn't have mattered to the crowds that Jaspal's father was a highly placed official in the Indian government. At his sister's wedding the year before, I had been astonished to see the president of India — Giani Zail Singh, a Sikh himself — walk right in front of me and congratulate the couple. The presidential palace was located in the center of Delhi and President Singh, ensconced in the Rashtrapati Bhavan, had to have known that his people were getting slaughtered.

"KG man, I need to find a phone," Jaspal said, his voice heavy with sadness. "I have to get in touch with my parents."

In 1984, the only means of communicating across the city was a landline telephone. Our hostel payphone, which barely functioned under the best of circumstances, had stopped working altogether.

Jaspal couldn't exactly walk out into the open and look for a phone. He also couldn't go home. On November 1, 1984, it would've been easier for a Sikh man in Delhi to travel to the moon than to cover the ten miles from IIT to his parents' house in central Delhi.

There was only one solution. I would have to drive him to the home of one of my father's childhood friends, which was located near our campus. That, however, would require us to leave the safety of IIT and venture outside, where mobs were running wild.

"Jaspal, we have to wait until it gets dark," I said.

"Okay," he replied quietly.

Under the cover of darkness, Jaspal crouched under the back seat of my car. I covered him with a dark-colored sheet and set off. I was counting on getting a pass from the crowds because I was obviously not a Sikh. The drive wasn't long, only ten to fifteen minutes, but if any of the wandering throngs had looked into my car, we would both have been in serious trouble. He for being a Sikh and I for being a collaborator. Heaven forbid the car should break down. I took the long way, staying inside the campus for as long as possible and turning on to the Outer Ring Road only at the last minute. The drive was extremely tense. I had my windows rolled up and continuously whispered to Jaspal where we were. I couldn't even begin to imagine the terror that he must've felt.

We made it to our destination and Jaspal finally had access to a phone. He made several calls and managed to locate his family at their friend's place. No doubt they were immensely relieved to hear his voice as well. We left shortly thereafter because I didn't consider the neighborhood safe, nor did I want his presence to endanger everyone else in that house. I drove back, with him once more under the sheet in the back seat of my car, breathing a sigh of relief upon entering the campus.

After I had deposited Jaspal safely back at the hostel, a group of us decided to go to the top of the IIT main building, a mile away. At ten stories high, it was the tallest structure around and the roof provided a panoramic view of the city. The roof was off limits to students but if there was ever a time to violate that rule, this was it. We took the elevator to the top floor, climbed two flights of stairs, and pushed open a creaky metal door to enter the vast open space at the top of the building.

All around us, near and far, flames shot up into the night sky. Sikh temples, also known as gurudwaras, were an easy target for the hundreds of gangs that had fanned out across Delhi. The sad part was that gurudwaras were open to people of all faiths and offered everyone a free meal. Under normal circumstances, the murderers would have been welcomed into the temples with open arms.

After torching Sikh places of worship, the perpetrators targeted Sikh-owned businesses along with their homes, setting entire neighborhoods on fire. Thousands of Sikhs were killed during that two-day period, and tens of thousands were displaced. Delhi was burning and the police were nowhere to be seen. We made the walk back to our hostel with heavy hearts.

The next morning, I was determined to see the carnage for myself and not rely on the heavily censored state television. No one else from the hostel was willing to join me so I went alone. This time, I left the car behind and ventured out on foot, walking north for a mile to the affluent neighborhood of Safdarjung Enclave. I felt safe despite the large-scale violence. No one was looking for me.

I passed packs of young men armed with iron rods, bamboo sticks, knives, machetes, and gasoline. As one of them walked past me, I just had to ask him.

"Kyoon?" Why?

"Unhone hamari mata ko maara. Hum unhe maarenge," he replied. They killed our mother, we'll kill them.

It was only then that I got a good look at the youth, about the same age as me. His bloodlust was matched by his bloodshot eyes, and his breath reeked of alcohol. Someone had not only fed him nonsense about Indira Gandhi being his mother-figure, they had also plied him with liquor. The true architects of the mayhem stayed in the shadows and had sent young men like him to do their dirty work for them.

I didn't say another word to him. Arguing with a drunk man holding a machete is never a good idea.

From the wide open main roads, I plunged into the narrow side streets of Safdarjung Enclave and saw a house on fire. It was a shocking sight, one that I hope never to see again. The white house was large, with a driveway on one side, and elaborate balconies on each of its three floors. The cars had burnt out already but the house was a raging inferno with flames darting out of every window. It looked so much like a scene from a disaster movie that I had a hard time believing it was real. I heard that the head of the household had owned a pistol and that he had tried to defend himself and his family. I shuddered to think what might have happened to them after he had exhausted his supply of bullets.

I stood in front of that house for what felt like a long time. I couldn't believe what had happened to India's capital city, the seat of its supposedly secular government. The assassinated prime minister's eldest son and heir apparent, Rajiv Gandhi, had been quickly sworn in as her successor, but there were no appeals for calm from him either. In fact, at an election rally just five days later, he appeared to justify the violence, saying, "When a big tree falls, the earth shakes." His mother was the big tree and India's Sikh community had been shaken to its core.

The next day, November 3, the army was deployed to restore order to the city. Military command decided to make IIT Delhi their temporary base, and for a few weeks, my engineering school was turned into a cantonment. Calm returned to the city in short order, albeit entirely too late for the victims. The ease with which the military was able to quell the violence led to an obvious question. Why had the government of India waited two full days before taking action?

After graduating from IIT, Jaspal and I both came to America. His older brother and sister were already here and, as soon as it was feasible, his parents also migrated to the U.S. The entire family left India for good.

Jaspal and I have stayed friends to this day, and yet we have never spoken about the events of those days.

CHAPTER 14

A Bee in the Oven

B y the time I had graduated from IIT Delhi, two things had become
abundantly clear. I wanted nothing more to do with electrical engineering and I wanted to leave India. The natural place to go was America,
the land of the free and the home of the brave. Seen through the lens of
movies and television shows, America seemed like a mythical place where
anything was possible. At least in my case, that reputation has turned out
to be richly deserved.

The grueling five-year IIT undergraduate program had left me exhausted,
and if it were up to me, I would never have attended another lecture or
taken one more final exam. However, the only path to America open to
me was via graduate school. So I took the GREs and applied to ten univer-
sities for a master's in computer science, a natural offshoot of electrical
engineering. Several offered me admission, and I chose the University of
Wisconsin in Madison because of its excellent reputation in the field. It
helped that the university had offered me free tuition as well as a monthly
stipend that would cover my living expenses. For the price of a one-way
ticket, I could leave both electrical engineering and India behind.

I landed in New York on August 15, 1985, which coincidentally was
also India's independence day. Despite arriving on these shores with only

five hundred dollars in my pocket, I was filled with anticipation. America had that effect.

My optimism notwithstanding, I was still concerned about how I would adapt to a new country, let alone tackle a new field of study. The Wisconsin weather was another source of worry. Winter temperatures in Delhi bottomed out at forty degrees Fahrenheit, whereas in Madison they reportedly went down to below zero, and even lower when something called "wind chill" was taken into account. Nevertheless, the die had been cast and I would have to deal with the consequences.

Jaspal had also received the same offer from the University of Wisconsin, and it was natural that we should become roommates. We rented a furnished one-bedroom apartment that was a ten-minute walk from the computer science department, splitting the $330 monthly rent down the middle. After winning a coin toss, I moved into the bedroom while Jaspal settled into the living room.

Unlike most of my IIT classmates, I hadn't come to America to spend five years on a doctorate or, if I could help it, even two years on a master's. Consequently, the first thing I did was to go through the computer science department's catalogue to figure out the quickest path to a master's degree. The document listed myriad ways a student could earn the diploma, some that required a thesis and a few that did not. After examining the various options, I was excited to discover a lightning-fast route that would allow me to complete the program in under a year, instead of the usual one-and-a-half to two years. That path would require me to complete eight of the toughest courses offered by the department, a daunting task given my limited background in computers. Jaspal thought the gamble was too risky so I went at it alone. I carefully planned the eleven-month roadmap to my degree — three high-level courses in each of the first two semesters followed by two more during the summer — and signed up for only advanced classes in my first semester.

The first few days of school proved challenging, and I felt lost in the advanced computer architecture class. A homework assignment handed out by the professor, *List the system requirements for a graphics workstation*, went completely over my head. What the hell was a graphics workstation anyway? It would have been safer for me to have taken the basic computer architecture course first, but that would have made a quick graduation impossible.

In addition to the challenges at school, we also had to figure out how to feed ourselves. The food at IIT had been awful but at least it was there. The task was made even more challenging by my being a vegetarian. During the 1980s, grocery stores and restaurants in America's Dairyland weren't very hospitable towards an Indian who didn't eat meat or cheese. Although I had been forced into it, I grew to enjoy cooking, an activity that had been off-limits to boys in India.

Laundry was another struggle. Putting quarters in the broken-down washers and dryers in the basement of our building felt like a game of roulette. If the ball landed on red, the clothes would come out clean. Otherwise the coins would disappear down a black hole.

At times, even sleep wasn't stress free. Late one night, a few days after moving into our apartment, I was jolted awake by a loud buzzing sound. I stumbled into the living room to find Jaspal sitting upright in his bed.

"What the hell is that noise?" I asked.

"No idea," he said.

"It's coming from near the front door."

Jaspal nodded in agreement.

In my addled state, I could only come up with one explanation for the infernal racket. "I think it's a bee."

"No way," he said.

"Nothing else buzzes like this. It has to be a bee," I insisted.

"But it's so loud."

"It's loud because it's trapped in the oven," I said. The oven was right by the door. Mystery solved.

Since he couldn't come up with a better idea of his own, Jaspal went along with mine.

"Go open the oven door and let it out," I said.

"No way! I'm not doing it." He wasn't going anywhere near a bee that was obviously very large and clearly very angry.

"C'mon, man," I implored.

"Nope."

"Fine, I guess I'll have to do it."

I tiptoed towards the kitchen, not wanting to make the bee any angrier than it already was. With one hand, I yanked the oven door open while at the same time using my other hand to fling open the front door. I thought this would provide the bee with an escape route. Having accomplished this dual feat, I rushed back to the other end of the apartment.

There was no bee of course. Had we bothered to examine the situation logically, we would have wondered how the bee got inside a closed oven in the first place. However, at two a.m. in a strange new country, neither one of us was thinking straight.

The buzzing now was twice as loud.

With the front door wide open, it became clear that the noise was coming from the hallway. I shut the oven door and stepped into the corridor, where at long last I discovered the source of the racket. A small red box just below the ceiling.

It was the fire alarm!

Jaspal and I panicked. There was a fire in the building and we were ten floors up. While we had never seen or heard a fire alarm before, we knew that you weren't supposed to use elevators. We grabbed our wallets and practically ran down the stairs, stopping only when we were outside.

The sidewalk was empty. The ten-story building housed at least a hundred residents. Where were the rest of them? We stood there for what felt like an eternity, shivering. In our haste, we had forgotten to pick up our jackets and the forty-degree weather chilled us to the bone. The fire alarm stopped buzzing after a few minutes, but that didn't put an end to our confusion. Should we go inside and risk a fire or stay outside and freeze to death? And where were the fire trucks? After a while, a good Samaritan on the second floor put us out of our misery.

"It was a prank, you fools. Go back inside."

Years later, when I told Kathleen the story, she almost died of laughter.

"A bee in the oven? What were you thinking?"

"Not much, apparently," I said.

A few weeks later, midterms loomed. The computer architecture professor had a reputation for being merciless and my grasp of the material was shaky at best. On the afternoon of the test, I was surprised to see that it consisted of just six questions. And in his generosity, the professor had allowed us to skip one problem of our choice.

As I glanced over the questions, I quickly realized that I didn't know the answer to any of the six problems. I stared at them for several minutes, unable to decide which five to answer. It was disheartening to look around the room and see everyone else scribbling furiously. Hoping for the best, I took a deep breath and attacked the questions one by one. While working on the third problem, I realized that my solution to the first question was incorrect. As I went back and redid the first problem, I was filled with doubt about my solution to the second one. While redoing the second problem, I became certain that I had answered the third question wrong. This nerve-racking process went on for two full hours with every question requiring repeated attempts on my part. Before the test was over, I felt that I had answered fifteen questions, not five. Luckily, I had brought an adequate supply of pencils and erasers.

I had found the midterm to be exhausting and wasn't looking forward to the results. The following week, before giving the tests back to us, the professor summarized the class's performance.

"Two of you scored below fifty, three between fifty and sixty, and six each between sixty and seventy and between seventy and eighty. Only one person was over ninety," he said. That last line irritated me. What kind of a maniac had scored more than ninety on that insanely difficult test?

I winced as the professor handed me my test, convinced that I was one of the two scores below fifty, and was stunned to see a ninety-five on the front page. Somehow, by repeated trial and error, I had arrived at mostly correct answers. I still don't know how I did it, other than refusing to give up.

At the end of my second semester, I was still on track for completing the master's degree in eleven months. I was stymied, however, when it came to the summer session. I was deeply disappointed to discover that a course that I needed to graduate was no longer being offered that semester. Having come this far, I wasn't about to give up and went to see the professor.

"I was counting on taking your course during the summer. That will allow me to graduate in August," I said in her office.

"I understand, Kamal, but you are the only one who signed up for it and I can't hold class for just one student."

There was only one way out of this predicament.

"In that case, how about this? You don't have to teach the class. I'll take it as an independent study and you can test me as you see fit," I suggested.

The professor was reluctant as she had never done this before. At the same time, she couldn't bring herself to refuse what was a reasonable request on my part. As far as I was concerned, I just needed to get through her class and go out into the real world. The grade was not important.

Two months later, I had completed the requirements for my master's degree with an A in the self-study course. The professor, in what turned out to be a pleasant surprise, had given me the same midterm and final that she had used in the previous semester. I had gone over those tests while preparing for my own.

After graduating from University of Wisconsin, I accepted a job offer from Honeywell's System and Research Center in Minneapolis. My salary was an astronomical $37,000 a year, or one million rupees annually, and I felt wealthy beyond my wildest dreams. I bought a brand-new, two-door silver Acura Integra, packed it with all my stuff, and headed out into the real world.

CHAPTER 15

Broken Heart, Broken Hand

As I surveyed the uptown Minneapolis apartment that was to be my home for the next three years, I felt an incredible sense of freedom. I had a new job, a new car, and now, my very own apartment in a new city.

"How much do you want for it?" I asked the rental agent.

"Four hundred and seventy-five dollars a month," she replied.

"I'll take it," I said.

Moving in was a cinch since all my worldly belongings were in the small car downstairs. I spread out a futon in the bedroom, lay down upon it, and gazed at the ceiling, breathing a sigh of relief at finally being able to live life on my own terms. I even felt a strange sense of comfort in not knowing anyone in Minneapolis. This is what I had come to America for, to make a fresh start.

There was just one problem. By the time I had completed my master's degree, I had lost all interest in computers. The Honeywell job was merely a stepping stone to the rest of my life, not a career choice. At twenty-three years of age, I didn't have the foggiest idea what I wanted to do with myself other than not sitting in a cubicle, writing software. Consequently, I would spend the next four years drifting from one distraction to the next, all the while searching for something that I could feel excited about. At work, I kept myself busy with computer games, and at night, I wandered through the bars and nightclubs in Minneapolis, playing pool. I learnt how to sail and bought a sailboat. In my search for an alternate career, I even moonlighted as a waiter at a small café. My first attempt at skiing turned into an unmitigated disaster, causing me to suffer not only a broken hand, but also a broken heart.

I had barely settled into my new apartment when Jaspal called.

"We're coming to Minneapolis on Friday."

"You'll have to bring sleeping bags," I told him. "I don't have any furniture."

"No problem," he replied.

The drive took my friends almost five hours and it was late in the evening by the time they reached my place. We were all tired and went to bed early with the three of them spread out across my living room.

I was fast asleep when Jaspal shook me awake. "KG, I think there's a fire in your building."

"Very funny, Jaspal. I suppose there's a bee in my oven also," I said and tried to go back to sleep.

"I'm not joking," he said, "take a look outside."

From my second-floor balcony, I saw several residents climbing out of their first-floor windows. I couldn't see a fire, but the situation was clearly serious. "We need to go!" I said and opened the door to the hallway after rousing the others. That door must have been unusually sturdy because, while there was no smoke inside my apartment, the corridor was filled with a dense, gray fog that stung our eyes and made it difficult to see anything. I led the way to the stairwell, with the three of them following close behind. Once we were safely outside, I went to look for the source of the fire and found it in the first-floor lobby of the sprawling complex, a safe distance from my apartment. It required several fire trucks and many hours to put out the blaze. We stayed outside till early dawn, shivering in the cool fall air. It was one year to the day since Jaspal and I had waited on the sidewalk in Madison. The one time that we could have used a fire alarm, it didn't go off.

"Great welcome, KG," remarked one of my friends.

Fortunately the fire caused no serious injuries. The lobby of the building, however, was a charred shell. The smell of smoke lingered in the hallways for months, long after the damage had been repaired.

My friends returned to Madison two days later and I went back to my routine at Honeywell. I soon discovered that my indifference to computers was matched by a complete lack of interest in climbing the corporate ladder. It didn't help that I had been paired with an officemate who hated the rigid corporate structure just as much as I did. Steve was a smooth-talking, long-haired Italian American from New Orleans with a sly sense of humor and a rebellious streak. In defiance of Honeywell's conservative culture, where many wore suits to work, he sported an earring.

The two of us spent long hours in the small office, bored out of our minds. That is, until we discovered Mex, a computer game similar to the hugely popular Tetris. The game caught our fancy, and we started a contest to see who could score the highest. We would shut the door to our office, lock ourselves in, and play Mex for a good part of the day. Through sheer practice, we mastered the game and went on to become pros at Tetris over the next twelve months. A couple of years later, on my first day at Oracle, I smashed the company-wide Tetris record to the shock of many.

"You've played this game before!" said the previous record holder.

"Once or twice," I replied dryly.

But Honeywell had not hired us to play video games and our managers expected us to write some software as well. My contribution to the group's project was to develop a module called Dynamic Object Space Management (DOSM). Even though I felt no particular affinity for my design, I was still shocked to learn that a senior member of my group had filed a patent for DOSM under his name. I couldn't have cared less about the recognition, but what this guy had done was blatantly unfair. Never one to shrink from a conflict, I marched into his office and told him as much. He apologized and added my name to the application, albeit in second place. I have no idea whether the patent was ever granted, nor do I care.

The billiards skills I had honed at IIT came in handy after work. Most smoke-filled bars in Minneapolis housed a pool table in the back and as long as you and your partner won, you could keep playing for free. Steve had grown up with a pool table and played a mean game of eight ball.

The two of us drew a lot of stares, and not just for our shooting abilities. Minneapolis in the eighties was overwhelmingly white, and a pool-playing Indian and his long-haired Italian partner were among the rarest of sightings.

The following summer, I tried my hand at sailing and signed up for classes at the nearby Lake Calhoun. As with snooker and billiards, I was fascinated by the physics of the sport. How on Earth did sailboats manage to travel against the wind? Over the next three months, I became a halfway decent sailor and, on a whim, bought a small sailboat at a liquidation store. My little boat and I drew a lot of attention. A lone Indian sailing on a Minneapolis lake was also a rare sight.

Still seeking my true passion, I took up cooking and fantasized about running a restaurant of my own. I was quickly cured of that notion after working for a few weeks at Mother Earth Café, a vegetarian Middle-Eastern restaurant owned by a burly Palestinian named Ahmed. Three times a week, I waited tables for the absurdly low pay of three dollars an hour plus tips. It was hard work but I found a certain satisfaction in making customers happy. My stint as a waiter came to an end when Ahmed found money missing from the cash register. Rather than figure out who had robbed him, he decided to fire the entire staff, including me. By then, I had seen first-hand how grueling the restaurant business was and had abandoned my fantasy.

It was inevitable that, in the long Minneapolis winters, I would try skiing. The first opportunity arose at a company outing to the Afton Alps ski resort, a somewhat ambitious name for a hill that was only three hundred feet high. I had two pursuits planned for that evening: to ask out a co-worker I had developed a crush on and to learn how to ski, in that order.

My first objective crashed and burned as soon as I arrived at the lodge. Mae-Lin had shown up with a boyfriend in tow, crushing my hopes and putting an end to any thoughts of asking her out. Luckily, she had no idea about how I felt and I was able to pretend everything was fine. It didn't help that she and the boyfriend were good skiers and that I was stuck in the lodge. The only way to salvage the evening was to learn to ski. But how?

"Come, I'll show you," said Adel.

I was surprised to learn that Adel, an Egyptian native and a senior member of my group, was an expert skier. I placed myself in his hands and got on the chairlift. Getting off it, however, proved to be a more difficult proposition. Holding two poles in one hand, I clutched Adel's jacket with the other, and gingerly put my skis down on the snow. The lift's momentum pushed me further than I had expected, but I managed to stay upright.

"See, I told you. No problem," said my instructor, beaming.

For the next few minutes, Adel showed me how to wedge my skis in a flat area near the chairlift. Soon, he was satisfied with my progress and said that it was time for us to ski down. That's when I noticed a large blue square next to the slope that he had picked out.

"Adel, this is an intermediate run. I think I should go down a bunny slope first."

"Don't worry, Kamal, you can just wedge your way down," he said.

I should have said no, but in my dejected state, I felt like tempting fate. That was a big mistake. Adel's faith in my ability to snowplow down the hill turned out to be grossly misplaced. I found myself gathering more and more speed and, in no time, I was completely out of control. By the time I got halfway down the slope, I had resigned myself to a spectacular fall. I didn't have to wait long. The skis came off and went flying in one direction, the poles in another, and I rolled down the hill a few times before ending flat on my face.

Adel came rushing down.

"Are you okay, Kamal?"

"I'm not sure," I said, taking stock of my person. As he helped me up, I cried out in pain.

Something appeared to be wrong with my right hand, and I knew that I needed to get to the emergency room right away. I walked down to the lodge and had a friend drive me to the nearest hospital, ten miles away. A quick x-ray revealed what I had suspected. It wasn't just my heart that had been broken that evening, my hand was also fractured in two places.

Back at the lodge, I received a great deal of sympathy from my co-workers, including from Mae-Lin. While I was glad for her attention, I felt that the price had been too steep.

Despite that disastrous trip to Afton Alps, I did manage to accomplish both of my goals for the evening, albeit in reverse order. The season was over by the time my cast came off but I learned to ski the following winter and continued skiing even after moving to San Francisco. Oracle had offered me a job and when Steve suggested that we use my move to California as an excuse for a road trip, I jumped at the opportunity. After the movers had picked up most of my stuff, the two of us got into my Acura and started driving west, making stops at Mount Rushmore, Colorado, the Four Corners, the Grand Canyon, Las Vegas, and Yosemite. One week and three thousand miles later, I arrived in San Francisco. It was August 1989.

Mae-lin broke up with her boyfriend and moved to the Bay Area shortly after I did. Having waited patiently for two years, I took the opportunity to ask her out. Our relationship lasted for a little over a year until it became clear that we were looking for different things in life. She wanted to make a million dollars and I wanted to play blackjack.

CHAPTER 16

Fire in the Sky

I n the fall of 1994, almost two years into my Wall Street career, a narrow escape from an airplane that had caught fire mid-flight forced me to take stock of my life and question my future.

I was flying back from Charlottesville, Virginia, when I noticed that the aircraft had started a rapid descent with LaGuardia Airport still more than thirty minutes away. The plane's steady loss of altitude was disconcerting, as was the worried look on the flight attendant's face. I gasped as yellow oxygen masks dropped from the ceiling and the aircraft went into a nosedive. My fear turned to panic when thick black smoke filled the cabin and passengers began to scream. There was a fire on board and we were still several thousand feet in the air. The only thing visible from my window was an expanse of green rushing towards us at two hundred miles an hour. For the second time in my life, I was forced to wonder if this was it.

Three years earlier, my first brush with death had lasted just seconds. I was driving south along the winding Pacific Coast Highway when I noticed a car speeding towards me in my lane. With no shoulder to speak of and the Pacific Ocean to my right, I made a split-second decision to cross the double yellow lines into his lane only to have the other driver realize his error and head for me once again — this time in his own lane.

A thought flashed through my head: *I'm going to die and everyone will think it was my fault.* In the nick of time, I managed to swing my Acura back into my lane as the other car flew past me at a hundred miles an hour, missing me by inches. I had to pull over at the next turnoff just so I could catch my breath.

Although the situation in the smoke-filled airplane was starting to feel increasingly desperate, I felt a glimmer of hope. I could tell that we were in a steep but controlled descent, and not in a freefall. At the last possible moment, a runway appeared in the distance, but I wasn't sure if the plane would stay in one piece long enough to reach it. The pilots banked the aircraft sharply to the left and landed at an unusually high speed, coming to a screeching halt on the tarmac. The flight attendant leapt from her seat and quickly opened the airplane's door, which produced a set of folding steps. To my great surprise, the pilot and the co-pilot rushed out of the cockpit and scrambled out of the plane before any of the passengers could.

Emergency vehicles surrounded the fifty-seat turboprop as I walked a safe distance away and sat down on the grass, half-expecting the plane to explode. I would find out later that the fire had started in the plane's batteries, which were located right under the pilots' seats. No wonder they had been in such a rush to get out.

A few days earlier, I had flown to Charlottesville to visit Dheerendra. A decade at AIIMS had transformed my high school friend into a neurosurgeon and he had accepted a fellowship at the University of Virginia to work on something known as the gamma knife — a cutting-edge technology for non-invasive brain surgery. He had arranged for me to meet the chairman of his department and America's preeminent neurosurgeon, Dr. John Jane, to discuss the subluxation in my neck. A decade and a half of arthritis had caused my cervical vertebrae to slide forward, fixing my head in a permanent downward-facing position.

Dr. Jane looked at my MRIs and delivered his verdict: "We need to operate on your neck."

Taken aback, I asked him why.

"Look, Kamal, if the bones in your neck keep moving, you run the risk of damaging your spinal cord. We need to fuse the top few vertebrae together to make sure that doesn't occur," Dr. Jane said.

"How will you do that?" I asked.

"With a metal plate."

The idea of a strip of metal being stapled to my spine was terrifying and something I wanted to avoid at all costs.

"Is it possible that my neck is already fused?" I asked the doctor. "I can hardly move it at all."

"That's impossible to know."

"And what if I don't get the surgery done?"

"You are gambling with your life," he said in a serious tone, causing me great distress. This was a decision that I could not take lightly, and I told the doctor that I would need to think about it.

"That's fine but don't take too much time," Dr. Jane said.

As I sat on the grass and watched firefighters wrestle with the still-smoking airplane, there was a lot on my mind.

For starters, Dr. Jane's grim diagnosis had placed me in a damned if I do and damned if I don't situation. The doctor had made it clear that the only reason I didn't have any neurological symptoms was because my spinal canal was unusually wide. The vertebrae in my neck had gotten close to my spinal cord but had not impinged upon it. I was quickly running out of room though, and the smallest of accidents had the potential of severing my spinal cord. At the same time, the thought of undergoing preventive surgery on my neck was frightening in its own right. Over the past fifteen years, despite having been in constant pain, I had managed to navigate life without ever having gotten down on myself. Dr. Jane's prognosis, however, had made it impossible for me to maintain a carefree attitude. I was faced with a difficult decision and had no idea how to go about making it.

Then there was Wall Street. My self-imposed two-year deadline was fast approaching and, at least by conventional measures, my time at Lehman Brothers had been a success. Despite all the abuse that I had suffered, it was widely acknowledged that I had caught on to the business at record speed. My pay had soared to multiples of what it had been at Ingres, and I had been promoted to vice president in just ten months. Despite that, I found it increasingly difficult to get out of bed in the morning and make my way to Lehman's offices. Even the fact that I had recently graduated to trading

CMOs from structuring them had made no difference. I felt as uninspired about my job as I had during my Honeywell days, but with one key difference. Unlike computers, I actually enjoyed working on the puzzle that was the mortgage market. It was the culture of investment banks and their business practices that I had a hard time with. The abusive and rapacious environment of the Lehman trading floor had filled my days with misery and no title or any amount of money was going to change that. I had come to New York to learn how to play a new game, not to become an expert at deceiving gullible clients.

I knew that I needed to put some distance between Wall Street and myself, if for no other reason than to gain some perspective. I decided that I had to leave the business, at least for a few months.

And finally, there was Kathleen. As that smoke-filled airplane hurtled towards the ground, I was filled with sadness at the thought that I might never see her again. I also couldn't help wondering how she would react to the news of the plane crash.

At the time, Kathleen and I had been together for a year and a half even though we were polar opposites in almost every way. I hailed from India whereas she belonged to an Italian American family. I was a strict vegetarian, an idea that was foreign to most Americans in the early nineties. I was brash and obnoxious while she was quiet and shy. She worked on healing patients and I worked in an industry that made people sicker, physically, mentally, and emotionally. She loved to travel and I preferred staying put, partly because of my aching joints. She had no interest in gambling or finance and I was squeamish at the sight of blood. She was diligent about obeying rules and I believed that rules were meant to be stretched, if not broken. The numerous differences between us, however, were easily overcome by just one facet of our relationship. We trusted each other.

The fire in the airplane was extinguished and it was time for me to find an alternate means of getting to New York. I stood up from the grass, dusted myself off, and made the biggest decision of my life. I would propose to Kathleen.

Once I was back in New York, I thought about nothing else for days. Even though I knew what had to be done, I had no idea how to go about doing it. This was my first time proposing marriage and, hopefully, it would be the last. After a great deal of deliberation, I sat her down one evening and told her about what had gone through my head during the ill-fated flight.

"What do you think that means?" she asked, a leading question if there ever was one.

"I think it means that we shouldn't waste any more time," I said.

"About what?" she asked, not making it any easier for me.

"In thinking about our future," I said, struggling to get the words out.

"How so?"

I fumbled for a few seconds and said, "It would be a shame if we weren't together."

By now, she had had enough of my beating about the bush and asked me point blank, "Are you asking me to marry you?"

"Yes, I am," I said, relieved at having said it at last.

"I will!" she said, without any hesitation and to my great relief.

It was only then that something occurred to her.

"By the way, where's my ring?" she asked.

"What ring?"

"You proposed without a ring?" She was likely wondering what sort of an idiot she had just agreed to marry.

"I didn't know what kind of a ring you'd like. I figured that if you said yes then we could go shopping for one afterwards."

"You seriously thought I might say no?" she said, shaking her head.

"I thought there was a chance," I replied sheepishly. I knew that my proposal had been clumsy at best, but the important thing was that it was done and that she had said yes.

The following day, we took a taxi to Manhattan's diamond district on 47th Street to buy an engagement ring. After passing through a series of locked doors, we entered a small chamber where a dealer laid out an array of stones before us. Kathleen picked out a three-quarter carat, pear-shaped diamond that we had set into a gold ring. More than twenty-five years later, that ring is still on her finger.

Now that we were engaged, we had a wedding to think about. I pleaded with her to elope with me to Las Vegas but she wouldn't hear of it. She wanted a proper wedding, as did our parents. While both families were equally thrilled that we were getting married, the gulf between the two sides was enormous when it came to planning a wedding. Kathleen's parents wanted us to get married in the Newburgh church they had been attending for years, Our Lady of the Lake. On the other hand, my parents were insistent upon a Hindu ceremony in New Delhi. Kathleen and I quickly realized that there was no possible way of bridging that gap and that we would need to get married twice, once on each continent. We picked two dates in April, one week apart. That would give us just enough time to get married in America, dash across the globe, and have another wedding in India.

With preparations in full swing in both countries, it was time for me to let Lehman know of my plans. It helped that Kathleen understood what I had been going through and was fully supportive of my taking an extended break. She also seemed wholly unperturbed by the idea of getting married to someone who could soon be unemployed.

One morning in January 1995, I marched into the office and told the head of Lehman's CMO trading desk that I was leaving, at least for a while.

"I'm taking some time off," I said.

"What do you mean? How much time?" he asked, thinking that I was going to ask for a week or two.

"Three and a half months," I replied.

"You're joking!"

I wasn't surprised by his reaction. It was unheard of for a trader to take an extended break. The fear of being replaced was too great.

"I'm serious," I said.

"Why?"

"I'm getting married," was the best excuse I could come up with. There was nothing to be gained by disclosing the real reason why I wanted to leave.

"What kind of bullshit is this? You're not the first person on the trading floor to get married. The most anyone has ever taken off is two weeks."

"I understand," I said.

"But you need more than three months?"

"Yes."

"When will you come back?"

"In May."

"Three and a half months is a long time."

"I know."

"You won't get paid."

"I figured as much." I didn't expect Lehman to pay for my soul-searching expedition.

At his wits' end, my boss played his final card.

"You know, Kamal, we may not have a job for you when you come back."

"That's a risk I'll have to take," I said quietly.

If my superiors had any idea about what was going through my head, they would have realized that this was an empty threat. Over the past two years, I had maintained a poker face on the trading floor and no one around me had any clue about the inner turmoil that I had faced on a daily basis.

Several of Lehman's senior managers tried to get me to change my mind, likely because they didn't want to see their two-year investment walk out the door. I, on the other hand, felt that I had paid handsomely for my Wall Street education and that I didn't owe the company anything. Even though it was made clear to me that my actions would lead to a lower bonus and could even spell the end of my career in high finance, I was not swayed.

And so, in the first week of February 1995, I walked away from Wall Street, not knowing if I would ever come back.

CHAPTER 17

A Wedding in Newburgh

I couldn't help thinking that I had let Wall Street get the better of me. The financial industry had not only beaten me, it had also crushed my spirit and turned me into something I despised. A quitter. I had been down in the dumps many times before but I had never turned tail and run. I realized that I had a choice to make. Would I let myself be bullied into leaving Wall Street for good or would I go back and fight once more?

After the rough and tumble of the Lehman trading floor, I was glad for the peace and quiet of my time off. Although I had managed to survive the two-year onslaught, it had taken a toll. The long hours at work — from seven in the morning to nine at night — had done a number on my neck and back. It seemed only natural that I should undergo physical therapy and that it be done at Kathleen's place of work, Mount Sinai Hospital. She, however, felt that it wasn't appropriate to treat her future husband and had one of her co-workers take my case. Out of the corner of my eye, I would catch Kathleen laughing as her friend Sari showed no mercy to her patient. For several weeks, Sari worked on my joints in an attempt to increase my mobility and correct my posture. After my sessions were over, I would linger at the hospital for as long as I could, watching Kathleen treat patients. Those idyllic mornings made Lehman seem like a distant memory.

A few weeks later, I retraced my steps and visited my old stomping grounds of Las Vegas and San Francisco. I had greatly looked forward to playing blackjack again and to beating the casinos one more time. Unfortunately, soon after landing in Las Vegas, I realized my heart was no longer in it, at least not in the way it used to be. The casinos were the same and so was the game, but I had changed. From Las Vegas, I continued onwards to San Francisco. As I walked around my old neighborhood of Haight-Ashbury, I finally understood the meaning of the saying "you can't go home again." Time either changes the home or it changes you.

After my lackluster trip out west, I was soon back in New York, where Kathleen had been busy planning the wedding with her parents. Before we could get married in the chapel though, the Catholic Church required us to perform two tasks. We had to first have a chat with the pastor and then attend a day-long Pre-Cana, a kind of marriage prep course for couples.

I had been inside the Our Lady of the Lake chapel twice before, for Christmas mass. Sitting at the edge of Orange Lake in the town of Newburgh, the low-slung white structure had a spire and an entrance on one end and an altar on the other. A series of stained-glass windows on either side allowed for light to filter into the hall, giving it a warm glow. The pastor was Monsignor Budwick, a tall, soft-spoken man with an avuncular disposition. He sat us down and gave us a serious talk about the responsibilities of married life. Of greatest concern to him appeared to be the fact that Kathleen was marrying someone who was obviously not a Catholic.

"You must promise that you will raise your children in their mother's faith," he turned to me and said.

I agreed reluctantly.

I wasn't particularly religious and had stopped going to temples when I was twelve, and I was uncomfortable with the monsignor's request. However, it was important to Kathleen's family that Father Budwick officiate our wedding, so I gave in. Much to everyone's relief, he gave us his blessings and agreed to marry us in his church.

The following Saturday, Kathleen and I attended a Pre-Cana class at a downtown Manhattan church. The class, held in the building's cavernous basement, was run by a couple who appeared to be in their seventies. Married for over forty years, they knew a thing or two about long-term relationships. They began the lecture by posing a question that has stuck in my mind to this day.

"What is the number one reason why couples get divorced?"

Many in the audience, myself included, assumed that the answer was infidelity. The elderly couple smiled and shook their heads.

"It's money," the woman said, "and it makes no difference how much money a couple has. The rich get divorced just as frequently as the rest of us."

What on Earth were they talking about then, I wondered.

"Couples get divorced because they can't agree on money matters, from how much is enough to how to spend it."

I was immensely relieved to hear this because, despite coming from different corners of the globe, Kathleen and I shared the same attitude towards money. We had both grown up in solidly middle-class households and had learnt the value of money early in life. Just as I had felt wealthy when I started working at Honeywell, she felt that her hospital pay was generous, enough to live in Manhattan and to travel around the world in her time off. Neither one of us had aspired to make a great deal of money or even considered it necessary. Had I cared about money, I wouldn't have walked out of Lehman and put my Wall Street career in jeopardy. And if she had considered money to be paramount, she wouldn't have been so understanding about it.

It is impossible to overstate how important this aspect of our relationship has been not only to our marriage, but also to my career. In an industry where self-worth is measured by the size of one's paycheck, having a spouse who was indifferent to money has given me the freedom to follow my own path. In fact, ten years later, Kathleen would insist that I choose a lower-paying job because she believed that it would make me happier. Money cannot buy that kind of understanding.

Two months flew by quickly and all of a sudden, it was our wedding day. I woke up in a Newburgh hotel to see flurries outside my window. Fortunately, the morning snow showers passed quickly and gave way to a beautiful spring day. The wedding at the chapel was to take place in the early afternoon followed by a reception at a nearby banquet hall. After a leisurely breakfast with friends and family, all of whom were staying at the same hotel, it was time to get dressed for the big day. My brother, Ami, was the best man and three of my friends had agreed to act as groomsmen. Dheerendra was one of them. We put on matching tuxedos, tied our bowties, and headed out to the chapel.

As soon as Kathleen stepped out of the limo in her white dress, I understood why the star attraction of any wedding was the bride. She looked absolutely stunning, and, at that moment, I felt very fortunate. The hundred or so people inside the church oohed and aahed as her father led her down the aisle. Father Budwick, clad in a long, flowing white robe and a blue sash, waited patiently in front of the altar as I stood to his left with the groomsmen. Kathleen's sister Gina, her maid of honor, stood on the other side of the pastor with the three bridesmaids, all wearing elegant blue dresses. My seven-year-old niece Aditi scattered rose petals in her role as the flower girl and Kathleen's cousin's six-year-old son Anthony acted as the ring bearer.

Once she had reached the altar, I lifted her veil and the monsignor began the ceremony. He talked about the holiness of the sacrament of matrimony and made us repeat after him, *in sickness and in health, in good times and bad*, and *till death do us part*. Before long, Father Budwick uttered the words we had all come there to hear.

"I now pronounce you man and wife." It was done. Kathleen and I were married. I breathed a sigh of relief, blissfully unaware of the dark cloud that was about to descend upon me.

For now though, everything seemed to be going well. Kathleen looked radiant and I felt terrific as we exited the church, walking past the long line of well-wishers. We spent the next hour or so having our pictures taken before heading out to the reception. The guests stood up and cheered as the DJ announced the first dance.

"For the first time, ladies and gentlemen, I give you Mr. and Mrs. Gupta!"

Kathleen and I walked to the middle of the dance floor as Elvis crooned "Can't Help Falling in Love" in the background. That's when I suffered the one and only panic attack of my life.

As we started the slow dance, I suddenly felt the weight of the whole world on my shoulders. Out of nowhere, a great fear took over me and my arms and legs felt as if they weighed a thousand pounds each. For thirty-odd years of my life, I had only myself to worry about; but now, I felt a great sense of responsibility towards Kathleen. My future remained uncertain at best. I was on my three-month hiatus from Lehman and I hadn't yet decided what I was going to do when it ended. I couldn't imagine going back to the computer industry or even to blackjack. My enthusiasm for gambling had waned and I couldn't see myself leading the life of a professional gambler as a married man. The idea of going back to Wall Street simply because I needed to make a living was also a crushing thought. What if we ended up having kids? How would I support them? Then there was my arthritis. Knowing that my condition was genetic, perhaps I shouldn't even have gotten married, let alone think about having children. Dr. Jane's dire warning was still fresh in my mind. What if an accident turned me into a vegetable? Adding to my sense of terror was the fact that, having broken my third vow to myself, I would never be able to live in India again. Did I want to close that door for good?

I had wrestled with these issues in the past but never all at once. In my panic-stricken state, I forgot that none of this was a mystery to Kathleen and that she had agreed to marry me regardless. She didn't care about my work situation and had faith that I would figure something out. More than anyone else, she understood the impact arthritis had on my life and the odds of passing it on to children. She, too, had been alarmed by Dr. Jane's diagnosis but we had agreed to postpone the surgery for the time being. And if it came down to it, she would even have considered moving to India. That I loved her deeply was without question but, in that moment, I couldn't even recognize the person in my arms. I also began to wonder why my parents were not there, having forgotten that they were busy planning a wedding in Delhi. My mind had gone blank and thoughts of *who am I* and *how did I get here* started to run through my head. I felt more afraid during that slow dance than I had in the smoke-filled turboprop.

Kathleen realized that something was wrong.

"What's the matter?" she asked, noticing that I was barely moving.

"I don't think I can do this," I said.

A look of shock and concern crossed her face.

"Kamal, this is not the time!" she said under her breath. "Everyone is watching us."

"I know, but I don't know what to do," I said, further compounding her misery.

"Just follow me," she said softly. "It'll be over in two minutes."

"I'll try."

I consider it a minor miracle that we made it through the dance without anyone in the audience realizing what had transpired between us. As Elvis sang about taking his hand, and his whole life too, she led me through the rest of the song. Everyone clapped and cheered while I mustered a weak smile. Thankfully, my panic subsided over the next hour and I returned to an almost-normal state.

Even though no one had noticed, I was deeply embarrassed by my reaction. It would be years before I worked up the courage to ask Kathleen how she had felt about my performance during the first dance. She did not mince her words.

"I thought that you were a coward."

Her verdict was harsh but deservedly so. It wasn't clear to her, or even to me at the time, what I had meant by *this*. Was it just the dance that I couldn't get through or was it the idea of getting married? While I couldn't change the past, I have made sure not to give her a reason to call me a coward again.

The celebration continued with the Indians and the Italians dancing to the biggest Bollywood hit of the year, "Tu Cheez Badi Hai Mast Mast." Lalit was an excellent dancer and he led the crowd, demonstrating bhangra moves for the song. The Indians danced just as enthusiastically when the Italians showed them the steps to the tarantella. It was only a matter of time before a conga line snaked around the banquet hall. I had never been one for dancing but I was relieved to see Kathleen enjoying herself.

After dinner, Ami gave a speech in his role as the best man. He had always had the gift of the gab and he held the crowd's attention, especially when he mentioned my gambling past and the role it had played in bringing Kathleen and me together. His speech gave me something to laugh about. How could I have imagined that a fifteen-dollar book would cause me to break all three of my promises?

The rest of the evening went off without a hitch. The next morning, after breakfast at the hotel with my friends and family, Kathleen and I rushed back to New York City.

We had a plane to catch and another wedding to be at, seven thousand miles away.

CHAPTER 18

A Wedding in New Delhi

As Kathleen and I prepared to board the Air India jumbo-jet for the twenty-hour flight to New Delhi, I could tell that she was nervous. Going to India for the first time was a daunting prospect in itself, let alone having to go through an Indian wedding. Although she was an intrepid traveler who had been to China twice, her past trips had been made as a tourist and not as a bride. I was a little worried too, mainly about how she would cope with the demands of a conservative Indian family. My brother and I had migrated to America, but the rest of our family remained rooted in tradition. Their ways frequently defied logic as well as explanation, especially when it came to weddings. For starters, my family's customs required Kathleen to spend the first three nights in a hotel.

"Why?" she asked.

"You're a single woman. The rules are that you can't sleep at my parents' place until we are married."

"But we are married!" she protested.

"Only my parents know that. As far as my relatives are concerned, the Indian wedding is the *real* one. Your staying with me overnight before the wedding would be a serious breach of protocol," I said.

"How would they even know?" she asked, which made me chuckle.

"They would know because twenty-five of my uncles, aunts, and cousins will be staying with my parents," I replied.

"Seriously? In a three-bedroom apartment? Where will they sleep?"

"They'll sleep wherever they can: in the bedrooms, on the living room floor, or in the dining room."

"Why don't they stay in a hotel?" Kathleen asked.

I laughed and said that staying in a hotel would be considered an insult for both sides, my parents as well as my relatives. Moreover, it was a celebration and everyone wanted to be together, no matter how great the discomfort.

"But *I* must stay in a hotel," she said sarcastically.

"Only until the wedding."

"I give up," she said, closing her eyes in an attempt to catch some sleep before we landed.

Two things hit you as soon as you step out of the Indira Gandhi International Airport in New Delhi: the heat and the crowds. We had landed at midday and April temperatures were already approaching a hundred degrees, a far cry from the snow flurries in Newburgh. As we jostled our way out of the airport, she could feel the eyes of hundreds upon her, a feeling she would have to get used to. My parents bundled us into a taxi and drove us to the south Delhi neighborhood of Saket.

That thirty-minute car ride was Kathleen's introduction to India. She sat glued to the window, watching the cab driver weave through nerve-racking traffic. Teeming with an assortment of vehicles — cars, buses, trucks, scooters, tempos, auto-rickshaws, and even a tractor or two — Delhi's roads are not for the faint of heart. The broken white line in the middle of the road seems meaningless and it isn't uncommon to see three or four vehicles riding abreast in a two-lane road. Motorists came perilously close to each other, causing Kathleen to wince every few seconds. And then there was the incessant honking. In America, beeping was a means of conveying displeasure, whereas in India, honking was simply a polite way of letting others know of your presence on the road.

More than anything else that she had witnessed during that car ride, Kathleen had been shocked to see a cow sitting peacefully in the middle of a busy road. No matter how dense or chaotic the traffic, everyone stopped and went around the animal respectfully. Cows are considered sacred in India and no one dared to harm a hair on its head for fear of causing a riot. Before long, Kathleen would learn to accept cows on the roads as a fact of life in India.

My parents' Saket apartment was small, about twelve hundred square feet, but felt larger because it was spread out over two floors. A spiral staircase connected the two bedrooms on the upper level with the living area and the bedroom downstairs. Three balconies, one off the dining area and two above, added to the feeling of spaciousness. My grandparents, amma and baba, both in their nineties, also lived in that apartment, which at present was filled with a host of relatives. They were all excited to meet Kathleen even though many of them didn't speak English. In that instant, I realized that my fears were unfounded. She had grown up in a large family with numerous uncles, aunts, and cousins and had no trouble dealing with mine. For their part, my relatives made Kathleen feel just as welcome as her family had made me feel. If the language barrier bothered her, she didn't show it. I did my best to translate but there was only so much I could do with ten conversations going on at once. The one thing that came through loud and clear to Kathleen was that all my aunts and cousins were thrilled that we were getting married. She wisely didn't mention that we already were.

With only three days to go until the ceremony, there was no time to waste. The first order of business was to procure a wedding dress. To that end, we drove across town to the famed Ram Chandra Krishan Chandra (RCKC) saree store, Delhi's go-to spot for bridal outfits. The store was a stone's throw from Springdales School and I felt myself growing tense as we went past.

After about an hour at RCKC, Kathleen and my mom settled on a red and green lehenga and choli — a two-piece garment that consisted of a skirt and a top — that was covered with golden embroidery. A sheer red dupatta, a shawl-like scarf, completed the outfit. In marked contrast to America, where the alterations to her wedding dress had taken months, RCKC promised to have them done in twenty-four hours. In another departure from our first wedding, it would have been unthinkable for Kathleen to be dressed in white. In India, white is the color of widowhood and therefore considered inauspicious at a wedding. Even the guests at an Indian wedding avoid wearing white.

With her outfit taken care of, it was time for Kathleen to check into her home for the next three nights. Unfortunately, my parents had selected a hotel for its location and not for comfort. The air conditioner in the room was out of order and the windows were bolted shut, turning the small space into an oven. Kathleen, who had a difficult time grasping why she had to stay in a hotel in the first place, had an even harder time understanding why she had to bake in this particular one. Changing hotels wasn't an option because it risked offending my parents. For my part, I made sure that we spent as much time as possible in the cool confines of the hotel's restaurant. We ordered dish after dish, making each dinner last for as long as we could. Kathleen would face numerous challenges in India, but food would not be one of them. She was not only an experienced eater of Indian food, she had also started to learn how to cook it. It was amusing to watch the waiter react to the American woman asking for dishes to be made extra spicy.

"Are you sure, ma'am?"

"Yes," she said.

The waiter looked helplessly at me, and I nodded as if to say, "Just do as she says."

The next day, we went shopping for jewelry in the posh South Extension market. As was the case at the saree store, the jeweler also plied us with chai and samosas in an effort to keep us there for as long as possible. The tea was too sweet for my taste but I had a couple of the potato-filled pastries. While munching on them, I couldn't help noticing how profusely the salesman was complimenting Kathleen's engagement ring.

"Madam, that is an excellent diamond. May I ask where you bought it and what it cost?" he said, in the most unctuous manner.

So I told him.

"I must say, sir, that was a fantastic purchase," he said, buttering me up further.

"Really?" I said. "Are you sure?"

"Very much so, sir!"

"In that case, would you like to buy it?" I asked the salesman, causing my mom to shoot me a look of disapproval. Kathleen wasn't pleased either, but she knew that I was only trying to keep the salesman honest.

"Are you serious, sir?" the salesman asked me, taken aback.

"Sure, what will you pay for it?"

"One moment, sir," he replied and disappeared into the back room. He reappeared a few minutes later, singing a very different tune.

"I am sorry, sir. The markups on diamonds in America are very, very high," he said, which made me laugh.

Despite that snafu, we walked out of the store with a gold necklace, earrings, and bangles. We bought several green and red churis as well, glass bangles to match Kathleen's wedding outfit. A set of silver payals, or anklets, was the final item on our shopping list.

With the dress and jewelry taken care of, it was time for mehndi, one of the more important traditions of an Indian wedding. Kathleen had to sit still while a professional mehndi artist filled a pipette with henna paste and applied it to her hands and feet, making intricate designs. As she waited for the paste to dry, Kathleen was unable to use her arms. My cousins held a cup of tea to her lips while my mom dabbed a mixture of lemon juice and sugar on the drying mehndi to give it a deeper color. A few hours later, with the mehndi completely dry, she washed it off, revealing a beautiful brown design on her light skin. For the next two weeks, that temporary tattoo would serve as a public announcement of her being a new bride. Everywhere we went — shops, restaurants, and even at the airport — people would stop her and ask, "Did you just get married?"

Three days was barely enough time to get ready for the wedding and they passed by quickly. Soon enough, and for the second time in a week, it was our wedding day. While my parents had been economical in choosing the hotel where Kathleen had spent three uncomfortable nights, they had gone all out in their choice of a wedding venue. They had picked The Claridges, a stately hotel situated in the heart of Delhi, as the site for the wedding. Furthermore, they had decided to hold it outdoors, on the hotel's pristine lawn. Both turned out to be wise choices. The hotel's imposing structure provided a majestic backdrop to the brightly lit garden, making the setting appear even grander than it was. The weather cooperated as well. The evening temperature was a comfortable eighty degrees and there wasn't a cloud in sight. On one end of the grounds, the hotel had erected a temporary stage that was topped with two ornate throne-like chairs. On the other end was a mandap, a temporary platform that would serve as the altar for the Hindu ceremony. In between the stage and the mandap was open space for the guests to mill about.

In an Indian wedding, the reception is held first and the ceremony afterwards, oftentimes late at night and with only the immediate family present. This allows guests to arrive leisurely as opposed to having to show up at the church at the appointed time. Also, unlike weddings in the west, it is impossible to get an exact head count since there is no concept of an RSVP and no way of knowing who your guests might bring along. Indian weddings tend to be free-for-all affairs where anyone with the slightest connection to the bride or the groom is welcome. To a smaller extent, the same had occurred during our wedding in Newburgh. Some of my friends from San Francisco had invited their New York area relatives to our wedding. The last-minute additions had played havoc with the seating chart — not that any of the Indians had paid much attention to it anyway. Much like the lane markers on Delhi's roads, they had treated the seating arrangement as a mere suggestion and had jumped freely from table to table. The Italians, on the other hand, wouldn't dream of straying from their assigned seats. It is perhaps for these reasons that Indian weddings serve a buffet instead of a sit-down dinner.

I broke out into a big smile when I saw Kathleen enter the garden wearing the lehenga, choli, and dupatta along with the gold jewelry and the mehndi. She looked just as terrific in red, green, and gold as she had in white. I overheard several of my aunts whisper approvingly, "She almost looks Indian." Although Kathleen had been Indianized, my outfit was not all that different from Newburgh. I wore a dark business suit with only a bright red turban on my head revealing my status as the groom.

Before taking our seats on the stage, we performed jaimala, a ritual thousands of years old that marks the beginning of a Hindu wedding ceremony. First Kathleen placed a heavy garland of fresh flowers around my neck and then I did the same for her. That minute-long ritual was the only portion of the wedding ceremony that most guests would witness. With jaimala over in a flash, we sat down on the oversized chairs with the garlands still around our necks. The 150 or so friends and relatives, many of whom I hadn't seen in years, came up to greet us one by one.

"This is the opposite of how it was in Newburgh," Kathleen whispered to me.

"Yes, and much easier on my joints," I said, the memory of having to go from table to table still fresh in my mind.

The guests at the wedding knew that we had met in New York, but many wondered how I had ended up on the east coast in the first place.

"Kamal, you were a computer guy in San Francisco. How did you go from there to working in finance in New York?"

The answer to that question was taboo. My parents had given me strict instructions not to mention my blackjack past to anyone in India. Even though I had gone legit and had started working on Wall Street, the shame of my having been a gambler had been too great for them to bear.

"I mailed a résumé to Wall Street and got hired," I replied, which was a factual statement, strictly speaking. That seemed to satisfy most of the guests. They would be shocked to learn the truth five years later when my parents finally gave me permission to talk about my gambling past.

During the reception, I was amused to see several tourists hanging about The Claridges lawn, enjoying tea and coffee. They had been drawn to the garden by a large sign that said, *Kamal Weds Kathleen*. The European guests of The Claridges were curious to see who this Kathleen was, who had been bold enough to subject herself to a traditional Indian wedding. I doubt if they would have been as interested if there had been two Indian names on the marquee. Many of the party crashers lingered to watch the wedding ceremony, long after most of the guests had left.

The ceremony started late, well after ten o'clock, and lasted until close to midnight. It was held under the mandap, a four-poster wooden canopy that was bedecked with marigolds and jasmine flowers. In the center of the mandap was a fire pit that served as the focal point for the ceremony. There were no chairs and everyone was expected to sit on the floor, which made matters particularly difficult for me. Kathleen and I sat side by side on two cushions and the purohit, the priest, sat across from us. Unlike the Catholic ceremony, which required guests to congregate in Father Budwick's chapel, the purohit would travel to wherever the wedding was being held, for a fee of course. He recited several shlokas, Sanskrit verses, that were incomprehensible to most in the audience. He translated some of them into Hindi, which were further translated into English by one of my uncles, for Kathleen's benefit.

It came as a great shock to Kathleen to see the members of the audience repeatedly heckle the purohit. At Our Lady of the Lake chapel, there was pin-drop silence while the monsignor had conducted the ceremony. At The Claridges on the other hand, harassing the purohit was not only accepted, it was expected. When he asked me to take a vow that I would turn over all my income to Kathleen, one of my aunts chimed in, "She also works! What about her income?" When the priest asked Kathleen to promise that she would drink alcohol only in the presence of her husband, murmurs of disapproval broke out. Virtually everyone in my family was a teetotaler and, in another major difference from our first wedding, there had been no alcohol served that evening. The purohit, who had undoubtedly been harassed at every wedding that he had presided upon, took it in stride and smiled at his hecklers.

After an hour of shlokas and numerous rituals that involved us throwing various things into the fire, we finally arrived at the climax of the ceremony, the saat phere, or the seven circles around the fire. Kathleen, holding a coconut in one hand, led for the first three and I for the last four. With each round, the purohit invoked a prayer for a happily married life. My relatives tried their best to get the priest to lose count of the number of times we had gone around the fire.

"That was only six pheras, not seven," they shouted.

"Behave yourself, or I will do an ulte phere!" the priest said in jest, threatening to reverse the pheras and thereby undo the entire ceremony. That silenced everyone.

At the end of the seventh round, everybody clapped and cheered, including the tourists. This was the *I now pronounce you man and wife* moment of the wedding. All that was left was for me to put sindoor, a red powder made of vermilion, in the part of Kathleen's hair. The red streak signified her status as a married woman. Single women in India do not wear sindoor nor do widows.

I was certain that by now my shoes would have disappeared. As required by custom, everyone had to take their shoes off before entering the mandap. In my family, there was a long-standing tradition of stealing the groom's shoes while he was busy getting married. The only way to get them back was to pay an exorbitant ransom to the thieves who, in this case, were my younger cousins. Kathleen watched the proceedings with a look of bemusement and chalked it up to yet another thing about India that she would never understand.

"We want dollars, not rupees!" my cousins demanded.

Since I was expected to negotiate for my shoes, I asked them how much.

"A hundred dollars," one said.

"I don't think so," I objected. "The shoes aren't worth that much."

"What do you mean?"

"You can keep the shoes," I said. "I don't need them."

"No, bhaiya! You cannot do that," they howled in protest.

I was only kidding. After needling them for a few minutes, I pulled out my wallet and paid up, bringing the evening to a close. Everyone was all smiles, including the bride and groom.

The next morning, Kathleen was formally welcomed into my parents' home, putting an end to her days of staying in a hotel. Shortly thereafter, we said our goodbyes and headed out to the airport to catch a flight to Goa.

After everything that I had put her through, I felt that Kathleen deserved a great honeymoon and the Fort Aguada Beach Resort did not disappoint. Set inside the ramparts of a sixteenth-century Portuguese fort, the resort was nestled against a hill overlooking the Arabian Sea. Despite not having a reservation, I managed to wrangle an elegantly furnished suite with a large balcony. Looking out of our room, we could see the beach on one side and the hotel's hexagon-shaped pool on the other. Kathleen loved everything about the resort, from the landscaping to the food. My favorite memory of the trip was the early morning breakfasts by the pool, watching the waves crash onto the empty beach. Her only complaint was that the Arabian Sea was murky and not crystal clear like the Caribbean.

A former Portuguese colony, Goa was replete with Catholic churches and we went to see a few, including the imposing Basilica of Bom Jesus. On Sunday, we attended mass at one of the smaller churches near Fort Aguada. As we made our way out of the chapel, Kathleen was surprised to see a large tree laden with hundreds of mangoes, one of her favorite fruits.

"Wow! I never realized mango trees grew this big," she said.

The tree was massive, almost sixty feet tall, and the fruit hung from it like ornaments on a Christmas tree. Like so many things that she had witnessed in India, it had never occurred to me that she had never seen a mango tree before.

"You know what, Kathleen," I said, sidling up to her.

"What?"

"Each and every one of those mangoes has a pit in it."

"Very funny," she said, pouting, understanding that I never missed an opportunity to remind her of her first encounter with a whole mango. Two years earlier, I had sliced one and given her both cheeks of the fruit.

"This is all I get?" she had asked, looking at the two oval pieces.

"Yeah," I said.

"And you get all that?" she said, pointing to the thick slab in the middle of the plate. It took me a while, but I figured out why she was questioning the way that I had divided the mango.

"Wait a second! Do you not know that there is a large pit in the middle?" I asked her.

"What pit?"

I burst out laughing and showed her. Ever since that day, whenever she has picked up a mango, I have made sure to warn her about the pit inside.

Kathleen's trip to India would have been incomplete without seeing the spectacularly beautiful Taj Mahal. To that end, we boarded an early morning train in New Delhi and arrived in Agra three hours later. As soon as she stepped out onto the Agra train station platform, she found herself surrounded by tour guides offering their services.

"Madam, hello!"

"Hello, madam!"

"Hello!"

Moments later, I exited the train and told them in Hindi that she didn't need one. They walked away muttering, "She came with a guide."

Our time in India was fast coming to an end, as was my three-month hiatus. We would soon be returning to New York and I would have to decide once and for all what I was going to do about Wall Street.

CHAPTER 19

Return to Wall Street

With just ten days left in my sabbatical, the question of returning to Wall Street loomed large. Despite their threats to the contrary, I wasn't worried that my Lehman bosses would not allow me to return. If the company had been willing to hire me when I hadn't even known what a tick was, it wasn't about to turn me away now. There was also the fact that they had tried hard to get me to stay, which meant that I had been of some use. The real question was whether I wanted to go back given everything that I had witnessed.

Right from the start, I had been struck by just how similar investment banks were to casinos, both in style and in substance. Neither industry *made* anything other than money. Casinos did it by offering games of chance while Wall Street trafficked in financial instruments. Bond traders took on the role of blackjack dealers, converting the house advantage into profits. Salespeople, akin to casino hosts, were responsible for bringing gamblers in and doling out comps in the form of dinners and show tickets. The heads of trading desks were the pit bosses of the trading floor, keeping an eye on the goings-on while making sure that the house bankroll was protected at all times. The back office was the cashier's cage, where the daily profits, or heaven forbid losses, were tallied. Clients such as money managers and hedge funds played the part of gamblers.

Both industries preyed on the weak. Investment banks had displayed no qualms about taking advantage of Orange County's treasurer, just as Harrah's had felt no compunction about taking my drunk friend's money. This willingness to exploit the vulnerable sets casinos and investment banks apart from other businesses. Most businesses don't ply their customers with alcohol in order to make them pay more for their products. Nor do they charge unsophisticated customers a higher price.

The realization that I had ended up on the wrong side of the fence was especially painful. At Lehman Brothers, I was employed by the house, an idea I would have found abhorrent in Las Vegas. However, I understood there was no other way for me to learn the game. Unfortunately, so far, I had been singularly unsuccessful.

For two years, I had tried to make sense of the CMO market and failed. It was a mystery to me why customers bought bonds that were so obviously overpriced. After racking my brain for months, I had concluded that there wasn't any logic to the CMO market other than the ignorance of its client base, especially when it came to understanding the implications of a steep yield curve.

A steep yield curve is one where long-term interest rates are higher than short-term ones, implying that rates in the future are expected (but not guaranteed) to rise. These future interest rates (also known as forward rates) are not apparent to the naked eye and the opaque structures of many CMO deals expose investors to unforeseen risks, especially if interest rates were to rise sharply. Orange County was a prime example.

During the 1990s, the Federal Financial Institutions Examination Council (FFIEC), an interagency body composed of five U.S. banking regulators, had restricted banks from buying high-risk CMOs. The guidelines had been designed to limit the banks' risk exposure to sharp fluctuations in interest rates. Our CMOs, like those of other investment banks, had been carefully engineered to pass the FFIEC test, but *only* at issuance. A combination of structuring ingenuity and rising interest rates would frequently cause them to fail the test in the future. The banks would then have to offload the offending securities and replace them with freshly created CMOs that passed the FFIEC test, at least on that day.

There were plenty of customers in the CMO market who understood forward interest rates, however they were not the ones that *drove* deals. Just like casinos would be forced to shut down their blackjack tables if every player followed basic strategy, the CMO market would have a difficult time producing new deals if every client understood the impact of a steep yield curve. A ten-dollar blackjack table would clear around twenty dollars per hour if every player adhered to strict basic strategy. That's not nearly enough money to keep the casinos in business. Likewise, if every customer were to learn a few simple facts about the yield curve, investment banks' profits would take a nosedive. The most damning proof of the CMO market's raison d'être was that whenever the yield curve flattened out — a scenario that implied that interest rates were unlikely to increase in the future — new deal issuance ground to a standstill.

While I was unsure about my return to Wall Street, I was certain about one thing. If the rest of the business was like the CMO market, then I wanted nothing further to do with the financial industry. I had no interest in being part of an enterprise predicated on the naïveté of its customers and where developing any sort of a methodology for long-term success was impossible.

I also realized that I was doing myself a disservice by lumping all of finance into the same category. There were plenty of sophisticated hedge funds and money managers in the marketplace, many that ran circles around Wall Street traders. Before leaving the business for good, I owed it to myself to find out what they did. Accordingly, I set a few conditions for myself before I would return to Lehman: I had to be in an area other than CMOs, and that area had to not only offer an even playing field to clients, it also had to make sense to me.

Having arrived at a decision, I went to see my bosses. As expected, my job on the CMO desk had been given to someone else.

"You can't go back to your old seat," said the head of Lehman's mortgage trading desk.

"Ah, that's too bad," I said, while breathing a sigh of relief internally. Going back to my old seat was the last thing that I wanted.

"We have an opening on the STRIPS desk though," he added.

I sat forward in my chair. This was great news. The STRIPS desk was one of the more coveted spots within the mortgage market and its traders were some of the sharpest on the street. Moreover, the customers who traded STRIPS — mostly hedge funds — were far more sophisticated than the clients who drove CMO deals.

STRIPS is an acronym for Separate Trading of Registered Interest and Principal of Securities, a phenomenon that is commonplace in the U.S. Treasury bond market. First introduced in the 1960s, STRIPS allow the interest and principal components of any bond to be traded separately as interest only (IO) and principal only (PO) securities.

I was attracted to the IO/PO market for two reasons. Firstly, there was no slicing and dicing of cash flows in mortgage STRIPS, only a separation of the interest and principal payments. Every month, as homeowners made their mortgage payments, the interest component was passed through to the IO holders and the principal portion to the PO holders. For example, a homeowner taking out a $250,000 thirty-year mortgage with an interest rate of four percent is required to make a fixed monthly payment of $1,193. The first month's payment consists of $833 of interest, which gets passed on to the IO holder, and $360 of principal, which is delivered to the owner of the PO. With every passing month, as the amount of principal owed by the borrower falls, the interest component of the monthly payment drops and the principal portion rises. Consequently, the price of an IO decreases with time and that of a PO increases.

As simple as they sound, IOs and POs are not without risk and are considered to be some of the most dangerous securities in the mortgage market. Those risks, however, stem from the behavior of homeowners across America and not from the nefarious actions of a structurer, as with many CMOs. Quick repayment of a loan is catastrophic to IO holders as no further interest payments are forthcoming; conversely, slower than anticipated repayments are devastating for PO owners. Predicting repayments with any degree of accuracy is almost impossible and Wall Street traders possess no greater insight into the phenomenon than do their clients. Consequently, the playing field in the STRIPS market is much more level.

Secondly, and more significantly, IOs and POs were a long-short market, whereas CMOs were a long-only market. The CMO market was rife with bonds that were priced artificially high, largely due to the lack of sophistication of its clients. Still, there was no mechanism available for an investor to bet that the price of those bonds would fall. The only option available to anyone in the CMO market was either to be long, a fancy term for owning a financial instrument, or to stay out of the market. The STRIPS market was different because an IO and a PO together made a mortgage bond, causing the following simple equation to hold true at all times:

IO price + PO price = price of the underlying mortgage

Since the market made it easy for an investor to lock in the price of the underlying mortgage, this equation all but ensured that buying an IO was equivalent to betting that the price of the PO would fall and vice versa. Hence, a long position in an IO was equivalent to a short position in the corresponding PO, with the reverse also being true. For a market to be free and fair, investors must be able to wager that prices will fall just as easily as they can bet that prices will rise. A CMO market, by its very structure, was neither free nor fair whereas the IO/PO market was both.

STRIPS and CMOs typified the differences between the two broad classes of financial assets, liquid and illiquid. True to their name, liquid securities are free flowing and change hands continuously. Microsoft stock is a good example. With tens of millions of shares trading daily, there is no mystery about what a share of Microsoft is worth at any time. Illiquid assets are the opposite. They trade infrequently and their prices are known only to a select few. This opacity makes them ripe for abuse. Illiquid securities were a significant factor in causing the 2008 financial crisis, which I'll address in depth in a later chapter.

Since the same IO was bought and sold several times a day, the STRIPS market was liquid. In contrast, once a CMO exchanged hands, it might not trade again for weeks or months.

For me, the choice between the two types of securities was an easy one. Only liquid bonds offered a level playing field where I could match my wits against others in the market. Moreover, the most liquid of mortgage bonds could be sold for a loss of as little as 0.015 percent, whereas the transaction cost of an illiquid security could be as much as a hundred-fold higher. That miniscule house advantage made liquid markets the closest thing to black-jack and consequently the only game worth playing.

My sabbatical had done its job. By allowing me to transition from CMOs to IOs and POs, my bosses at Lehman had unwittingly met the very conditions that I had set for my return to Wall Street. There was just one downside to my joining the STRIPS desk. I would have to surrender the modicum of seniority that I had gained. That, however, was a small price to pay for being able to escape from CMOs as well as taking a big step forward towards my ultimate goal: mastering the game of finance.

Looking back, I now realize that the spring of 1995 was a pivotal moment in my life. In addition to getting married, the three months that I had spent away from Lehman gave me a chance to look at the business with a fresh pair of eyes. At the end of my break, I returned to Wall Street with a clear goal. Under the guise of working as a bond trader, I would devote all my attention to developing an investment methodology for beating the mortgage market. If successful, I would use that system to manage money at a hedge fund. If not, my time in the business would come to an end. Much like I had done at Ingres, my job would serve as cover while I set about transforming myself into a player of the game. The name of the game was mortgages, and this time the house was Wall Street itself. All I needed was a method that would turn the odds in my favor, a system for counting cards in financial markets.

So I returned to Lehman Brothers in May 1995 with a renewed sense of purpose. I would either develop an investment framework for beating the mortgage market or die trying.

CHAPTER 20

The Artful Dodger

"How long are you staying this time, Gupta?"

Not surprisingly, my return to the trading floor was met with a stream of taunts. Many of my co-workers resented me. Some because I had left and others because they wished they could have taken a few months off. The prospect of a lower bonus, coupled with the possibility of moving further away from the power seat in the center of the aisle, ensured that no salesperson or trader left the business for an extended period of time. The loss of status didn't bother me. As with the computer industry, I had no interest in scaling the Wall Street corporate ladder. My plan was to work at an investment bank until one of two things happened: I would create a method for beating the mortgage market and use it to manage money at a hedge fund, or I would get thrown out of the business. Coincidentally, both events occurred within twenty-four hours of each other four years later.

In my new role on the IO/PO desk, I was free of Fred but not from torment. My latest persecutor was a senior trader known as Dodger for his wily ways. While Dodger didn't routinely hurl homophobic slurs at me, his compulsive lying and incessant bullying made my life difficult none-theless. Although we were both part of the same trading desk, Dodger and

I trafficked in different types of securities. I was a junior STRIPS trader, whereas he traded derivatives that were a byproduct of CMO deals.

It didn't take me long to realize that Wall Street trading desks viewed their business as a zero-sum game. Just as in Las Vegas, where a player's loss was the house's gain, in New York a client's loss was a trader's profit. On more than one occasion, I had observed head traders stand up in the morning, rub their hands together while looking around, and muse loudly, "So, who are we going to rip off today?" A few traders stretched that principle to the extreme. Chief among them was Dodger. In the dog-eat-dog atmosphere of the trading floor, he had no qualms about taking a bite out of his co-workers either. It wasn't long before I found his teeth on my leg.

One morning, shortly after my return to Lehman, Dodger asked me to do him a favor.

"Gupta, can you sell me twenty-five million Fannie Mae 235 IOs?"

Fannie Mae was short for Federal National Mortgage Association (FNMA), one of the largest issuers of mortgage-backed securities, and 235 was the series number of the IO. Normally, Dodger would have asked Jon, the lead IO trader and the head of our desk, but he was out visiting clients that day and had left the book in my care. A few days earlier, Jon had purchased three hundred million of the 235 IOs from a Florida hedge fund, a substantial trade that had required preapproval from higher-ups. As with any large trade, Jon had managed to extract a significant concession from the seller. His plan was to distribute the bonds in a piecemeal fashion over the next few weeks, which made me reluctant to trade them in his absence.

"I don't think so," I told Dodger. "We should wait until Jon comes back tomorrow."

"Please, Gupta, I really need those bonds," Dodger pleaded.

"I have no idea what to even charge you for them," I demurred.

"The price in the system is fine. Trust me," he said.

The words *please* and *trust me* out of Dodger's mouth should have set off alarm bells, but I was oblivious to what was happening. Jon owned three hundred million of the bonds and I foolishly assumed that selling a small amount wouldn't hurt. So I sold Dodger the IOs.

First thing the next morning, Jon demanded to know why some of his bonds had gone missing.

"Gupta, where did those twenty-five million 235 IOs go?" he asked.

"I sold them to Dodger yesterday," I confessed.

"At what price?"

"The price from the night before," I replied.

"You fucking moron!"

I was no stranger to abuse but this took me by surprise. What exactly was my offense? All I had done was to help out a fellow member of the desk.

As he continued with his tongue lashing, Jon told me that he had lowered the mark (the financial industry's term for the daily closing price of a security) on those bonds two nights ago, something Dodger had been aware of. He also knew that I didn't know. I had unwittingly sold twenty-five million bonds at a below-market price, a cardinal offense on any trading desk. Out of the corner of my eye, I caught Dodger smiling. He had to have known that he wasn't going to get away with stealing his boss's bonds. So why had he done this? The only reason that I could come up with was that he wanted to show me up.

"Doesn't he also deserve some blame?" I asked, pointing to Dodger.

"Absolutely not! I left you in charge. It's your responsibility to know who you're dealing with," Jon snapped.

He had a point. Even though we were on the same team, I should have known better than to trust Dodger. I should also have taken the trouble to find out the correct price for the bonds instead of simply relying upon the price in Lehman's computers. In addition to being gullible, I had also been lazy. While I accepted responsibility for my stupidity, I found it remarkable that Dodger's thievery was so casually accepted by everyone.

Despite his character flaws, or perhaps because of them, Dodger was a highly profitable trader. In his search for a quick buck, he displayed no scruples about taking advantage of customers as well.

A client needed to raise a few million dollars, so they asked Dodger for a bid on one of their bonds. The bid side on any financial instrument is the price at which a trader is willing to buy it and the offer side is the price at which he will sell it. The difference between the two prices, known as the bid-offer spread, is the house advantage.

A Wall Street trader's job is to make what is known in the industry as a two-way market. At all times, he is expected to have a bid as well as an offer on any security, which allows a client to either sell at the lower price or buy at the higher. Under normal circumstances, the fair market price lies somewhere between the two prices. In practice, however, that is often not the case, especially for illiquid securities. Traders frequently shade their markets depending on which way they expect the client to go, shifting it higher for a buyer and lower for a seller, all the while maintaining the illusion of providing an honest two-way market.

Dodger was certain that the client asking for a bid was a seller, so he started with an unusually low price, confidently telling the customer, "I'll pay you 106."

I was surprised to hear the bid. I knew that Dodger owned the same bonds and that he had marked them in our systems at around 116. Under normal circumstances, Dodger should have been willing to buy the bonds at 115 and sell them at 117, thereby earning a bid-offer spread of two points. His 106 bid meant that Dodger had either overpriced the bonds at Lehman or he had grossly underpriced them for the customer.

"That's very low. We thought it should trade around 115," said the portfolio manager.

"No chance," Dodger replied. Then abruptly switching tactics, he continued, "In fact, I own the same bond. You can have it at 108."

I was shocked by the offer. It meant that he was willing to sell his holdings at a substantial loss, something traders were loath to do. Before long though, it began to feel like Dodger was attempting a daylight robbery. He had offered his bonds at 108 as a ruse in order to create doubt in the customer's mind. How could the bond be worth 115 if the Lehman trader was willing to sell it at 108? By making his two-way market as 106/108, he had shifted the bond's perceived fair value downwards by nine points, from 116 to 107. If, on the other hand, a client were to announce as a buyer of the same security, he would no doubt have moved prices substantially higher, as we would soon see for ourselves.

If Dodger could persuade the customer to sell at the lowball price of 106, Lehman would make an extra three-quarters of a million dollars in profit. That in turn would boost his year-end bonus by fifty thousand dollars. Not bad for a few minutes' worth of trickery.

The gambit didn't work. Unbeknownst to Dodger, the dumb client had hired a smart consultant who also concluded that the bond was worth 115. The consultant was flabbergasted when he heard that Dodger was willing to sell the bonds at 108. He advised the client to buy them. They tried.

"We will buy it at 108."

Dodger did a double take, as this wasn't part of the plan. He was supposed to rob the customer blind, not the other way around.

"What do you mean? Buy mine? How?" he sputtered.

"We think the bond is worth 115. You obviously disagree. So we'd like to buy yours at 108," the client said innocently.

Dodger was caught in his own trap. Selling at 108 would mean losing hundreds of thousands of dollars and not selling would lead to a loss of face. The choice was easy. His face wasn't worth all that much.

"Sorry, I'm no longer a seller there," he said.

"Where will you sell it?" the portfolio manager asked, probably expecting him to say 109 or 110. Even at that price, the bond would have been a good purchase.

What happened next took my breath away. Realizing that the jig was up, Dodger pulled the most egregious bait and switch that I have ever witnessed. Without displaying an iota of shame, he jacked the price by a whopping fourteen points!

"You can have it at 122," he said without skipping a beat.

It had taken some time but the customer had finally wised up to Dodger's game. The portfolio manager was furious at the attempted mugging, but no one at Lehman seemed to care. Not Dodger and not our bosses. If anything, the managers had continually encouraged Dodger's piggishness as they fed off the same trough themselves. To my amazement, this blatant attempt to rip off a client earned Dodger a standing ovation from the desk. In honor of this audacious maneuver, Jon gave him a new nickname, Mr. 106/122. Dodger embraced the moniker with enthusiasm and moved on to his next victim.

Even after I had watched him operate for several months, Dodger remained an enigma to me. I was unable to fathom why he felt compelled to run over everyone, and everything, in his path. One evening, on our way to a client dinner, my curiosity got the better of me.

"Can I ask you a question?" I said.

"By all means," Dodger replied cheerfully. He had had a good day and was feeling buoyant.

"Why are you such an asshole?"

In the backseat of the taxi, Dodger roared with laughter. A normal person would have been offended by my question, but not him. He was proud of his boorish ways and wasn't bothered in the least by my presumption that he was indeed an asshole.

"There's a very good reason, Gupta," he said, in a tone that reminded me of Gavin's lesson about fear and greed. It was clear that Dodger also wanted to tell me something.

"My father-in-law is worth fifty million dollars," he said, in a hushed tone.

"So what?" I didn't understand what a rich relative had to do with his obnoxious behavior.

"And my wife is an only child," Dodger added, grinning from ear to ear, "capeesh?"

Suddenly, everything made sense. Dodger had his FU cash locked in. Wall Streeters were obsessed with the amount of money that would make them financially secure for the rest of their lives. Like inmates looking forward to their release date, traders frequently talked about the number that would set them free. Once they had it, they were free to say FU to the whole world. Fifty million was more than enough. In Dodger's mind, that gave him the license to act as he wished. If anyone didn't like it, to hell with them. It had never occurred to him that just because you could say FU to everyone, it didn't mean that you should. He also failed to consider the possibility that the odd FU might boomerang and hit him on the head.

The following year, I had had enough. I left Lehman for a rival firm that was smaller in size and in reputation. My tormentor was ecstatic at having taken another junior employee down. He needled me nonstop.

You loser!
Your company sucks.
Your career is finished.
Next stop, washing dishes.

You buffon. (His spelling, not mine.)
Are you enjoying eating your boss's dingleberries?

I had never heard the word *dingleberries* before and had to ask around for its meaning. When I found out what it meant, I was furious. I made up my mind there and then that Dodger had to be punished, but not just yet. Retaliating against his messages was futile; he was never going to stop. Instead, I filed away the taunts, the put-downs, and all of his insults, biding my time. If revenge was a dish best served cold, then I hoped to prepare something frozen for Dodger.

I believe that if you are going to fight a pig then you might as well learn to enjoy rolling around in the mud. Otherwise, the pig wins. If I were to have any hope of beating the Dodgers of this world, there was no other choice. I would have to get down and dirty.

I waited patiently for two years, until Lehman let the scoundrel go for committing the gravest of offenses. He lost money.

Wall Street traders, as long as they are profitable, are treated like minor deities. Every infraction is forgiven. A loss, on the other hand, leads to a swift ejection from the arena. In an instant, fame and fortune are replaced by obscurity and unemployment. There are no fallback options for the real-life Sherman McCoys.

With his FU check still years from being cashed, Dodger now needed to find a job. To my great surprise, he turned to me for help. He was interested in a job at my firm, a company that he had mercilessly derided not too long ago. I desperately wanted to tell him off, but the gratification would have been short-lived. Instead, I agreed to meet him for drinks, and a changed Dodger showed up. Gone were the bluster and the cockiness, replaced by a newfound humility and affability. The lion had been miraculously transformed into a lamb. I played my part too, without letting on that my sympathies were equally insincere, as was my offer of help.

Like many money-losing traders before him, Dodger sought refuge in sales. He felt that it would be far less stressful to be a casino host than to be a dealer. I introduced him to our sales manager, Harold, and watched in silence as the two men got along fabulously. Several rounds of interviews followed and, with each visit to our office, Dodger became increasingly more confident of landing a job. His high hopes were justified except for one small problem: me.

When Dodger was on the verge of being offered the job, I made my move. I revealed the truth about his character to Harold. I also disclosed the 106/122 incident and encouraged the sales manager to ask Dodger about it. As an added insurance, I gave him an ultimatum.

"If you hire him, I'll quit."

"Are you sure, Gupta?" he asked.

"Absolutely!"

Harold was baffled. On one hand, I had introduced him to Dodger and on the other, I was threatening to resign if he was hired. Regardless, he yanked the job offer, leaving Dodger bewildered. *What happened? It was all going so well.*

It would be two more years before he discovered the answer to that question. By then, I was a client and Dodger was a salesman at a European-owned investment bank. When he found out that I had blocked him from becoming our sales coverage, he tried to bully me once more. This time, however, the tables were turned and his huffing and puffing got him nowhere. Frustrated, he sent me a message: *Now that I think about it, you were probably the reason why I didn't get that other job either.* He had finally figured it out.

Dodger should have paid attention to the adage, "Be nice to people on your way up because you might meet them again on your way down." In a karmic twist, he got divorced a few years later and likely never saw any part of the fifty million dollars.

CHAPTER 21

Yin and Yang

S ean Murphy paused, took a long puff from a freshly lit cigarette, and delivered his verdict.

"You're not a trader. You're a portfolio manager."

With just eight words, Lehman's head of mortgage trading had summed up my predicament. I tried to argue with him, but deep down, I knew that he was right. I was on the wrong side of the fence.

Financial markets are composed of two distinct and complementary sides, the sell side and the buy side. Investment banks, since they are in the business of selling financial products, are known as the sell side. The consumers of those products — money managers, bank portfolios, and hedge funds to name a few — are collectively known as the buy side. The two sides are the yin and yang of the market universe. One cannot exist without the other. A gambler needs a casino just as much as a casino needs gamblers.

It may come as a surprise to many that Wall Street trading desks operate like a department store, albeit one that deals in financial products. Just like department stores divide their floors into sections, the aisles of a trading floor are divided into stocks, bonds, currencies, and commodities. Every area is further subdivided into specialized trading desks such as government, corporate, or mortgage bonds. A trading desk is staffed by several traders, each buying and selling specific instruments in countless transactions with their clients.

The key to success for any store, physical or virtual, is flow. The greater the amount of product moving through a store, the greater its profit. It is not a coincidence that Jeff Bezos named his company after the river that transports the largest volume of water in the world. Likewise, investment banks judge their traders by how "in the flow" they are.

The limiting factor for flow is storage capacity. Even the online giant Amazon, despite its seemingly limitless inventory, is constrained by the size of its fulfillment centers. Similarly, the activities of an investment bank are restricted by its balance sheet, the maximum amount of product that the company can hold at any given time. A larger balance sheet leads to more flow and higher profits while also magnifying losses in a market downturn.

The balance sheet limit extends to every trading desk as well as to individual traders. At large investment banks such as Goldman Sachs or Morgan Stanley, a trading desk's balance sheet can be as high as several billion dollars. Traders are expected to constantly replenish this resource by buying and selling securities as rapidly as possible and making money on the bid-offer spread. Bonds that sit on the books for too long are considered to be aged inventory and are disposed of in a clearance sale.

A sell-side trader's primary responsibility is to trade with customers. He is expected to know who is buying or selling which security, when they are doing it, and in what quantities. The why is of no consequence. A good trader positions himself between customers, buying the product on the bid-side and selling it on the offer-side. Capturing the bid-offer spread is the key to profitability on a trading desk, not understanding the game. Some of the most successful traders I have known make it a point to avoid learning the reasons for their clients' actions. A blackjack dealer doesn't care why a player wants to stand on twelve. His job is to finish the current hand as quickly as possible and deal the next.

The bid-offer spread earned by a sell-side trader varies by product. For the most liquid of bonds, the spread can be as little as one sixty-fourth of one percent or half a tick. As long as there is enough flow, that seemingly minute house advantage can yield a profit of almost a million dollars per day. Investment banks pay their traders top dollar to keep this engine of profit running.

A portfolio manager is the antithesis of a sell-side trader. Instead of turning over his inventory in a matter of hours or days, he (portfolio managers are also mostly male) takes a significantly longer view. He buys an asset that he considers to be undervalued and waits for market conditions to turn in his favor. Since it is impossible to know when the change of fortune might occur, he might be forced to wait for weeks, if not months. During that time, it is possible that the market turns even more adverse, and the position suffers a loss. A successful portfolio manager needs to not only understand the game well, but also employ a trading strategy that can withstand market shocks.

Portfolio management was not the business of Lehman Brothers. Sean expected his traders to buy and sell as much as possible, and as quickly as possible. The goal was to make a small profit on each transaction and make it up in volume. By clogging the desk's balance sheet for months, a portfolio manager violated the sell side's raison d'être. Investment banks, contrary to what their name implies, are not in the business of investing in financial instruments. Investing is the business of the buy side.

As Sean finished his smoke, I made a half-hearted attempt to argue that I wasn't a portfolio manager, and that I was indeed a trader (which I still was then, back in the spring of 1996). However, both of us knew that wasn't true. I had no interest in dealing the cards or in earning the bid-offer spread. I couldn't care less about which client was buying what security and when. Instead, I had focused on the fundamental value of every bond, seeking to buy the ones that were undervalued and to sell those priced too high. In short, I was acting like a portfolio manager, just like Sean had said. What I needed to do was to stop pretending and move to the buy side. But the path to the other side of the fence remained murky at best.

Sean stubbed out his cigarette and I walked out of his office, feeling downcast. I wouldn't have been quite so despondent had I known that I would make it to the buy side three years later. And that I would spend two decades managing money for hedge funds, the pinnacle of high finance.

Hedge funds sit atop the buy-side community, both in skill and in compensation. In 1992, George Soros had famously bet against the British pound, brought the Bank of England to its knees, and pocketed a billion dollars in the process. Unlike the sell side, where political games abound, the hedge fund industry is the closest thing to a meritocracy. You perform and you thrive. You don't and you are out. It is that simple. Hedge fund investors and owners are also color blind. They don't care whether you are black, white, or brown, just as long as you make them some green.

The defining characteristic of hedge funds is their use of borrowed money, also known as leverage. Leverage, however, is a double-edged sword, increasing returns on one hand and reducing the margin for error on the other. The history of hedge funds is littered with bodies of those who borrowed too much and invested in a strategy gone awry. During my sell-side years, many would blow up right in front of my eyes. I was determined to avoid their fate at all costs.

But before I could cross over to the buy side, I needed a "system." With no *Million Dollar Blackjack* to show me the way, I would have to start from scratch. I set myself one simple goal: find a way to consistently beat the market. No ifs, ands, or buts. As in Las Vegas, I was only interested in playing the game for the long haul and not in making a fast buck. To survive for any length of time at a hedge fund, I would need a method that tilted the odds demonstrably in my favor. To accomplish that, I would not only need to gain a deep understanding of the mortgage market, but also develop a disciplined trading strategy as well as a method for managing risk. I didn't know it then, but I was searching for the holy grail of investing.

I slowly walked back to my desk, fearful that Sean's pronouncement had doomed my prospects. To be known as a portfolio manager is the kiss of death on the trading floor. In addition to limiting your career prospects, it also makes you an object of ridicule. However, the more I thought about it, the more I realized that it was futile to disavow my true self. Instead, I decided to embrace the scarlet letters PM and redoubled my efforts to create a methodology. That decision had a profound impact on my immediate future.

I didn't waste time cozying up to clients, or wining and dining them with the goal of separating them from their money as efficiently as possible. I stopped asking customers what they were buying or selling. Instead, I told them what they *should* be doing. I expressed my opinions about markets and securities without restraint, even at the risk of offending clients. This wasn't an exercise in vanity. I wasn't doing this to be smart or show off; I was still trying to educate myself about mortgages and about markets. The average customer was far more experienced than I was and their reactions, both positive as well as negative, proved highly educational as I set about creating an investment framework.

In many ways, I felt very fortunate. I had once again found a purpose in life. Mortgages became an obsession, much like blackjack had once been. I was as determined to beat Wall Street at its own game as I had been to beat the casinos of Las Vegas. I thought about nothing else during the day and stayed awake many nights, trying to decipher the mysteries of the mortgage market. Developing a methodology that would stand the test of time was an exceptionally difficult undertaking, one that would take me years to accomplish. In the meantime, I tested my hypotheses by putting on small trades across the mortgage market. Some of those trades worked and many did not, but they all taught me valuable lessons.

My outspokenness proved to be both a blessing and a curse. While it offended many clients as well as several of my co-workers, it also won me a small but loyal following. A few customers were willing to look past my impertinence and focus on what was important; that I was right more often than I was wrong. Three years later, one of those customers would be instrumental in facilitating my passage to the buy side.

Ironically, in the decade following our pivotal conversation, Sean would try to hire me twice, once as a trader and once as a portfolio manager. I would turn him down on both occasions.

CHAPTER 22

The Mortgage Puzzle

By far, the hardest problem that I have ever tackled is the mortgage puzzle. In retrospect, it's not surprising that it took me almost seven years to come up with a solution. In blackjack, the optimal move can be determined with certainty given the state of a shoe. Not so with financial instruments. They are far too complex for such clear-cut answers. There were times when I didn't even know where to start.

I had shown up on Wall Street not knowing the first thing about finance. Nor had I heard the expression "mortgage-backed security" before. Those three words, however, were destined to play an outsized role in the next twenty-seven years of my life.

A mortgage is simply a loan made with the purpose of facilitating the purchase of real estate. Although properties can range from office buildings to shopping malls, the vast majority of mortgages in America are used for the purpose of buying a single-family home. A homeowner puts up a small down payment, often around twenty percent of the purchase price, and borrows the rest from a bank. The loan is paid off via a series of monthly payments that can last for as long as thirty years. Given that owning a home lies at the heart of the American dream, mortgage finance is a cornerstone of the U.S. economy.

"Security" is another word for a financial instrument that can be freely bought and sold. Stocks and bonds are good examples. A mortgage-backed security (MBS) is a bond backed by a collection of loans. For instance, forty $250,000 loans can be pooled together to create a ten-million-dollar MBS, which can then be sold to investors around the globe. The pooling of a large number of loans, sometimes as many as several thousand, protects investors from the risk of lending to a single borrower. The idea is, there is safety in numbers.

The bulk of mortgage-backed securities in America are issued by three agencies of the U.S. government: Federal National Mortgage Association (FNMA), Federal Home Loan Mortgage Corporation (FHLMC), and Government National Mortgage Association (GNMA). In Wall Street vernacular, they are referred to as Fannie Mae, Freddie Mac, and Ginnie Mae, respectively. Created by an act of the United States Congress, they are charged with promoting home ownership and making housing more affordable. To that end, the agencies act as financial intermediaries for the housing market by purchasing loans from originators, repackaging them into mortgage-backed securities, and selling them in the open market. If a homeowner were to fall behind on their payments, the agencies make up the shortfall to the investor, ensuring that an investor will not lose their principal. Despite that principal guarantee, mortgage-backed securities contain a fair amount of risk. While an investor can rest assured that their principal will be returned, they have no idea when that might occur. It may come back in six months or take longer than ten years.

This unpredictability of cash flows is the result of an option embedded in most home loans; the homeowner can repay any part of the loan early. With a thirty-year loan being the most common mortgage in America, this uncertainty can last for decades. Complicating matters further, the principal is almost always returned at the worst possible time.

Take a $300,000 thirty-year loan with a fixed rate of five percent. In order to repay the loan, a homeowner will need to make a monthly payment of $1,610 for 360 months, making the total amount with interest almost $580,000. A drop of one percent in the mortgage rate, to four percent, would reduce the monthly payments to $1,432, leading to savings of $65,000 over the life of the loan. Even at the cost of several thousand dollars, a homeowner would be well advised to refinance (pay off the old loan and take out a new one). In this scenario, the owner of the five-percent MBS would see a premature return of principal, forcing them to reinvest it at a lower interest rate.

If, on the other hand, interest rates were to rise by one percent, monthly payments would increase to $1,799. The homeowner, having locked in a below-market rate for thirty years, would now make only the minimum payment required. With the return of principal delayed, the MBS holder would be prevented from earning the higher prevailing rate.

Investors expect to be compensated for this risk and are paid roughly one percent more than the rate on the ten-year treasury note. However, that advantage is scant protection in volatile markets.

The homeowner's option to pay off a loan early, known in the industry as the prepayment option, makes it extremely difficult to determine what a mortgage bond is worth. Valuation is affected by a large number of variables, some that can be quantified and many that cannot. The quantifiable variables consist of interest rates, shape of the yield curve, volatility, and prepayments. Interest rates are fundamental to the pricing of any bond and mortgages are no exception. When rates go up, the price of a mortgage falls and vice versa. The shape of the yield curve is indicative of interest rates in the future, a significant factor in determining not only what future cash flows are worth, but also homeowner prepayments. Volatile markets are detrimental to mortgage investors because they increase the uncertainty about future homeowner behavior. Lastly and most importantly, the absolute rate of homeowner prepayments is a critical factor in determining the price of a mortgage. The higher the prepayments in a low-interest-rate environment, the worse it is for the holder of a mortgage-backed security. The same is true for low prepayments in a high-interest-rate scenario.

It would be impossible for anyone to come up with a complete list of the non-quantifiable variables that affect the mortgage market. Simply put, there are just too many. For starters, the list would need to include any economic indicator that could affect housing prices: unemployment rate, inflation, personal income and spending, commodity prices, population growth, and household debt, to name a few. Government intervention in the mortgage market and unexpected changes in regulation make the task even harder. In addition, systemic changes in leverage and financing, also impossible to foresee, only add to the complexity of the problem, as do innovations in mortgage lending and changes in the risk profiles of financial institutions. Then in 2020, an entirely new variable roiled the mortgage market — a pandemic.

Despite the risks involved, the agency MBS market was, and still is, one of the largest and most liquid bond markets in the world. In the mid-1990s, there were several trillion dollars' worth of mortgages outstanding and tens, if not hundreds of billions changed hands daily. Consequently, the bid-offer spread for the most frequently traded mortgage bonds, called passthroughs because they passed the monthly homeowner payments through to investors, was as little as 0.015 percent. The razor-thin house advantage made trading passthroughs especially attractive, and they would form the foundation of my investment framework.

If I were to have any hope of beating the market on a consistent basis, I knew that I would need to first understand the risks contained in an MBS, and then neutralize them one by one. Given the sheer number of variables involved, the task seemed almost impossible. Nevertheless, I started by examining how others had tackled the problem before me.

There were two schools of thought about how mortgages should be valued. One looked to the past and the other to the future. I would eventually discard both methods, choosing to focus on the present instead.

Historical analysis, as its name implies, attempts to fit today's prices into a historical context by running a series of correlations and regressions. I found this to be a lazy way of managing money. Correlation is not causation and it is impossible to predict when the relationships between the variables might break down. Regressions assume that the world will go back to the way it was and are unable to detect paradigm shifts, which also occur regularly. For instance, a model that applies regression to buggy whip prices would be useless in a world transitioning to motor cars. Furthermore, the choice of a regression time period, whether three months or two years, often produces different results. By focusing solely on prices, regressions also fail to take into account the key risk for mortgages: changing prepayment patterns.

One of the more glaring examples of the flaws in a regression-based methodology occurred during my buy-side years. Morgan Stanley's head of passthrough trading, armed with a new statistical model, urged clients to sell a particular trade. When I asked him why, he replied, "My regression model tells me so."

A few months later, with prices substantially higher, the same model concluded that the trade was now worth buying. I burst out laughing because *sell low, buy high* is not a winning strategy in any market. I couldn't help asking the model's creator if he saw the obvious inconsistency between the two trade recommendations.

"No," he replied, without a trace of irony.

To this day, it remains a mystery to me why reputed money managers swear by this methodology. I myself have never run a regression in my life.

The second approach to valuing mortgages focuses on predicting the future. Math PhDs perennially find their skills in demand as hedge funds (and dealers) are continually building complex models to predict prepayment rates ten, twenty, and even thirty years into the future. In reality, predicting homeowner behavior is an unsolvable problem. While homeowners tend to refinance their loans when interest rates fall, exactly how many will do so is unknowable. Lower interest rates are typically caused by economic downturns, which are often accompanied by a decline in home prices. To refinance an existing loan, a homeowner would have to make up the difference between the old appraisal and the new. Furthermore, recession-related job losses make it even harder for a borrower to qualify for a new loan, no matter how low the rate.

Conversely, higher interest rates don't always suppress refinancing activity. Rising home prices allow cash-strapped homeowners to use their house as an ATM. By refinancing into a larger loan, they can take cash out of the house and use it for a variety of purposes: make home improvements, go on a vacation, or retire their credit card debt, to name a few.

I considered any methodology that relied upon forecasting the future to be, in a word, foolish. Predicting prepayment rates was as difficult as forecasting the weather, if not more so. No meteorologist would dare predict the New York City weather for June 20, 2035. Prepayment models on the other hand suffer from no such scruples and would confidently forecast a high of 87.3 degrees.

These future-based models failed every few years, and yet hedge funds swore by them. Each claimed to have the best model, which made me wonder if it was a marketing tool in disguise. The boom-bust cycle that the mortgage market had become famous for was most likely the result of an overreliance on such models.

Since forecasting prepayments was an impossibility, there was only one way forward. I would have to be immune to them. This stood in sharp contrast to almost every other hedge fund manager who believed that great rewards lay in assuming prepayment risk, not in neutralizing it. While their method worked from time to time, it was doomed to failure in the long run. I had no interest in pursuing a methodology that worked only part of the time.

As I had done with correlations and regressions, I stayed away from forecasting prepayments as well. Instead, I trained my sights on a problem that I considered to be far more manageable: *How sensitive is the price of any mortgage-backed security to changing prepayments?*

By quantifying the effect of prepayments on the price of any mortgage bond, I aimed to create a prepayment-neutral portfolio by mixing and matching bonds with opposite sensitivities. Unfortunately, this was easier said than done. It required me to go beyond the IO/PO market and plumb the depths of the broader mortgage market, especially passthroughs. My goal was to create a theoretical framework where every mortgage bond would fit neatly into a jigsaw puzzle. I was keenly aware that, in reality, that would almost never be the case. A robust theoretical framework was necessary, however, to identify the pieces that stuck out.

While I refused to trust prepayment models to make investment decisions, they proved invaluable in developing a methodology. A construct truly independent of prepayment risk would also be independent of the projections of any prepayment model. A trade that was genuinely mispriced would look mispriced in every model, from the slowest to the fastest, from the rudimentary to the most sophisticated. To mimic a variety of models, I simply took the one that was easily available and modified it every which way. It was hard work but I plugged away at it and, after years of effort, was able to come up with a broad framework.

Before it could be used in the real world, however, the system needed to answer four questions:

1. What types of mortgage bonds would I trade?
2. With those bonds, what sorts of trades would I put on?
3. How would I enter trades and how would I exit them?
4. How would I protect myself from changing financial conditions, notably in leverage and financing?

The answer to the first question was easy. In the world of mortgage-backed securities, only two markets were considered liquid, passthroughs and STRIPS. Both instruments allowed investors to be long as well as short, making it possible to bet on prices rising as well as falling. They also carried the lowest bid-offer spread, half a tick for passthroughs and four ticks for IOs. Consequently, in two decades of managing money, I have only played in those two markets.

The second question posed a considerably harder problem. After much deliberation, I decided that, instead of attempting to determine the absolute value of any mortgage bond, I would try to create a relative value (RV) methodology. As implied by its name, a relative value trade is a bet on the price relationship between two or more bonds such that their absolute prices become irrelevant. This forced me to concentrate on a handful of trade constructs — coupon swaps, butterflies, IO swaps among them — whose fair value I felt was knowable. The RV method severely restricted the types of trades that I could execute, but at the same time, it also sharpened my focus. Interestingly, my search for an investment method had also become a quest for fairness, this time between the prices of various bonds.

The methodology for entering and exiting trades, a complex topic in its own right, also required a fair amount of thought. It forced me to clearly explain (to myself) why mispricings occurred in the mortgage market in the first place, and how they would correct.

It took me a while, but I figured out that pricing anomalies in the mortgage market are the result of a narrowly focused client base. Investors in mortgages range from government institutions (U.S. Treasury, the Federal Reserve, overseas central banks, and the mortgage agencies themselves) and financial intermediaries (banks, insurance companies, mortgage originators) to investment firms (money managers and hedge funds). Each investor class utilizes the mortgage market for a specific purpose, without any regard for how their trade fits into the overall market. For instance, the Federal Reserve buys vast quantities of mortgages in an attempt to drive mortgage rates down — a process known as quantitative easing. Overseas central banks utilize the mortgage market to park the dollars earned from their trade surplus with America. Bank portfolios use mortgages as a repository for customer deposits. Hedge funds use them to speculate.

It was hard to believe, but I didn't know of any buy-sider that was solely focused on identifying and exploiting mispricing across various mortgage sectors. Nor was I aware of any customer who insisted on being prepayment neutral at all times. Investors in the mortgage market had gotten used to the fact that they were at the mercy of volatile markets and the whims of homeowners, a fate that I refused to accept.

Once I had determined why mispricings existed in the mortgage market, I turned my attention to how they might be corrected. There were two possible ways for prices to come back in line, either through a repricing of risk or via a phenomenon I call "shared experience."

The repricing of risk occurred if and when other market participants came to the same realization as I had. They would either buy the bonds that I already owned or sell the ones that I was short. In either case, prices would move in my favor, allowing me to exit my position in a matter of days or weeks. The vast majority of my trades, however, required several months of shared experience.

All my constructs were composed of two or more bonds whose prices were out of line with respect to one another. Such a mispricing could exist if a market participant had sold the first bond at too low a price or another investor had paid too much for the second bond. If I had calculated correctly, both could not be right. It is important to note that I never choose sides in a conflict. I couldn't care less who won and who lost.

The winner would be determined over the next several weeks and months. During that time, no matter how divergent their initial views were, both sides in this conflict would be subjected to the exact same market conditions and the loser would have to capitulate. For instance, a market participant betting that interest rates would rise could withstand only so much pain if rates were to fall steadily instead. There is nothing like sustained losses to make your bosses pay attention and ask you to exit your position, if not the building. At the very minimum, adverse market moves cause customers and dealers alike to rethink their original ideas. While markets are frequently irrational in the short term, it is my firm conviction that they are incredibly logical in the long run. This is the fundamental tenet I formulated, the cornerstone of my money management philosophy: *the market's short-term irrationality creates opportunities and its long-term rationality creates profits*. It may take some time, but the true odds will eventually be realized. If this were not the case, developing any sort of methodology would be a waste of time. In other words, if the fourth ace does not come out by the end of the deck, the game is not worth playing.

This led me to a fairly straightforward yet highly disciplined method for entering and exiting trades. I always start small, no matter how attractively a trade is priced. My sizes are minute in the context of the larger market, and it is highly unlikely that the trade would turn around the moment I chose to get involved.

Nine times out of ten, my first trade loses money.

I then reexamine the idea from every possible angle, and if there is no reason to change my opinion, I double down.

Seven times out of ten, my second trade loses money.

This process repeats itself until one of two events occurs: I discover a market bottom — usually after the seventh or eighth iteration — or I realize that I have made a mistake. Whenever the latter occurs, I immediately liquidate the portfolio. As in blackjack, there is no room for emotion in managing money.

There is also a third possibility, that I reach my position limit and am unable to add to the trade. Every hedge fund restricts how much balance sheet a portfolio manager can use as well as how much risk he can take, as measured by something known in the industry as value at risk (VaR). VaR is a price-based measure of the riskiness of an asset; the more volatile a security's price, the greater its VaR. For instance, an investment in bitcoin will have a considerably higher VaR than the same amount invested in short-term U.S. Treasury bonds. Furthermore, a portfolio manager is also subject to a drawdown limit, the maximum amount of money he can lose before he gets liquidated, if not fired. In my case, careful trade sizing has ensured that I have never come close to breaching any of my limits in two decades of managing money, a fact that has continually irked my bosses.

I have often wondered if I could skip the first few trades and avoid the agony of losing money. But over time, I have come to accept that a temporary loss of money is integral to my method. Countless losing streaks in Vegas had made me realize that nothing made me focus like underperforming. That focus allows me to either discover an error or have renewed confidence in the idea. In both cases, the course of action is obvious. Successful money management is not about becoming adept at making difficult choices. It is about avoiding situations where one might be forced to make them.

I add risk *only* when my trades are losing money, and *never* when they are going my way. Losing money is synonymous with a construct moving further away from its fair value, thereby increasing not only its profit potential but also the probability of success. Both reasons demand that more capital be deployed.

The opposite is true when a trade outperforms. The profit potential as well as the probability of continued success both fall. While that often causes momentum investors to jump in and buy, I take a step back and do nothing. And when the trade reaches anywhere close to fair value, I take it off. Completely.

Although I add risk incrementally, I subtract it in one fell swoop. When I take a trade off, I don't sell a part of it. I sell everything. Even though I have done so for decades, I am not quite sure why. My best guess is that adding risk feels like stepping out into the wilderness — something that needs to be done carefully. Subtracting it, on the other hand, is akin to returning home. I know the way and there is no reason to be bashful.

The final piece of the puzzle was figuring out how to protect myself from the ever-changing financial landscape and guard against systemic changes in leverage and financing, risks that affect hedge funds more than any other investor class. Hedge funds use leverage to amplify returns, which requires them to borrow vast sums of money. The amounts borrowed as well as the rate of interest are critical in determining the performance of any hedge fund. Looser financial conditions lead to an increase in available leverage, causing asset prices to rise. So does easier financing. A financial crisis has the opposite effect. Markets seize up, credit disappears, and asset prices fall, pulling the rug out from those making a living from borrowed money.

I racked my brain but was unable to find any means of predicting changes in leverage and financing, which meant that I would have to hedge out this risk as well. It took me a while, but the solution turned out to be deceptively simple. I simply needed to make sure that my mortgage longs and shorts were in the same amounts. As long as the net market value of my mortgage portfolio was zero, systemic changes would affect both sides of my position equally. This led to the elimination of the most popular trade in the mortgage market from my repertoire. Basis trading, as the trade is known, is the buying or selling of passthroughs against U.S. Treasury bonds. I had long felt that the relationship between the two markets, mortgages and treasuries, was tenuous at best and could not be relied upon during periods of stress. Despite its poor risk/reward ratio, investors continue to swear by the strategy and basis trading remains widespread to this day.

My rigid approach to money management would lead to regular debates with industry colleagues. Buy- and sell-siders alike argued against my opposition to basis trading and to regressions and correlations. One of the largest money managers in the world, despite having based their entire methodology on historical analysis, was unable to articulate why it was the correct approach. Nor did they care. As far as they were concerned, the ends justified the means. Logic and reason be damned.

When the money manager pointed to their past profits as a justification for their method, I could not resist firing back.

"From time to time, two plus two equals five can make you a lot of money in the markets."

CHAPTER 23

Hedge Funds Behaving Badly

The Russian financial crisis of 1998 caused many mortgage hedge funds to not only lose a great deal of money, but also their minds. The market gyrations of that summer led to the downfall of Long-Term Capital Management (LTCM), the famed Connecticut hedge fund that was led by Nobel Prize–winning economists and much-celebrated Wall Street traders.

That year also provided the first real test of my investment framework and it came through with flying colors. For the past three years, I had tested my theories by putting on test trades across the mortgage market. The performance of those trades had led me to believe that I was on to something. Although it was still young, my framework allowed me not only to sidestep the incredible market volatility of 1998, but also to profit from it. Success proved to be bittersweet, however. My outspokenness led one hedge fund to blame me for their losses and, as the year drew to a close, yet another tried to bully me into revealing my method. Both failed.

I was still stuck on the sell side, employed as a dealer, and playing just one game: interest only (IO) and principal only (PO) securities. As discussed before, an IO and a PO are two complementary pieces of a mortgage bond and they are considered to be some of the riskiest securities in the agency mortgage market. A refinancing boom, usually caused by lower mortgage rates, has a devastating effect on IOs as no further interest payments would be forthcoming on existing loans. Similarly, a rise in interest rates is catastrophic for PO owners. Hence, the prices of IOs and POs are extremely sensitive to interest rates as well as to the behavior of homeowners across America.

My job required me to perform a narrowly defined task: trade IOs and POs with clients and make money for the company. Nevertheless, I had decided to expand my horizons to the broader mortgage market. I knew that the creation of a robust investment framework would require an understanding of all the pieces of the jigsaw puzzle, not just IOs and POs. As it turned out, a bird's eye view of the mortgage market also made it easier for me to determine what IOs and POs were worth.

In early 1998, I came to a startling conclusion. After looking at the market from every angle, I became convinced that IOs were overpriced by at least twenty percent, if not more. In the bond market, mispricings of that magnitude were extremely rare. This was by far the biggest trading opportunity of my career.

While there were a number of reasons for my findings, three in particular stood out: the recent fall in interest rates, a rise in housing prices, and the pricing of risk in other areas of the mortgage market. A financial crisis in Asia had caused interest rates to fall steadily in the second half of 1997, until they hit a local bottom in January 1998. The accompanying fall in mortgage rates signaled an impending refinancing boom which, if realized, would clobber IO prices. Moreover, an increase in home prices had caused the newly issued mortgages to have significantly larger loan sizes than their older counterparts, by almost thirty percent. This made refinancing a loan even more attractive for a homeowner as their monthly savings would increase by the same percentage. Consequently, I expected mortgage prepayments to be considerably higher than what the IO market could handle.

I shared my concerns with a New York money manager who was heavily invested in IOs. There would come a time when I would no longer feel the need to discuss mortgages with others, but I wasn't there yet.

The money manager decided to teach me a lesson.

"Kamal, you're not getting it," he said, in a tone that implied that he was about to school me in something important.

"What am I not getting?" I asked.

"Loan sizes have gone up, sure, but so have people's incomes," he explained.

"Yes, I know that."

"Since the average homeowner has more money in his pocket, he would need a greater dollar incentive to refinance," he continued.

"So what are you saying? Loan sizes have no impact on prepayments?" I asked him, just to be sure.

"Yes. That's exactly what I'm saying," he said and hung up the phone.

I was floored by what the guy had said. He was effectively claiming that a rise in one's income would make it less likely that they would pick up a dollar bill off the street. Refinancing a mortgage was the closest thing to free money that I knew of, and I was certain that homeowners in America would jump at the chance to lower their monthly payments. To be fair, it wasn't just him. My views about higher loan sizes leading to higher prepayments were almost universally mocked. I never even got around to discussing the biggest reason I felt the way I did about IO prices.

That reason — how risk was priced in other mortgage assets — formed the foundation of my investment philosophy. While I was highly confident in my views about IOs, I also realized that there was a nontrivial probability that I was wrong. That's why, for every mispricing that I saw, I sought confirmation from other areas in the mortgage market. A significant part of my last three years had been spent looking for ways to decode the prepayment risk priced in various mortgage bonds. I would then buy bonds that had priced in a high degree of risk and sell the ones that had done the opposite. It was hard work, much harder than learning to count cards, but also incredibly satisfying. Being hedged against the possibility of being wrong was the number one reason I felt I had an edge in the market.

The irony was that, contrary to what their name implied, most hedge funds did not hedge. Led by the LTCMs of the world, hedge funds had transformed themselves into the high rollers of high finance, relying on fancy mathematical models to assume more and more risk. While this high-risk strategy carried with it a higher financial reward, it also increased the probability of a career-ending blow up, something I was determined to avoid at all cost.

Once, at a dinner with one of LTCM's many clones, I asked the hedge fund's portfolio manager a simple question.

"Do you really make all your investment decisions on the basis of your model?"

He gave me an icy stare and replied, "Our models represent the sum total of our wisdom. So yes, that's how we make our decisions."

Well before LTCM's collapse in the fall of 1998, I knew that was a flawed approach. I had used models on a daily basis as well, but only as a sanity check. Moreover, I had worked extra hard to make sure that the success of my trades was not dependent on any model's predictions. Coincidentally, LTCM had also been heavily invested in IOs just as I had determined that they were grossly overvalued.

One of my duties as a trader at an investment bank was to send out a morning commentary. Throughout January and February 1998, my message was brief and to the point.

Sell IOs if you have them. Sell them even if you don't.

My views made me deeply unpopular, especially with hedge funds that owned large amounts of IOs. For the umpteenth time in my life, I felt that the world had lined up against me. Also for the umpteenth time in my life, I stuck to my guns.

One hedge fund was especially vocal, Forward Point Capital (FPC). FPC's portfolio managers didn't just ignore my commentary, they did the exact opposite, buying IOs hand over fist. It was astonishing to me how two people could look at the same information and arrive at diametrically opposite conclusions. Over time, I would realize that it is this phenomenon that makes markets. For every buyer, there must be a willing seller or the market ceases to exist.

IO prices rose throughout January and for most of February, partly due to Forward Point's large-scale buy program, causing me to suffer losses in my position. That did little to shake my conviction and I added to my trade every time prices went up, albeit in small increments. It was against this backdrop that I visited the hedge fund's offices in upstate New York, and urged them to sell their holdings. The firm's portfolio managers were sitting on a tidy profit and feeling pretty good about themselves.

"I really think you should get out of your IOs. I fear that March and April prepayment data won't be kind to them," I warned.

"We're not worried," they said.

This made no sense. While they were within their rights to disagree with me, I felt that not worrying was a luxury that a hedge fund could not afford.

"Why is that?" I asked.

"Even if you're right, Kamal, and IO prices do crash, that will be good for us," they said, leaving me dumbfounded.

"How will that be good for you? You're buying them now. Won't you lose a great deal of money?" I asked.

"True, but then we'll be able to buy a lot more at lower prices."

I let out a long and audible sigh, amazed that the hedge fund was unaware of the glaring hole in their game plan. *If prices fall, then we'll buy more* sounds great on paper but rarely works in real life. It's one thing to talk about losses in an abstract sense, but it is entirely another to experience them firsthand. I had suffered plenty of losing streaks in Las Vegas and in New York, enough to know the damage they can do to your psyche. Their bravado notwithstanding, I didn't believe that Forward Point's portfolio managers would be able to retain their confidence in a market downturn. More importantly, even if they were somehow able to maintain their conviction, the same could not be said for their investors. Hedge fund investors are an impatient lot who are quick to withdraw their funds from underperforming managers, forcing them to sell their assets into an already depressed market.

In short, that's what happened to Forward Point.

The bump in IO prices gave way to a steady downward slide during spring, caused by the higher prepayment rates that I had feared. As the summer of 1998 rolled around, prices went into freefall. Far from buying more in the downturn, Forward Point was one of the sellers.

One morning, as the IO market continued its march downwards, I heard a voice over my shoulder.

"Goopy, the guys at Forward want to talk to you."

It was Gregory Andrews, the hedge fund's salesperson at our firm. We had become friends despite my not having shown him any mercy when it came to business.

"Greg, I begged them to sell but they wouldn't listen. There's nothing left to talk about," I replied.

Greg had seen for himself how the hedge fund's portfolio managers had dismissed everything I had said about IOs. Now it was too late. The fat lady had sung and I saw little point in rehashing the matter. Greg, however, was a salesman and it was his job to keep the client happy.

"I know, Goopy. They lost big. I don't know why, but they want to talk to you. It won't take more than a few minutes. Just do it, please."

I put down my pencil and warned him, "Fine, I'll talk to them but you're making this call at your own peril."

Greg understood the risks but dialed anyway. The conversation began with the hedge fund's portfolio managers bemoaning the market move. I knew full well how great their loss was, so I kept my mouth shut — until the point where they started blaming me for their losses.

"Wait a second," I interjected, "you think I'm responsible for your losing money?"

"Well, kind of . . ."

I cut them off, "How? Did I not ask you again and again to sell your IOs?"

"It was your morning commentary. Day after day, week after week, you said sell, sell, sell!" they said.

I couldn't believe what I was hearing.

"Are you serious? My morning commentary is to blame for the crash in IOs?" I asked, my voice rising.

"Yes."

To say that I was incensed would be a gross understatement. Forward Point's portfolio managers, who should have been looking inwards for flaws in their investment process, had chosen to cast blame on a small dealer's market commentary instead. Greg knew that I wouldn't take the accusation lying down and waved his hands wildly, motioning me to let it go. I ignored his flailing. A charge like this could not go unanswered. Just like their game plan from three months ago, Forward Point's argument had a gaping hole that needed to be pointed out.

"If my commentary is so damn powerful then how dare you not follow what it says?" I shouted and slammed the phone down, leaving Greg to clean up the mess. Incredibly, the portfolio managers were at a loss as to why I was so irate. I was angry because they had refused to take responsibility for their actions. They had to have known that no commentary was that powerful, least of all mine. And if they didn't know that, they had no business running a hedge fund.

The IO market, in the meantime, had turned into a runaway train. There was no telling where it would stop. I had covered my shorts in IOs (by selling all the POs that I had owned) and sat on the sidelines until the collapse of LTCM in fall of that year. There was widespread pain in the market and hedge fund after hedge fund suffered huge losses. In a remarkable turn of events, the same IOs that I had found to be twenty percent overpriced in the spring were now fifteen percent underpriced. My morning commentary in late October said *buy IOs*, causing a Rhode Island hedge fund to send a message to my firm: "Kamal has picked the top and the bottom of the IO market this year." It was high praise indeed.

I ended 1998 feeling upbeat. My system had performed admirably and, after six long years on the sell side, I felt that I could see the light at the end of the tunnel. Unfortunately, there were a few more obstacles before I could escape from it.

"Gupta, Mark wants to go to dinner."

It was Harold, the sales manager who had been the instrument of my revenge against Dodger. Mark was the founder of a medium-sized hedge fund that had also had a disastrous 1998.

"Are you sure?" I asked, as I was surprised to hear this.

"Yup, and we'll even go to a restaurant where a lettuce-eater like yourself can get something to eat," said Harold.

My relationship with this hedge fund had also been fraught. Mark had made it clear that he did not approve of my market views, which in itself was not a problem for me. I took issue, however, with the hedge fund's repeated attempts to nudge IO prices higher by making it seem like they were a buyer when they really weren't. In one particularly heated exchange, Mark had even asked me directly, "So are you saying that we're not a buyer and that we're just pretending?" By then, I was fed up with their shenanigans and told him flat out, "Yes, that's what I'm saying." To say the least, he was not amused and our relationship had turned even frostier.

At a golf outing that summer, Mark had remarked to a friend of mine, "If IOs fall in price by another two or three percent, we will buy a billion!" Over the next two months, in a repeat of what had happened to Forward Point, Mark was forced to sell as prices dropped not by two, but by another ten percent. The hedge fund's aggregate losses in 1998 had amounted to a nine-digit number.

I had no desire to go to dinner with Mark, but I didn't have the option of saying no. One of the curses of working at an investment bank was that if a client wanted to go to dinner, you not only went but you also paid for it. The only good thing was that Harold had picked a midtown Italian restaurant instead of a steakhouse.

At dinner, as was customary for him, Harold lubricated us with bottle after bottle of expensive red wine. I was starting to get settled in when the conversation turned towards a topic that made me decidedly uncomfortable.

"So, Kamal, you were convinced last spring that IOs were greatly over-valued?" I knew that Mark had posed the question rhetorically. Everyone in the market knew where I had stood.

"I was," I replied, wondering where he was going with it.

"Why?"

I froze. It suddenly became clear to me why we were all there.

"Excuse me?" I mumbled.

"How do you look at these bonds?" Mark said, removing all doubt about what he was asking.

I felt my hackles raising.

"Sorry, what?" I said, in an attempt to buy time and get my thoughts in order.

"I'd like to understand your methodology. How do you decide when to buy or sell?" Mark said calmly as if he were discussing the weather.

The buzz from three glasses of wine vanished in an instant and I found myself jolted back to reality. In many ways, the situation reminded me of my first barring at a casino. Mark had admitted defeat just like the Bally's shift manager had. Once again, a fleeting feeling of satisfaction was swiftly replaced by a growing sense of horror.

The distinguishing feature of hedge funds is that they are notoriously secretive about their methodology and go to great lengths to keep it concealed.

Every hedge fund has a secret sauce, a recipe that determines their trading strategy and keeps them in business. Just like diners in a restaurant wouldn't have the temerity to ask a chef for the recipe for their favorite dish, no one would dare ask a hedge fund about their methodology. Unfortunately for Mark, I felt the same way about mine.

Even though I understood that he must have swallowed a great deal of pride before casually asking me *why*, I was never going to answer that question. It had taken a great deal of pain and suffering for me to create an investment framework and I wasn't about to give it up.

"I'm sorry, but I can't discuss that with you," I replied and put down my fork in preparation for the backlash.

"Why not?" Mark demanded.

"My method is private and I'd prefer to keep it that way," I said.

This was the worst-case outcome for Mark. He had been loath to ask me in the first place and my refusal had only added insult to injury. Harold looked like he was about to have a fit.

"Gupta, stop being so difficult. Can't you see that Mark is paying you a compliment?" he said.

Compliment or not, I knew that it was only a matter of time before I went to a hedge fund. Educating a future competitor would be downright foolish.

"I'm sorry. I can't do it," I said.

It didn't take long for Mark to revert back to form.

"If you won't disclose your method, how do I know that you're not simply guessing?" he said, goading me further.

This tactic wasn't going to work either. Mark knew full well that there was a careful thought process behind my decisions. So I fired back.

"Maybe I am guessing. But if my guesses turn out to be right more often than not, then perhaps you should follow them."

Mark was starting to get annoyed with me. He made one final attempt to strong-arm me into giving him what he wanted.

"You can't afford to take this high-and-mighty attitude, Kamal. You're a small dealer. You need customers."

His not-so-subtle threat to cut me off from future business pushed me over the edge.

"I don't think so! If the past twelve months are any guide, customers need me more than I need them!" I retorted.

That shut him up. I never heard from Mark again.

Many years later, a Turkish-born mortgage trader offered me fifty thousand dollars an hour to teach him how to value mortgages, something Mark had demanded for free.

I refused him too. The price was too low.

CHAPTER 24
Escape from the Sell Side

The hits kept on coming. Having gained a small measure of recognition for my calls during the Russian crisis, I found myself under attack from all sides. Clients as well as competitors hounded me with questions about methodology. The Florida hedge fund that had sold the three hundred million 235 IOs dispatched their head of research to New York. My refusal to answer his questions infuriated not only the hedge fund and their salesperson at our firm, but my bosses as well.

I was keenly aware that my attitude wasn't winning me any friends, but I refused to be distracted from the task at hand, which was to fine-tune my method for use in the real world. With every passing day, I acted more and more like a portfolio manager instead of the trader that I was supposed to be. I was thereby sowing the seeds of my own downfall, which came in the fall of 1999 when I was fired from the sell side. The timing could not have been more perfect: I had secured a job on the buy side the day before.

Another side effect of my performance during the Russian crisis was the periodic attempts by rival investment banks to recruit me. One such feeler came from Morgan Stanley, the perennial also-ran of the mortgage market. At the behest of a customer, I agreed to have a drink with the company's sales manager. After an hour-long conversation, he asked me to come to their headquarters for a longer interview.

"I don't think so," I said, afraid changing jobs would delay my passage to the buy side.

He implored me to reconsider.

"What do you have to lose?"

As it turned out, my dignity.

One evening after work, I walked into Morgan Stanley's Times Square offices, expecting the company to roll out the welcome mat. The head of sales had practically begged me to come, a fact I had assumed all his colleagues would have been made aware of.

I could not have been more wrong. Far from rolling out the red carpet, Morgan Stanley set a pit bull upon me instead. Right from the start, I found myself under attack from Chip, a mid-level manager in their mortgage business. He charged at me with the one question that I had grown tired of.

"Tell me how you look at mortgages," he demanded, his tone making it clear that he expected me to comply.

I mumbled, "Excuse me?"

"You claim to have a method. What is it?" There was no beating about the bush for the pit bull.

I was stunned by his presumptuousness. It was one thing for a client to ask me that question, but surely Chip knew that it was inappropriate for a competitor to do so. If he knew, he didn't act like it. So I told him that I wasn't going to discuss it.

He jabbed me further, wondering out loud, "How else are we supposed to judge if you know your stuff?"

"Ask your clients," I said, knowing full well that Morgan Stanley had already done so, even before my drink with the sales manager.

Chip was not pleased and he went on the offensive, alternately mocking and threatening me. That windowless office, in a remote corner of the trading floor, started to feel increasingly claustrophobic. I would find out later that this was standard operating procedure for him. He especially enjoyed badgering fresh Ivy-league graduates searching for their first Wall Street job.

Unfortunately for Chip, I was neither a fresh grad nor did I need a job. I had also dealt with enough bullies in the industry by then and the hound of Morgan Stanley didn't scare me. I figured that the time had come for me to straighten him out.

"I think I know what the problem is, Chip. You seem to be under the impression that I'm here looking for a job," I said.

"Well, you're here, aren't you?" he sneered.

That was the final straw. I put my palms on the desk separating us, stood up, and barked back.

"You're right, Chip. I am here. But with every passing second I'm beginning to wonder why!"

That shut him up. He realized that he had overplayed his hand and that I was on the verge of walking out. He dashed out of the office and went to fetch some grown-ups. They tried their best to salvage the situation, but it was too late. The sales manager's apologies rang hollow. There was no way for me to know whether Chip's tactics had been a mistake or a part of Morgan Stanley's plan. Regardless, I was done with the company.

"Take my name off the list of candidates," I said and stormed out.

One year later, Chip apologized profusely, but not because he had had a change of heart. I had moved to the buy side and he was afraid that I might cut his firm off. As always in this business, it came down to dollars and cents.

After Morgan Stanley, it was a large New York money manager's turn. That investment powerhouse had recently hired a highly-ranked researcher as their head of mortgages. Protocol required that every dealer pay their respects to the new hire. Customers were the lifeblood of the sell side's profits and this money manager was among the biggest. I was looking forward to the meeting, as my disillusionment with Wall Street research was still a few years away. The guy had a sterling reputation and I figured that he could teach me a thing or two.

One afternoon, a five-member contingent from my firm marched over to their offices in midtown Manhattan. We crammed into a closet-sized conference room along with eight of their best and brightest. The researcher, befitting his status, sat at the head of the table and I secured a seat around the corner from him. Half the people in the room were forced to stand. Led by our saleswoman, the passthrough traders made a pitch for more of the company's business. Then came the CMO traders and, finally, me.

"I trade IOs and POs," I said.

"Interesting. Are there opportunities in that market?" the researcher asked. I thought that the question was odd — every market has opportunities, it's just a question of finding them — but I let it pass. I then made a catastrophic error. I mentioned my methodology, unsolicited.

"Yes, especially if you take into account the relationship between STRIPS and passthroughs," I replied, causing the passthrough traders to roll their eyes. They had heard it all before.

"What do you mean?" the researcher said.

The blank look on his face told me all that I needed to know. Apparently, he had no idea what I was talking about. I had only brought up the matter because I was convinced that he knew a lot more about mortgages than me. His reaction, though, made me regret what I had done. I tried to put the cat back into the bag, but to no avail.

"Well, it's complicated. It depends on the shape of the yield curve, the volatility surface, and the risk premium in the market. It'll take me a long time to go through it," I said, backpedaling furiously. I couldn't think of any other way to extricate myself from the situation other than to throw out buzzwords.

It didn't work. He ignored the eleven other people in the room and trained his eyes on me, firing question after question. I spewed meaningless jargon in the hope that he would give up, but he was undeterred.

"Go back to your office and write a document describing your system. I want to see it," he said, to my great shock.

I found it breathtaking that the top mortgage professional at a top money manager had asked me to hand him a methodology. While I was never going to do it, I took comfort in the fact that if the great researcher wasn't aware of my method, then it was highly unlikely that anyone else would be either. I escaped from the conference room and promptly forgot about his request. He, however, would not be denied. The saleswoman harassed me nonstop for the write-up. After a few days, I told her straight up that I wasn't going to do it. In return, she complained to my bosses, who ordered me to comply. I was left with no alternative but to start typing.

As I stared at the blank page on my computer, a way out dawned on me. Nobody had any idea what I was talking about. Not the researcher, not my superiors, and certainly not the saleswoman. They had all asked for a method and I would give them one.

Just not the right one.

It took me a day and a half to come up with a plausible scheme. The logic was deeply flawed and the framework was full of holes. But it would get the saleswoman and my superiors off my back. They didn't know any better. The money manager was a different story. I fully expected the mortgage head to spot the inconsistencies in my report, but I figured that I would cross that bridge if and when I came to it.

To my great relief, despite his repeated requests for my write-up, the researcher had no response to it. Upon reading it, he must have thought that I was an idiot. I wouldn't have blamed him. I would have thought the same if someone had sent me that drivel. From my perspective, it was much better to be thought of as a fool than to give up the goods.

While I had refused to discuss my framework with virtually anyone, there was one client that I freely shared it with: Max. It turned out to be a wise choice because, a few years later, he would open a door to the buy side for me.

Max ran a proprietary trading group at the Swiss bank Credit Suisse. A proprietary trading group, for all practical purposes, functions like a hedge fund, but with one significant difference. Whereas a typical hedge fund has tens, if not hundreds of investors, a proprietary trading group has only one. Consequently, the group's profits belong solely to the parent company and so do the losses. LTCM had its origins in Solly-Arb, a proprietary trading group at Salomon Brothers, the legendary bond trading house.

Max had been in the business for a long time, a lot longer than I had, and I found his counsel immensely useful. Despite our vastly different backgrounds, we had become friends. We set up a dedicated phone line between our desks and I used it constantly to run ideas by him. We didn't always agree and the discussions often turned heated, but our friendship endured.

In early 1998, Max had done what Forward Point's portfolio managers hadn't. He had paid attention to my commentary and had established a large short in the IO market. During that time, I found myself in the strange situation of buying vast amounts of IOs from Credit Suisse and simultaneously selling them back to Credit Suisse. The Swiss bank, not satisfied with just one in-house hedge fund, had set up another and called it the Credit Suisse arbitrage desk (CS-Arb). I had bought hundreds of millions of IOs from Max's CS-Prop and sold them to CS-Arb, and no one was the wiser. It made me chuckle that one side of CS was short IOs and the other side was long, ensuring that the company would not make or lose money. Even though the firm's profit was guaranteed to be zero, CS would have to pay out the winning side, which had turned out to be Max.

In fall of 1999, Max was lured by the largest and the most prominent of Swiss banks, UBS, to set up an operation similar to CS-Prop. UBS had recently launched its own internal hedge fund and named it the Principal Finance Group (PFG). The group was run by Michael "Hutch" Hutchins, an old-timer from Salomon Brothers. Before joining UBS, however, Max asked that Hutch hire me as well. Hutch said that he would need to interview me first.

The interview was short, only about thirty to forty-five minutes. Hutch began by asking me the question that I had spent the past seven years preparing for.

"What is it that you want to do?"

"To produce the best risk-adjusted return in the mortgage market."

It was a bold statement, but I felt qualified to make it. By now, I was convinced that my method gave me an edge and that it would allow me to beat other participants in the market. To my surprise, Hutch didn't grill me on mortgages. He must have decided to take Max at his word that I knew what I was talking about. Before ending the conversation, however, he posed a question that threw me for a loop.

"Let's say you work here for five years. What would you want people to say about you then?"

Given everything that had happened in the past five years, I had no idea what to expect from the next five. Despite that, I wanted my answer to ring true. I thought about it for a few seconds.

"All I want for people to say is, *who* is that guy?"

That was indeed all I wanted. I had no desire to be the most popular person in the mortgage market or even the richest. I simply wanted to be the one who made people wonder, what makes *him* tick?

Hutch nodded approvingly and said that he would hire me. I heaved a huge sigh of relief at having finally landed a job on the buy side.

In hindsight, it was fitting that my time as a dealer should come to an ignominious end. From the moment that I had arrived on Wall Street, I had displayed no interest in performing the job of a sell-side trader. It was a minor miracle that I had managed to survive for almost seven years before the ax had fallen.

The signs were all there. In the single-minded pursuit of an investment framework, I had managed to infuriate many customers along with most of my co-workers. The CMO traders hated me for my dismissive attitude towards their market. They had tried to argue with me, but it was useless. My views about CMOs were based upon two years of experience and their claiming otherwise wasn't going to change them.

The passthrough traders hated me for the fact that clients as well as salespeople had begun to solicit my opinions about their market. I had spent a great deal of time analyzing passthroughs and freely expressed my views, which were often contrary to theirs. The final straw was my one-minute conversation with a large bank portfolio.

"What do you think of Fannie 7s?" the bank's portfolio manager had asked me. Fannie 7s were passthroughs issued by FNMA that carried a seven-percent coupon.

"I think they're the cheapest mortgage but also the most vulnerable if volatility goes up," I replied, giving him my honest opinion.

"Fuck volatility," he said.

"In that case, I would buy them," I said, not thinking anything further about the conversation.

The next day, when the price of Fannie 7s shot up, I still didn't think anything of it. The passthrough traders, however, were furious when they learnt that the bank portfolio had not only bought billions of Fannie 7s, but also discussed it with me the day before.

"You should have told us!" the passthrough traders said angrily.

"Told you what?" I asked.

"That the bank was interested in Fannie 7s."

"Why?"

That made them even angrier. They couldn't admit that had they known about the bank's interest, they would have gone out and bought Fannie 7s themselves. That practice, known as front running, was against the rules.

The list of colleagues that hated my guts was long and continued to grow. The mortgage derivative trader joined their camp after his purchase of an inverse floater, one of the hardest mortgage bonds to value. The trader had bought the bond from a bid list, sell-side lingo for a client auction, and he asked me to take a look at it.

"What did you pay for it?" I asked.

"Ninety-nine."

"Sorry, man. I think it's worth ninety-five," I said.

Even though I was only expressing my honest opinion about the bond, the guy felt that I was calling him incompetent. Wall Street traders, their bravado notwithstanding, are notoriously thin-skinned. No matter how he felt about what I had said, the fact remained that he had paid too much. A few weeks later, he was forced to sell the bonds for ninety-five and a half, thus proving my point. The loss of a few hundred thousand dollars made him dislike me even more.

Salespeople weren't thrilled with me either. My refusal to kowtow to customers had caused many to complain behind my back, "It's so hard to do business with him." Clients routinely asked for my opinions, but that made no difference to a salesperson. An opinion was not a sale, and it did nothing to help their bonus.

It was only a matter of time before all this hatred caught up with me. Fortunately, it happened the day after I had gotten the job offer from UBS.

That fateful afternoon, I was summoned to a conference room upstairs. I went up the stairs, not knowing that this was to be my last day on the sell side.

"Your association with this firm has come to an end," said my boss, a lady from human resources by his side.

I smiled inside while maintaining a grim look on the outside. If they had waited for twenty-four hours, I would have quit voluntarily. Now it was going to cost them.

Haste, as it often does, proved expensive for the company. They agreed to pay all my deferred compensation — investment banks typically hold back one-third of an employee's bonus and pay it out over three years — along with part of my bonus. UBS had also agreed to make me whole for my withheld pay and the thought of double-dipping briefly crossed my mind. Instead, I called Hutch and told him to not worry about my deferred compensation. He was ecstatic and I simply walked across Park Avenue to my new job.

There was a small hiccup along the way. It came in the form of an innocent question in the UBS employment form.

Have you ever used an alias?

I answered yes, which almost derailed my buy-side career before it had started. UBS's human resources were taken aback by the yes, and my explanation — I had used fake names while gambling in Las Vegas — alarmed them even further. Max, who had been aware of my blackjack history, said, "Why did you say yes? No one was going to check this." I told him that I didn't want to start my money management career with a lie.

The storm passed. UBS's lawyers concluded that I hadn't used an alias, at least not legally speaking. Had I bought property or opened a bank account under a fake name, they would have felt differently about the matter. I breathed a sigh of relief when they gave HR the green light.

Seven long and difficult years after counting a deck on the Lehman trading floor, I finally had my chance to play the game. The stakes could not have been higher. My method would either allow me to swim, or I would sink.

There was nowhere left to hide.

CHAPTER 25

The Buy Side: Life of a Hedge Fund Manager

Walking into the offices of UBS, I felt like I had on my first trip to Reno. A decade had passed, but the memory of losing big was still fresh. I could not allow myself to suffer the same fate again.

I had desperately wanted to move to a hedge fund, and yet I was worried about much that could go wrong. The stakes had risen dramatically — the average trade in the passthrough market was in the hundreds of millions of dollars — and my system was unproven in the real world. Fear notwithstanding, I was thrilled to finally be on the right side, where I could place bets on the table, instead of standing behind it.

The first thing that struck me about UBS was the silence. Although the relationship between investment banks and clients was akin to that between the house and gamblers, the bets in this casino were placed over the phone (today increasingly over the internet). In contrast to the commotion of the trading floor, the atmosphere at PFG seemed almost meditative. I quickly realized that the life of a money manager, much like that of a gambler, was a lonely one.

That suited me just fine. I had no use for the hustle and bustle of a casino or that of a trading floor. I much preferred to be left alone, to play the game as I saw fit.

The sell side, however, had other plans. My phone rang all day long. The past seven years had made me realize that every outgoing phone call from an investment bank was made with the express purpose of putting more money into their own pocket. Nevertheless, every salesperson would insist that it was for the client's benefit.

"I want to share some market information with you" was a much-used opening line. Under the guise of sharing information, the salesperson tried to figure out which way a client was leaning. That information would get passed on to the traders, who would find a way to monetize it.

"I have a great trade idea." This was a far more dangerous line of attack. Most salespeople wouldn't know a good trade if it hit them in the face. Their job was to get clients to buy whatever bonds their traders wanted to sell or vice versa. It was, however, far easier to pretend that it was in the customer's interest to buy the security than to say, "We want to sell because we are afraid that the price will fall."

Fielding sell-side calls was a waste of time. Silencing the ringer didn't help either. I found the flashing red light impossible to ignore. To combat the problem, I instituted a do-not-call rule and insisted that salespeople limit their communication with me to the Bloomberg terminal, the most widely used messaging system on Wall Street. I promised that I would respond if I had a trade to do. Salespeople resented being treated like telemarketers, but they complied. The customer, after all, was always right.

One salesman took it particularly hard.

"How can you stop me from calling you?" said Bruce, a wiry and high-strung former colleague.

"Why? What's the problem?" I asked.

"How are we going to do business?"

"I told you. I'll call when I have something to do," I replied.

"Yeah. But what if my traders have a great trade idea?"

"In that case, Bruce, they should keep it to themselves. You don't need to tell me about it."

"I don't understand your attitude, Kamal. I thought the way to manage money was by listening to everyone's opinions and then making up your own mind," he said, indignantly.

The last thing I needed was a salesman telling me how to do my job. A casino host does not tell a gambler how to play the game.

"Bruce, if I were to multiply the number of trades with the number of opinions out there, I would be forced to sift through hundreds every day. Instead, how about this crazy idea: I don't listen to anyone and just do whatever I think is right?"

This wasn't arrogance on my part. The sell side's ideas were poorly thought out and their motives questionable at best. Eliminating annoying phone calls from them made it considerably easier to focus on the task at hand.

Much like I had done at the Golden Nugget, I set up a routine at UBS, one that I would adhere to for the next twenty years. I arrived at work early, before seven a.m., and spent an hour analyzing the mortgage market. My goal was to formulate a game plan before the market opened and to be ready by the time traders arrived at their desks. Wall Street trading desks had grown to expect an early morning call from me: "Where can I buy . . ." A few traders balked, saying, "Market hasn't opened yet. Go back to sleep." The Goldman Sachs passthrough desk went so far as to put up a sticker above their computer screens: *Adjust prices for overnight market moves for Kamal.* I found it exhilarating to be able to call one of fifteen dealers and buy or sell bonds at will.

I did most of my trading in the morning. The rest of the day was spent watching the market and reacting to its moves. By late morning, I would invariably turn my attention to lunch. For twenty years, I have gone out to a restaurant for lunch virtually every day. During my sell-side days, I had been forced to attend countless dinners with clients, a practice that I ended shortly after arriving on the buy side. I much preferred meeting salespeople and traders over lunch, where the absence of alcohol kept the discussion more business-like. In addition to being a welcome break from the action, lunch took place during work hours and did not interfere with my evenings. Despite leaving my post unattended for an hour (sometimes two) at midday, I have rarely if ever missed out on a market opportunity. Also, lunch was exempt from my do-not-call rule. A salesperson was permitted to call me at any time to make lunch plans.

I started my money management career much like I had played black-jack — by placing small bets. As I grew more comfortable with the market,

I upped the stakes. However, my sizes would not go up in perpetuity. After about two years at UBS, once I had reached the happy medium between profits and being able to sleep at night, I refused to increase them any further. Moreover, I would keep the stakes constant for the next eighteen years, which has infuriated my bosses. Even though every hedge fund I worked for urged me to take more risk — in some cases by a factor of ten — I saw no reason to do so. The incentive "you will get paid more" held little attraction for me. I simply wanted to play the game for as long as possible and had no interest in increasing the probability of a career-ending blow up. Wanton risk-taking had caused an endless number of hedge funds to bite the dust. No matter how much my "wimpiness" irked my bosses, I insisted on staying in my comfort zone.

In casinos, my bets had been sized to limit the probability of losing my bankroll to under five percent. I have followed the same script on Wall Street. In an industry where everyone tries to make the most amount of money, I have followed the opposite path. I have consistently aimed to make the *least* amount of money that would keep me in the game. While that has lowered my pay, it has given me something far more valuable in return: peace of mind.

In addition to the troubles that I faced in the markets, I also had to worry about dealers. Investment banks, like casinos, were a necessary evil. I needed them to play the game, but I was also determined not to become another of their victims. As much as I would have wished it otherwise, I knew that conflict with dealers was unavoidable. Sell-side traders were shameless — you gave an inch, they took a mile — and regular disciplining would be required.

One of my earliest spats left me smiling. It started with me asking Credit Suisse, the Swiss investment bank that was a leader in mortgage trading, for a bid on a coupon swap.

"Where can I sell 260 by 200 of Fannie 7.5/7 swap?" I asked the salesman on our dedicated phone line.

A coupon swap is the sale of one passthrough against another, usually in weighted amounts. In this particular trade, I was looking to sell 260 million Fannie 7.5s against buying 200 million Fannie 7s. The 1.3 ratio was determined by the relative interest rate sensitivities of the two bonds, also known as their durations. A higher coupon mortgage typically has a lower duration than a lower coupon one, which required me to sell more 7.5s to stay interest-rate neutral.

I overheard the salesman shout to his trader.

"Where can Kamal sell 260 by 200 of the 7.5/7 swap?"

"Two and sixteen," the trader yelled back, two and a half points.

"That works," I said to the salesman. "Can we use 103-16 and down?"

The strike price mattered because my purchase and sale were in different amounts. I had proposed that I sell the 260 million Fannie 7.5s at 103-16 versus buying 200 million Fannie 7s at 101-00, thus making the price spread 2-16.

That was enough to set the CS passthrough trader off. I heard him screaming at the salesman, who had forgotten to mute the phone.

"No fucking way will I let him set the prices! I'm the trader. I set the strikes!"

"Okay fine," I said, "what strikes would he like to use?"

Amazingly, the trader said, "101-01 and up," making the two prices 101-01 and 103-17.

I was floored. CS was net buying sixty million more bonds. It was in their interest to use as low a price as possible. By shifting the strikes one tick higher, the trader had gifted me almost nineteen thousand dollars.

"You win," I said quietly. "We can use your prices."

"Done!" said the salesman, happy to have consummated a trade with a new client.

I waited for five minutes before calling him back.

"Seriously, man. How stupid are you guys?"

The salesman was mortified when he realized what he and his trader had done. Giving money away was just about the worst sin on the trading floor.

"Kamal, can we please go back to the prices that you had suggested?" he pleaded.

Even though I was under no obligation to do so, I agreed to change the prices to 103-16 and 101-00. It was early days and I wanted CS to know that I wasn't trying to rip them off. More importantly, they needed to understand that I wasn't to be trifled with.

I had many such skirmishes with dealers, each of which caused Max and Hutch great amusement. They gave me a nickname, Kamal "don't fuck with" Gupta. One afternoon, as Hutch and I stood in the pantry, waiting for the coffee machine to finish brewing, he asked me a question.

"How upset would you be if a dealer ripped you off for fifty thousand dollars?"

"Forget fifty thousand," I said, "I'm not willing to tolerate five thousand dollars."

"Why?"

"Because, if they can get away with cheating me out of a small amount, what's to stop them from stealing a larger amount in the future?" I replied.

"Good," Hutch said approvingly. "By the way, Kamal, why do you bring your own coffee mug to the office? We provide cups," he wondered as I filled my cup with fresh, hot coffee.

"Yes, Hutch, but your cups are made of styrofoam," I said.

"So what?"

"Styrofoam doesn't let you feel the temperature of the coffee. Your lips might get burned if the liquid is too hot," I explained. The famous McDonald's hot coffee lawsuit was caused by a styrofoam cup.

"Hmm." Hutch smiled. "I'm glad that I hired a careful mortgage guy."

No matter how careful I was, there were times when my defenses would get breached. One afternoon, while I was still new to the buy side, a hyper-aggressive salesperson from one of Wall Street's smaller investment banks hounded me to buy some IOs. By a twist of fate, their trader was the *same* five-foot, five-inch bully that had shouted expletives at me eight years earlier.

I gave in and bought the bonds, the first and the last time I would trade under duress. Before hanging up the phone, though, I happened to ask the salesperson if they had bought the IOs from a servicer. Mortgage servicers collected monthly payments from homeowners and passed them along to investors in mortgage-backed securities. They were the Goliaths of the STRIPS market whose trades had the potential to crush IO prices.

"No, we didn't," replied the trader.

That wasn't true. He had indeed bought them from a servicer and, moreover, the seller was none other than the bank portfolio manager who had once asked me about Fannie 7s. He had recently assumed the responsibility of managing the bank's servicing portfolio as well. Unfortunately for the trader, I was scheduled to have coffee with my friend that evening.

"Oh yeah, we sold those IOs today," he said, confirming the dealer's identity.

I simply shook my head, but my friend was angry. By sheer coincidence, he was having dinner with the same investment bank that evening and the IO trader was going to be present.

"You're coming with me," my friend said, refusing to take no for an answer.

As soon as the trader saw us together, he realized that he had been busted. He mumbled something that I took to be an apology of sorts before taking his seat at the far end of the table. I had long believed that lying to customers was standard operating procedure on the sell side and didn't make a big deal out of the incident. The same could not be said for my next run-in with the company, however, which turned into an all-out war.

It started with a message from the firm's mortgage head.

"Buy IOs now or regret it for years," he had said.

It was an astonishing claim, especially because I believed the exact opposite. Had I written a missive, it would have been titled "Sell IOs now or regret it for years." Both of us could not be right. While I was confident in my views, I still wanted to understand how someone had reached the opposite conclusion. A twenty-minute conversation revealed that his claim was based on a mythical prepayment model, which only reinforced my views further.

The fact that the mortgage head held the opposite view did not bother me. However, it was impossible to know whether the firm's wild assertions were rooted in belief or in a desire to book profits and get out.

Despite the bank's best efforts, IO prices suffered a dramatic fall over the next two months. I had earned a tidy profit, and yet I was angry. If there had been a shred of intellectual honesty in his write-up, the firm's mortgage head would have sent out a follow-up detailing where he went wrong. Instead, he simply vanished. I demanded that the company publicly acknowledge the failure of their trade, but to no avail.

I harassed the company daily: *Where is the mea culpa?* I was enough of a pest that my salesperson arranged for me to have breakfast with the firm's CEO. As I climbed the steps of the Four Seasons Hotel on 57th Street, I found myself wound up. No sooner had I sat down than I unloaded on the CEO.

"You cannot go around making wild claims like this, especially if the claim is based upon some ridiculous model. And if you are going to recommend a trade in such a public fashion, don't you have to acknowledge its failure in a similar manner?"

The CEO tried to calm me down. As I picked at my overpriced waffle with strawberries, I realized that he wasn't a neutral party in the conflict. If the trade had worked out for the investment bank, it would have boosted his pay as well. I argued for a while and gave up. My rantings were not going to change this business. Upton Sinclair was right. It was indeed difficult to get a man to understand something when his salary depended on not understanding it.

CHAPTER 26

The Buy Side II: Dealers Behaving Badly

W orking at a hedge fund meant being in a constant state of alert. The interests of my opponents — the markets, the dealers, and sometimes even my bosses — were rarely aligned with mine. These forces repeatedly tried to derail my plan, which was simply to play the game well and beat the market, over and over. I understood that I needed to make money to prove that I was indeed beating the market. However, I felt that beating the house on a twenty-five-dollar table was enough. I didn't feel the need to move up to a hundred-dollar table. Moreover, I was never in a rush. I knew that the odds were in my favor and the longer I played the game, the greater the likelihood that I would come out ahead. Hedge fund owners, on the other hand, were focused on making as much money as possible and as quickly as possible, an objective that was often at cross purposes with mine.

I particularly enjoyed doing battle with the Goliaths of the mortgage market — large money managers, bank portfolios, and even the Federal Reserve, to name a few. While most in the market were intimidated by their size, I viewed their high-volume trades as an opportunity. These lead-footed mammoths were slow in adapting to changing market conditions, something a minnow like me could do far more nimbly. Whenever new information came to light, or if prices moved sharply in either direction, I could turn on a dime. I had gone from being a buyer to a seller (and vice versa) in a flash more times than I can count.

A Merrill Lynch trader was to discover this the hard way. One morning, he sent out an "ax," dealer speak for expressing a strong desire to buy or sell a security.

"I am a seller of this PO at 75-16."

As far as I was concerned, this was not an ax. It was a wish. Under normal circumstances, an "axed" dealer would offer the best price in the market, which was not the case here. The correct price of the PO on that day was one point lower, or 74-16, and I assumed that the trader had simply made a mistake.

"Justin, I think you have a handle error. The price should be seventy-four and a half, not seventy-five and a half," I told my Merrill salesman.

I knew Justin from the sell side, when he was a trading assistant and I was a junior trader. Now I was working on the buy side and he had become a full-fledged salesman. He said that he would check the price with his trader and come back, which he did five minutes later.

"No error, Gupta. Seventy-five and a half is our price," he said.

"Are you sure?" I said, giving him one more chance.

"Yes, absolutely sure," he said.

"I'm sure you know what comes next."

"Yeah."

Justin knew that my next question would be: "If that's your offer then what's your bid?" In this business, the only way for a client to keep a dealer honest was to ask for a two-way market, a bid to go along with the offer.

"Do you have to, Gupta?" Justin wasn't thrilled at the prospect of having to confront his trader even though making two-way markets was a trader's job.

"You know the rules, Justin. At seventy-four and a half, I'd consider buying the bond. But if you insist upon offering it at seventy-five and a half, then I have to ask you for a bid," I said.

"Okay. Lemme check," Justin said.

This time it took him a lot longer to return with an answer. Fifteen minutes is an eternity in financial markets.

"We will buy it at seventy-five and we will sell it at seventy-five and a half," Justin said sheepishly.

The width of the market, half-a-percent, was twice what it should have been. Nevertheless, a bid of seventy-five was still too high. Even though I believed the fair value of the bond to be considerably higher, I had to sell it to him. There were plenty of other POs in the sea. I could always buy another that offered even better value. I could also have walked away from the situation and left the Merrill trader alone. However, after having given him repeated warnings — a courtesy investment banks rarely extend to their clients — I felt a moral responsibility to teach him a lesson. Making a small profit wouldn't hurt either.

"Fine. I'll sell it to you," I told Justin, without skipping a beat, believing that the trade was as good as done. As long as a customer responded to a bid on the wire — within thirty seconds and without hanging up the phone — a dealer was obligated to buy the bonds. Not this time though. In a clear violation of the rules, the trader refused. I complained to Justin and his boss, the sales manager, but without success. The trader escaped unscathed, but not for long. His cavalier approach to prices caught up with him two years later.

By then, the Merrill trader had moved to another investment bank that was the most aggressive of Wall Street's trading houses and also my least favorite dealer. My poor relationship with the company notwithstanding, I sold seventy million bonds to their new hire. The price was 24-20, or twenty-four and five-eighths in Wall Street lingo. While jotting the trade on his blotter, the trader carelessly wrote down twenty-four and five, or 24-05, instead of twenty-four and five-eighths. The error was discovered two weeks later when there was a $330,000 difference between what UBS expected to receive and what the dealer expected to pay.

In a first for me, the investment bank's managers pulled out the audio tapes of my conversation with their trader. Once they were satisfied that the price had indeed been 24-20, and not 24-05, they paid the difference. But not before they had fired the trader. An error of this magnitude could not be tolerated, especially if the trader had failed to make money.

I have always had a difficult time feeling sorry for fired traders. Most traders, and for that matter salespeople, had no qualms about taking advantage of a customer. Hence, I felt that they weren't deserving of any mercy either, especially when they touted the virtues of a trade that they were desperate to unload. It would drive me crazy whenever a trader tried to sell a bond while at the same time refusing to buy it, a condition that seemed to afflict Merrill Lynch more than any other dealer.

The firm's self-styled maestro of the mortgage market once sent out an unusually exuberant message.

I LOVE THIS TRADE!!!

I had seen enough shills in Las Vegas to know that this was a thinly veiled device to lure customers. The more vociferously a trader argued that a security was attractive, the more anxious he was to sell it.

In this instance, I was convinced that the Merrill savant had gotten it wrong. So, to prove it, I tried to sell his beloved trade back to him, but to no avail. He ran away, saying, "Not gonna happen." In retaliation, I barred him from sending me messages in the future.

Merrill Lynch was hardly the only dealer guilty of this offense. The geniuses at Deutsche Bank (DB), the German banking giant, created a truly abominable structure called prepayment linked notes (PLN). While going through the PLN write-up, I discovered that this product was nothing more than a repackaged IO. The only difference was the price, which had been jacked up by twenty percent. In an audacious move, DB had taken a liquid security, inflated its price, and turned it into something illiquid. If a customer happened to be foolish enough to buy the note, DB would get them twice; once at the time of the sale and then again when the client tried to unwind the note.

Just for fun, knowing full well that they would refuse, I tried to sell the PLN back to DB, leading to a panicked phone call from their head of mortgage trading.

"Kamal, how did you get this write-up?" he asked in a hushed tone.

"From our London office," I said. "Why does that matter?"

"Dude, you were not meant to see it," he said.

"Why not?"

"We are only marketing PLNs to overseas clients," he said, which made the memory of the kitchen-sink deal come rushing back. New York traders have always considered European and Asian clients to be an easy mark.

Once in a while, though, a dealer would unwittingly reveal the truth. Jon, my Lehman ex-boss who had once lambasted me for selling bonds too cheaply to Dodger, called in with a new line of attack.

"KG, I want to discuss a bond with you," he said.

Jon was a master at steering clients into trades that he wanted them to execute to further his own interests. He was far too sophisticated to use transparent language like "I love this trade" or "Buy it now or regret it for years." Instead, he would deftly plant a worm inside the customer's brain and let the worm do his work for him.

"What kind of bond?" I asked.

"An inverse floater."

"I'm not interested," I said. Jon knew as well as anyone that I didn't buy inverse floaters.

"I know. I know. I'm not trying to sell it to you. You're a smart guy. I just wanna know what you think of my rationale."

In one fell swoop, Jon had managed not only to flatter me, but also to pique my curiosity. I couldn't help admiring the tactic and let him have his say. For fifteen minutes, he tried to convince me of the inverse floater's virtues, but made no headway. Exasperated at not getting anywhere, he gave up, but not before he had made the most honest statement that I have ever heard from a sell-side trader.

"Looks like you're not going to buy this bond," Jon said. "Let me go find some other moron to sell it to."

I had to laugh as he hung up. He had been trying to sell it to me all along. I wasn't a smart guy. I was just the first moron that he had called.

Bad behavior in markets was not the sole prerogative of dealers. Clients were often guilty of it as well. Sometimes a customer would indulge in what was known in the industry as a drive-by. They would lie to a trader, saying, "We're only coming to you," even as they were flooding the market by selling the same bond to five other dealers at the same time. The resulting fall in price would frequently prove painful for traders.

At other times, large money managers would "squeeze" a bond by cornering the market and artificially inflating its price, causing widespread pain on both sides of the fence. While there was much that I found objectionable in the conduct of money managers and hedge funds, one particular tactic of theirs would drive me up the wall. It occurred when these so-called clients banded together with a dealer and attempted to manipulate prices by "painting the screens."

The screens in question were managed by inter-dealer brokers, the most prominent of which was Cantor Fitzgerald. For a small fee, the brokers allowed dealers to trade with each other via tiny computer monitors known as "green screens." Any dealer could ring Cantor and ask the broker to put up bids and offers on the screen. Those prices would then be visible to every other dealer, but not to clients. A flashing price indicated a live transaction. Most of the time, though, the numbers just sat there, quietly.

Even without any live trades, the green screens had enormous influence on the market. The numbers on the screen determined the nightly marks for every bond, the industry-wide price for any security. For instance, a quote of 24-16 x 24-24 on the IO screen would cause dealers to price it at 24-20. That price determined the performance of hedge funds and money managers which, in turn, determined their compensation.

The screens were meant strictly for dealer use, but some customers could not resist interfering with them. They would ask a complicit dealer to put up a "picture" and try to nudge prices higher or lower. Unbeknownst to the brokers or other dealers, the posted prices would belong to the customer and not to the dealer that had put them up. So would the trades. If another dealer were to transact on those prices, the trade would get passed through to the client. In effect, the first dealer had effectively surrendered control of the screen to a customer, allowing them to paint whatever picture suited them best.

One afternoon, when I learnt that the IO trader at a large bank was painting pictures for a hedge fund, I confronted him directly.

"I want you to stop putting bids and offers on the screen that aren't your own. The screens are meant for dealers, and clients aren't supposed to have access. I don't want to make a big deal out of this. So, if you stop now, I'll let bygones be bygones."

The trader was young and didn't realize the full impact of what he was doing. I knew that because I was a young IO trader once and had been guilty of the same offense. Back then, it had taken me a while to realize that the money manager who had asked me to post prices for him could have used another dealer to do the same. The two dealers could have allowed him to trade with himself at an artificial price by using one dealer to put up a bid and asking the other to quickly "hit" it, street talk for selling a bond. Theoretically, a hundred million bonds could trade at an off-market price, which would cause every dealer to price the bond accordingly. Mission accomplished.

I deeply resented this activity. In my book, clients were supposed to execute their trades and wait for prices to move in their favor. Instead, some money managers and hedge funds took matters into their own hands and tried to force prices one way or the other. The dealers, who were often naïve and inexperienced in these matters, submitted to their clients' request and gave them access to the screens, thereby opening the door to potential market manipulation.

The IO trader paused and said, "Let me come back to you."

The poor guy didn't realize that, in doing so, he had confirmed what I had suspected. Otherwise, he would have said, "What are you talking about? I'm not putting any pictures for a client."

He came back a few minutes later and delivered his response in a monotone: "We have discussed this matter with our lawyers and they say that everything we're doing is proper."

"Are you serious?" I asked him.

"Yes."

"Look, man," I said, "I was hoping to resolve this matter amicably but it looks like that's not going to happen. I'll give you one more chance to reconsider."

In the meantime, the head of his trading desk had gotten involved in this matter as had the salesperson I dealt with there. When he called me about it, I carefully walked him through my logic.

"What exactly do you want?" the salesman asked, cutting to the chase.

"I want you to stop doing this. That's all," I replied.

"Understood. I'm going to go talk to the traders and find out what's going on."

"Fair enough."

He returned with a made-up story.

"K, you're right. We put prices on the screen for a client. A customer gave us an order to buy as well as sell those bonds. We first tried to execute the order with our clients. When we failed to do that, we put the picture on the screen in the hope that we could fill the order with other dealers."

I knew this was a fabrication.

"So let me get this straight," I said. "First you tried to transact with clients, and you put pictures on the screen only after you failed to get any customer interest. Is that what you're saying?"

"That's what they're telling me," he said. I could tell that he was nervous. He knew me well enough to know that my question was a set-up.

"They're lying," I said, not mincing any words.

"How can you say that? You have no way of knowing what they did or did not do."

"I can prove to you in one minute that's a lie."

"K, how can you?"

"You have a minute?"

"Of course."

"Let me start by saying that if they have done as you claim then there's no problem. However, I'm also saying that they did no such thing. They took the prices from a hedge fund and immediately put them on the screen," I said.

"You don't know that," he protested.

"I do," I said. "Let's just take the first of the three bonds."

"What about it?"

"You're claiming that the desk tried to fill the hedge fund's order with clients first, right?"

"Yes."

"In that case, it's fair to assume that your traders would have called the client, who is their number one counterparty for that bond," I said.

"Yes."

"You wanna take a wild guess as to who that is?"

The light finally came on for him. "Oh no, K. It's you, isn't it?"

"Yup!"

"And no one called you about it?"

"Nope!" I said. "So the only logical conclusion is that your traders didn't call any client on any of the bonds. They gave screen access to a hedge fund, just like I said."

He hung up the phone and went running to his trading desk, returning two minutes later.

"The desk agrees to all your demands. We'll do whatever you say."

This was quite a capitulation. The desk was beaten and they knew it. They must have hated having to give in, but a bruised ego was a small price to pay for being caught in a lie. Nevertheless, from that day onwards, the bank stopped giving screen access to its customers.

CHAPTER 27
It's Not Research, It's Marketing

M y skirmishes with investment banks were not limited to their salespeople and traders. From time to time, they involved research, the third leg of the Wall Street trinity.

Every client knows that a trader's year-end bonus is determined by his profits. Similarly, a salesperson's compensation is a function of his sales credits, an annual score based on the amount of product that he has sold. It is widely understood that their jobs are to make money and that they have a vested interest in every transaction.

Research is different. Analysts are considered to be the brains of the sell side and are not burdened with the daily drudgery of buying and selling securities. Instead, they are left free to ponder weighty issues such as valuation, risk, and portfolio management. Having unlocked the mysteries of the financial universe, the wise men (researchers are also overwhelmingly male) of Wall Street stand ready to dole out advice to any client lost in the wilderness.

In reality, this is all an illusion. Research is nothing more than an extension of the business of making money. Every action taken by an analyst is also geared towards increasing the firm's bottom line, a fact that many clients seem to be unaware of.

The most important task for a researcher is to accompany salespeople and traders on client visits. These trips, whether to a client across the street or halfway around the world, are made with the sole purpose of luring the customer into doing more business, and research serves as bait. Some investment banks keep track of every contact, no matter how trivial, between analysts and clients. How else will you know if the fish are biting?

Research is also expected to publish regular reports, usually once a week, about market matters. These write-ups purportedly contain valuable insights, and yet every investment bank distributes them free of charge. Not surprisingly, you get what you pay for. For years, it was customary for traders to ask for an analyst's help in selling bonds, especially those that had been sitting on the books for too long. The "impartial" analyst would insert a narrative about the bond's virtues into the next weekly, thereby allowing the trader to offload the position to an unsuspecting client. While this practice has largely ceased in recent years, research remains subservient to sales and trading.

Wall Street research is not research. Real research is conducted behind the scenes and is not published on a preset schedule. Nor is it disseminated widely for your competitors to discover. Sell-side research should not even be called research. The right term for it is marketing. Perhaps in a belated acknowledgement of this fact, J.P. Morgan recently combined its sales and research functions under the leadership of one individual.

The word "research" imbues what amounts to a marketing effort with an aura of authenticity, which is further enhanced by the annual Institutional Investor (II) survey, or the Oscars of Wall Street research. Top-ranked research analysts gain publicity, which leads to a boost in their box-office receipts. Every spring, just as movie studios canvas the Academy of Motion Picture Arts and Sciences, investment banks lobby customers for their vote in the secret II ballot. Since the II vote is nothing more than a popularity contest, the path to research riches lies in keeping the voters happy. Consequently, Wall Street researchers find themselves in a year-long political campaign, trying to curry favor with customers. Confronting a client, no matter how wrong or unreasonable they are, is out of the question. You don't win votes by fighting with the electorate. Moreover, not every voter is treated equally in the II poll. The results are weighted by the size of the assets managed by a customer, which effectively turns the contest into one dollar, one vote. Hence, research analysts are far more responsive to the Goliaths of the market.

My scuffles with research began early, while I was still on the sell side. The first scrap started with our head of research making an incorrect statement during the morning meeting.

"Prepayment fears are growing in the market because, in the recent rally, Fannie 7s have outperformed Fannie 8s," he had said.

The research head claimed that the market had displayed a marked preference for the lower coupon mortgage, implying that investors were concerned about prepayment risk in Fannie 8s. Had this been true, his conclusion would have been correct. In reality, though, the opposite had occurred. I knew this because I had suffered the consequences. My test trade, where I had been long Fannie 7s and short Fannie 8s, had gotten clobbered. I felt obligated to set the record straight because I knew that no one else would.

"That's not true," I said from across the conference room, jolting a few people from their slumber.

"Who said that?" The research head scanned the room as he tried to figure out who had had the audacity to challenge him. The room was crowded, but it didn't take long for him to discover that it was me.

"Fannie 7s have underperformed Fannie 8s. This means that prepayment fears have receded, not increased," I elaborated.

"Absolutely not," he said. A look of anger flashed across his face.

No matter how strongly he said it, he was still wrong. I tried to explain why, but he was in no mood to listen.

"You have no idea what you are talking about!" the research head shouted.

The thirty or so salespeople and traders jammed into that room couldn't have cared less who was right. They just wanted to get back to their desks and start their day. Knowing this, Dean, the head of mortgage trading, intervened.

"You two, meet me in my office. I don't want a screaming match in my meeting."

Dean was my boss. He was also the tallest man I knew and his presence made me feel small. I left the conference room and walked down a flight of stairs to his office. Dean showed up shortly thereafter, but the head of research made us wait for ten minutes. I was getting ready to leave when he came barging into the room, carrying a sheaf of papers. He held the pages in one hand and gesticulated wildly with the other, as if he were making a speech on the senate floor.

"You can stop there. I agree with your prices," I said, hoping that he would sit down.

"Aha!" he said triumphantly and turned to Dean as if to say, "I told you so."

But the game had only just begun. The head of research was cutting the net down prematurely.

In the NBA's Pacific division, during the 2017–18 regular season, the Golden State Warriors and the Phoenix Suns had nearly opposite records. The Warriors ended the year with 58 wins and 24 losses whereas the Suns finished 21-61. Consequently, whenever these two teams played each other, the market expected the Warriors to win. The Las Vegas betting line had the Warriors up by as much as fifteen points. A loss by just seven points would mean that the Suns had outperformed expectations. The punters betting on the Suns didn't need them to win the game. They only needed their team to lose by less than the line.

The equivalent of a betting line in the mortgage market is called the hedge ratio. In the trade in question, I had sold Credit Suisse 260 million Fannie 7.5s versus 200 million Fannie 7s because their relative hedge ratio was 1.3. The widely accepted ratio between Fannie 8s and Fannie 7s was two to one, implying that for every one percent change in the price of Fannie 8s, the market expected the price of Fannie 7s to change by two percent.

Over the previous few weeks, the price of Fannie 7s had gone up by one-and-a-half percent. During the same period, Fannie 8s had appreciated by one percent, beating the line by a quarter-percent.

"Wait a second," the head of research said, "so you agree Fannie 7s have increased in price by a larger amount?"

"Yeah, everyone knows that," I said.

"So I'm right and you're wrong," he said.

I was shocked that the head of research would make such an infantile statement. From his perspective, the Warriors had won and that was the end of it. The fact that the score was 107-100 did not matter to him. I tried to explain that everyone, including me, had expected the Suns to lose, but not for the game to be that close. Yes, the price increase in Fannie 7s was greater than for Fannie 8s; however, Fannie 8s had unquestionably outperformed the market's expectation of a 0.75 percent gain.

I turned to Dean with a look that said, "What the hell is this guy talking about?" My boss was a trader who understood hedge ratios as well as anyone. He could have set the research guy straight. Instead, he took the easy way out and declared a draw.

"You're both right. It depends on how you look at it."

I was incredulous. There was only one way to look at it and Dean knew it. I couldn't help wondering if his call had been a political one. Perhaps he did not want to antagonize a senior member of the firm. The head of research was a managing director whereas I was only a lowly vice president.

The research head walked out of Dean's office with a huge smile on his face. A draw was as good as a win for him. I, on the other hand, felt that the referee had rigged the game.

What really bothered me about this situation was the utter lack of intellectual honesty. Even a junior member of a trading desk knew what a hedge ratio was, let alone the head of mortgage research. It seemed obvious that he was being willfully ignorant simply to win an argument. And the head of trading, who knew better, had allowed him to get away with it.

It's not research. It's marketing. Facts and logic just get in the way.

That maxim was stretched to the limit by one of Wall Street's smaller trading houses where the head of mortgage research managed to gain widespread recognition using a simple yet misleading scheme: a model portfolio.

This particular researcher's approach to the mortgage market was to reduce its extraordinary complexity to a handful of easy-to-understand variables. Even though I had no use for his analysis, I couldn't help admiring the genius in his technique. He had figured out that simple-minded clients required a simple method. So he gave them one. To my great surprise, and despite glaring holes in his system, several money managers and hedge funds became his loyal followers.

That following was cemented via a model portfolio, in which he executed a series of paper trades. As with everything else that he published,

I considered the model portfolio a marketing effort and paid no attention to it.

I was forced to take notice, however, when the researcher circulated a write-up claiming that his model portfolio had a win-loss record of 47-3. His near-perfect performance was stunning, even if it were only on paper. A sixty-five percent hit ratio will get you far in financial markets; ninety-four percent was unheard of.

This 47-3 track record became not only his calling card, but also his employer's. The investment bank's traders and salespeople touted it endlessly and trotted the researcher out in front of clients. The message was that anyone not doing business with the firm was missing out on a mastermind who could make them incredible amounts of money. Aided by the firm's marketing effort, he steadily rose in the II rankings, gaining fame and fortune.

For years, I had ignored his publications (as I had done with every other Wall Street researcher), but I couldn't get this 47-3 out of my head. Hedge funds would have paid dearly for anyone who was right even two-thirds of the time. So why did he stay on the sell side, year after year, earning a relative pittance? To find the answer to that question, I decided to take a closer look at his track record.

The rules governing the model portfolio were deceptively simple. Every trade had a ninety-day horizon with no stop-loss. Furthermore, there was no target profit and he was free to unwind a trade whenever he wished.

As I went through the fifty trades, the first thing I noticed was that the winning trades had an average holding period of three to four weeks whereas the losing ones had stayed on the books for almost the entire ninety-day duration. It appeared to me that the scheme in the model portfolio was to unwind the winning trades as quickly as possible while letting the losers run for the full term. In order to confirm my hypothesis, I created my own model portfolio, one that was the mirror opposite of the researcher's. I replaced all his buys with sells and sells with buys. I followed the same rules that he had set for himself: ninety days, no stop-loss, and no target profit. Like him, I unwound the winning trades quickly and let the losers run out the clock.

It was hard work. I had to pull out the one-year price history for every liquid mortgage bond and compute the nightly performance of fifty trades. When I finished tallying the results, I burst out laughing.

The win-loss ratio was still 47-3!

A portfolio that was the exact opposite of the famed model portfolio produced the same hit ratio, ninety-four percent. How was that possible?

The answer to this conundrum lay in the rules governing the model portfolio: ninety days, no stop-loss, and no predetermined target profit. While the parameters sounded innocuous, they were anything but, especially the last two.

It is a well-known fact in the financial industry that everyone has a stop-loss. Whether self-imposed or mandated by the company, a loss limit is a vital tool for avoiding catastrophic losses. Without it, the researcher could simply wait for a trade to go in the money, which the vast majority of trades did at some point within ninety days. His argument for getting rid of the stop-loss — "I don't allow myself to double down either" — was also misleading. A loss limit is the reason to add risk incrementally. Once that pesky restriction is removed, a portfolio manager can simply max out his position on day one. There is no need to double down.

The absence of a target price was also problematic. A portfolio manager must be able to define the upside in a trade as well as the downside *before* entering into it. Otherwise, he lacks an understanding of the most fundamental concept in finance: risk versus reward. More importantly, the absence of a target price permitted the researcher to take a trade off whenever he saw fit, often within a handful of days.

I concluded that the 47-3 track record represented the time difference between the holding periods of his winners and his losers. In fast-moving markets, that nine-week differential was equivalent to several lifetimes. To me, the mirror portfolio had shown that the ninety-four percent hit ratio was a function of the rules governing the model portfolio, and not the actual trades in it. With this simplistic (and unrealistic) method, any investor could achieve the same hit ratio, at least on paper. Not only was his track record meaningless, it could never be replicated in the real world.

I confronted the investment bank and the researcher with the results of my investigation, only to have them turn into the proverbial three wise monkeys. My analysis was evil and they had no interest in seeing, hearing, or speaking about it. Everyone at the firm, from senior managers down to the trading assistants, had swallowed the 47-3 Kool-Aid. Questioning it was blasphemy. Even my friends at the company, and I had several, lined up behind their guy. Instead of presenting any arguments for their point of view, they simply said, "Let it go, Gupta." Upton Sinclair was once again proven right.

While I strongly disagreed with the researcher's methods, I understood his motivation. Once you replace the word "research" with "marketing," every action of his makes sense. I was, however, unable to figure out why so many customers were willing to suspend disbelief and go along with rules that they knew to be fiction. In taking their cues from Wall Street research, these highly paid managers of money had effectively outsourced their jobs. Did they not realize that accepting investment advice from a company that was in the business of selling financial products was a contradiction in itself?

The researcher persisted with his model portfolio for years. Despite consistently maintaining an outstanding hit ratio, he left the financial industry without ever having worked on the buy side. I believe that, deep down, he knew that he was involved in a marketing effort and had the sense not to drink his own Kool-Aid.

I don't read research reports. I am not willing to let someone else play the game for me. I do my own research, and keep the findings to myself.

CHAPTER 28

House of Cards

I n the fall of 2004, my blissful existence at UBS came to an end with the realization that I wasn't working for a bank or a hedge fund, but a house of cards. I became convinced that the largest of Swiss banks was nothing more than a ticking time bomb. I needed to get out.

Until then, my first buy-side job had been everything that I had hoped for. I had been given free rein to manage money as I saw fit as well as come and go as I pleased. The shackled existence of the sell side was quickly forgotten as I set about mastering the game. My system had performed splendidly, allowing me to weather numerous storms in addition to compiling a stellar five-year track record.

The realization that UBS was headed for disaster was particularly distressing given that, for the first time in my life, I felt like I belonged. I had never been happier in a job.

My halcyon years at UBS contained just one discordant note. I was continually pressed to take more and more risk. First it was Hutch who asked me to do "more." After he left PFG to run the bank's bond trading businesses, his deputy Ken took over. At the end of every year, I was forced to come up with an excuse for why I hadn't even tried to make more money, just to keep them at bay.

After the first year, my scorecard stood at 12-0, twelve months of profit and zero months of losses. Hutch was delighted with his new hire and asked me to "grow the business" by increasing the sizes of my trades. I said that I would even though I had no intention of doing so.

Twelve months later, he was annoyed at my having kept the risk profile the same as the year before. I apologized and said that I would increase it the following year. His displeasure notwithstanding, I was in no danger of being fired because my monthly track record was now 24-0.

During my third year, I got lucky. The mortgage market presented opportunity after opportunity and I was able to do as he had asked. Hutch was pleased with my progress, but he still ended our year-end conversation with, "Do even more next year." I realized then that no matter how much I did, it would never be enough.

In the fall of 2003, at the end of my fourth year, it was Ken's turn. When he demanded to know why I hadn't "grown the business" from the previous year, I came up with a truly preposterous reason.

"I am not yet fully confident in my system," I said.

With a track record of 48-0, my claim was laughable. But Ken was in no position to argue. He had no idea about what I did or how I did it. Nevertheless, he complained that I wasn't "taking full advantage of the seat." I found the remark strange because the seat at a hedge fund has no value. Value lies in a method that resides inside a portfolio manager's head.

One year later, with my monthly track record at 60-0, Ken finally figured it out.

"I know what your problem is, Kamal. You are happy with what we are paying you. You don't even want to make more money," he said, as if it were an insult.

Ken had hit the nail on the head. It had taken five years, but I had finally been discovered. How could anyone not be satisfied with playing a game that they loved while getting paid seven figures every year? I had found my comfort zone and had no plans of leaving it.

I could have pushed the envelope in one of two ways. I could either have increased the sizes of my trades or ventured into riskier areas of the mortgage market. The latter was unthinkable. Abandoning my proven system to try my hand at a new game would have been downright foolish, especially given how well it had performed. I did give serious consideration to the former but decided against it as well. The only benefit of assuming more risk was the possibility of getting paid more, something I had little interest in. I had no desire to spend sleepless nights worrying about my position and increasing the probability of a blow up. Consequently, my strategy would stay unchanged from 1999 to 2019.

An investor once asked me if I was bored with playing the same game for so long. I replied that while the game did not change, every day presented a new challenge. No one would ask Roger Federer if he was bored playing in the same seventy-eight-by-twenty-seven-foot rectangle, year after year. Every tennis match is different and so is every trading day.

There was no point in explaining any of this to Ken. Firstly, I didn't expect him to understand that someone might not care for more money. Secondly, and far more importantly, I had already decided to leave UBS.

My decision was the culmination of a sequence of events that had been set into motion by a casual comment from him a few months earlier.

"You have the highest hit ratio of anyone in PFG. And yet, everyone else here makes more money than you," he had said.

In a single stroke, Ken had managed to pay me a compliment as well as put me down. For the past five years, I had buried my head in the sand and focused on my own performance, paying little attention to the goings-on around me. Ken's comment, however, jolted me from my complacency and I decided to take a closer look at how all of this money was being made.

I focused on two businesses in particular, collateralized debt obligations (CDOs) and subprime mortgages, both of which caused me great alarm. I didn't know it then, but CDOs and subprime mortgages would also be the catalyst for the 2008 financial crisis.

When I first joined UBS, the plan was for me and Max to manage money together. A few months later, however, he began working on a new project and left me to my own devices. That project was none other than CDOs, a little known product that would soon take the world by storm.

In its simplest form, a CDO has two components, the collateral backing it and the debt issued as its obligations. The debt fell into three broad categories or tranches — equity, mezzanine, and super-senior — based on their cash flow priorities. The proceeds from the sale of the debt were used to purchase the deal's collateral which ranged from corporate bonds to emerging market debt. In certain CDO deals, as was the case with many of Max's, the collateral consisted of derivative contracts instead of actual securities.

Every month, the cash flow generated by the underlying collateral first flowed to the super-senior tranche, followed by the mezzanine, and finally the equity piece. Defaults were felt in the reverse order, with the equity suffering the first impact. After the equity was exhausted, any additional losses flowed through to the mezzanine portion of the deal. The super-seniors were the last to take a hit and, as a result, considered to be extremely safe. As long as there were no defaults in the bonds backing the CDO, the debt holders received a steady income.

In many ways, CDOs reminded me of CMOs, especially the kitchen-sink deal, but with one key difference. In a CMO deal, sooner or later, every tranche was sold off. Profit was determined by the difference between the amount paid for the deal's collateral and proceeds from the sale of its bonds. In contrast, UBS had decided to retain a significant portion of the super-seniors from its CDO deals. The deal profit was computed by fanciful models that relied on historical analysis to estimate the probability of default. These backward-looking models assigned a very low chance that the super-seniors would ever lose money. Consequently, they were blessed with a high "mark," the price at which they would sit on UBS's books.

One evening, I was stunned to hear that the latest CDO deal had produced an instant profit of thirty million dollars.

"My god, Max! If these deals are that profitable, why doesn't everyone do them?" I asked.

"I have no idea," he replied tersely, indicating that the conversation was over.

I discovered soon enough that the profit was a function of the mark assigned to the super-senior. A mere 0.01 percent increase in its yield would have lowered the deal's profit by almost one million dollars. The deal had produced immediate profits, but it had also left UBS vulnerable to years of credit, market, and funding risks. The margin of error was uncomfortably narrow. UBS, like any other large investment bank, was highly lever-aged and relied upon large-scale borrowings to fund its holdings. A slight increase in the funding rate would make it impossible for the bank to hold the super-seniors without losing money. Moreover, the CDOs had bought back only a fraction of credit protection, thereby leaving the firm vulnerable to defaults in the underlying collateral. The modelers had determined that to be adequate insurance, based upon past experience.

I had always considered historical analysis to be a deeply flawed methodology. Every investment brochure states that "past performance is no guarantee of future results," and yet historical analysis runs rampant across the financial industry. In UBS's case, I became worried that a credit crisis or a liquidity crunch would lead to catastrophic losses. The firm was saddled with these risks for the next decade and beyond, ample time for one of those events to occur.

It was a crushing realization. And it didn't stop there.

As I looked around, my fears about UBS's future skyrocketed. Many of the strategies employed around me were a variation of the "carry" trade. A carry trade is a strategy in which an investor borrows money at a low interest rate in order to invest in an asset that is likely to provide a higher return.

Carry, contrary to popular belief, does not come for free. It is compensation for risks undertaken by an investor. The more risky (or illiquid) the security, the greater its carry. Someone had wisely referred to carry trades as equivalent to "picking up pennies in front of a steam roller."

One of those strategies was subprime mortgages. Unlike the agency-backed mortgages that I traded, these privately issued subprime mortgages carried no principal guarantee. Subprime loans were made to borrowers with poor credit histories and carried a substantially higher interest rate. Asking a cash-strapped homeowner to pay more interest was a contradiction in itself and unrestrained subprime lending would become one of the root causes of the 2008 financial crisis. I had stayed far away from these types of mortgages because I had thought them to be extraordinarily dangerous. In contrast, the person seated to my left owned a few billion subprime mortgages.

It had taken me a couple of months, but I finally had answers to the two questions that Ken had raised: how others in PFG made money and the so-called "value of the seat."

Most traders around me were running a carry book, something that requires very little skill. You just load the firm's balance sheet with high-yielding securities, cross your fingers, and collect fat paychecks. That is, until it all blows up. And if there was one company that should have known better, it was UBS. Carry trades had been a contributing factor in the 1998 collapse of LTCM, a disaster that had cost UBS almost $700 million and had led to the ouster of its chairman.

I found it insulting that Ken had compared my carefully risk-managed strategy with a carry trade. I had started work at UBS with a clean slate, holding no assets, and would leave the firm the same way, having sold all my holdings. Consequently, every penny of my profits was real. The same could not be said for the substantially larger "profits" earned by many in PFG, as would become clear over the next few years. (My frustrations would be captured perfectly in the April 2008 Shareholder Report on UBS's Write-downs, which concluded that "employee incentivisation arrangements did not differentiate between return generated by skill in creating additional returns versus returns made from exploiting UBS's comparatively low cost of funding in what were essentially carry trades.")

It also dawned on me that the "value of the seat" lay in exercising what was known in the industry as the "trader option." It allowed a trader, on either side of the fence, to gamble wantonly with the firm's capital. If the bet worked out, the trader would get paid handsomely. If not, he would get fired. No matter the outcome, he would not lose a penny of his past bonuses. The trader option on Wall Street went all the way up the chain, from a line trader to the CEO. I myself have never had any interest in exercising the trader option. It didn't matter who had bankrolled me. Whether it was a hedge fund urging me to take more risk or Vinh insisting that I play on a twenty-five-dollar-minimum table, I have consistently tried to minimize my chance of ruin, not maximize my pay.

In late 2004, I had mistakenly believed that the CDO and subprime problem was confined to UBS. A 2005 conversation with Morgan Stanley's Howie Hubler, who himself would be held responsible for losing nine billion dollars during the financial crisis, would make me realize that it wasn't just UBS. The entire financial universe had lost its mind.

CHAPTER 29

Fleeing the Titanic

Like Tom Cruise's character in *The Firm*, I spent the last few months of 2004 in a state of controlled panic, desperately hunting for a way out of UBS.

It had taken five years, but my eyes had finally been opened to the reality of UBS's profits, leaving no doubt that the Swiss bank was headed for disaster. I watched in dismay as traders around me recklessly added to their positions, thereby exposing the bank to greater and greater peril. The music played and everyone danced, with no thought or concern for how the party was going to end. Short-term profits ruled the day, long-term risk be damned.

I didn't share in their greed and I was equally determined not to share in their downfall. It had taken a great deal of discipline and hard work for me to get through my five years at UBS without suffering a single losing month. I could not allow my spotless track record, and for that matter my reputation, to be sullied when this enterprise was exposed in the light of day. With every passing week, I found it more and more difficult to deal with my co-workers. I was afraid that they could see right through the disgust that was written all over my face. Every night, I breathed a sigh of relief at having made it through another day without my true feelings having been discovered. My dream job had turned into my worst nightmare.

I thought about becoming a whistleblower but decided against it. There was no one to blow the whistle to. The UBS business plan had been sanctioned at the very top of the organization and complaining internally would have been pointless. Nor could I have turned to the regulators outside the company. In the halcyon days of 2004, they would have laughed at one man's complaints about CDOs and subprime mortgages. Harry Markopolos had repeatedly tried to warn the SEC about Bernie Madoff, only to be ignored. There was only one plausible exit strategy. I needed to find a job, any job, and quickly. It didn't matter which lifeboat I used to flee the *Titanic*, as long as I was far away when it hit the iceberg.

I could have simply walked out of UBS and looked for a job afterwards; however, abruptly quitting mid-year would have appeared suspicious and might even have caused prospective employers to wonder if I had lost money. What other possible reason could there be for my leaving the vaunted Principal Finance Group so suddenly? I was also keenly aware that my negotiating position would be stronger while I still had a job. Under normal circumstances, potential employers would have had to work much harder to hire me away from UBS, much more so than if I were sitting at home.

Fortunately, Sean Murphy and Adam Miller threw me a lifeline. Over lunch at my favorite midtown Italian restaurant, San Pietro, they offered me a job managing parts of the Hongkong and Shanghai Banking Corporation's (HSBC) fledgling mortgage trading desk. Just like that, a way out had landed in my lap.

I had known both Sean and Adam for over a decade, going all the way back to my Lehman days. They had been hired by HSBC, one of Europe's largest banks, to build a mortgage business to compete with the likes of Goldman Sachs. Eight years earlier, it was Sean who had said to me *you're not a trader*. I found it ironic that he was now asking me not only to trade, but also supervise other traders. Adam had been the head of a trading desk at Lehman where I had helped him recruit traders from rival investment banks. The most dramatic of those hires involved hijacking a young Citigroup trader from a taxi as he headed uptown to join Morgan Stanley.

Despite being thrilled to bits at the job offer, I listened impassively as Sean and Adam made their pitch for me to join HSBC. I had to let them believe that they needed to talk me into leaving UBS in order to negotiate the best possible deal for myself.

Unbeknownst to both of them, I knew a thing or two about negotiating. Over the past five years, I had helped a great number of traders and salespeople negotiate against an assortment of Wall Street firms.

I had learned how to negotiate at an early age by watching my mom bargain with shopkeepers in New Delhi. Putting her negotiating skills to full use, she managed to buy fruits and vegetables at prices that were considerably lower than what the non-negotiators had paid. It was an early lesson in the saying "You don't get what you deserve, you get what you negotiate."

My mom negotiated because she needed to save money; however, I did it out of a sense of fairness. I felt that the playing field was unfairly tilted in favor of corporations and against individuals. My assistance gave the person a fighting chance and, far more often than not, allowed them to extract significant concessions from the company involved.

One of the first people to use my help was none other than my friend and colleague Greg Andrews. A few months after the Forward Point fiasco, a small broker dealer had offered to pay him $750,000 a year for two years to entice him over. While I felt that he would be better off staying where he was, an offer of this magnitude could not be wasted. We decided that we would use it to get Greg a comparable deal from our current employer.

I had him gently inform his boss Harold about the job offer while making sure not to disclose the amount or the identity of the small broker dealer. Harold and his superiors were not pleased; however, they quickly admitted that they didn't want Greg to leave and made him a counteroffer. In doing so they had carelessly revealed their cards, causing me to go on the offensive.

"Greg, tell them that you need $950,000 a year for two years."

"Goopy, are you crazy? There's no way they'll pay that!" Greg protested.

"With an attitude like that, they certainly won't. Now go do it!"

Even though it went against all his instincts, Greg followed my advice. The blowback from senior management was immediate and severe: "Are you nuts? We can't pay you that much!" Somehow, in the face of all this yelling and screaming, Greg managed to stand firm, forcing them to capitulate. But as they waved the white flag, the bosses threw in a last-minute wrinkle. "It's almost two million dollars. An amount this large needs to be approved at the highest levels of the company. We'll need a few days to draw up the paperwork."

This was a transparent attempt by the company to buy time, something that I could not allow. Verbal agreements are meaningless and we needed a signed contract without delay. A lot can happen in a few days. The managers at the small broker dealer could change their mind, as could Harold and his bosses. So I sent Greg back into the lion's den with an ultimatum.

"I need the paperwork within twenty-four hours or I'm leaving."

This was a bluff, but only a partial one. If push came to shove, Greg was prepared to leave the next day. The bosses were livid, but there was precious little they could do about it. The next morning, Harold handed Greg a fully executed contract, thereby putting an end to years of his being underpaid. Greg was thrilled with the result, as was I. All that had been necessary was an ability to read the opponent's cards correctly while keeping ours hidden. That and a stiff spine.

After the dust had settled, Harold couldn't help himself. He took Greg aside and asked, "What happened to you? You used to be a nice guy. When did you turn into such an asshole?"

Greg was still a nice guy but he wasn't the one negotiating. Harold didn't know it but, all along, he had been negotiating with me. I was the asshole.

Despite the large sums of money involved in these deals, I have never made a penny from helping others negotiate. My reward was simply knowing that I had played the game well. In many ways, negotiating contracts made me feel like I was back in Las Vegas, engaged in a secretive battle against a powerful adversary while trying to separate it from some of its cash. That the cash went to someone else made no difference. I negotiate for others with the same zeal with which I negotiate for myself. The corporations never learned of my involvement and, to my great amusement, frequently complimented the individual for being a good negotiator.

I have long believed that the best strategy for a contract negotiation is the exact opposite of how chess is played. The key to a successful outcome is a single-minded focus on the next move, and *only* the next move. Thinking any further ahead is a waste of both time and effort.

A chess player has to abide by strict rules; a bishop can only move diagonally and a rook only sideways. A negotiation, on the other hand, is not governed by any rules whatsoever. It is virtually impossible, and frankly unnecessary, to predict your adversary's next move. Instead, when it's my turn, I consider all available information and formulate a careful response. Once I have delivered it, I wait patiently for the ball to return. Only when it arrives back in my court, and with new information from the other side, do I start thinking about my next move. The ball bounces back and forth between the two sides until the game concludes, either with an agreement or with the court being abandoned.

My unwillingness to speculate about future moves, both ours as well as our opponents', is invariably met with bewilderment and confusion. It is a struggle, but I insist upon maintaining a focus on the move in front of us, without the distraction of what-ifs. I have always found that as long as every small move is made carefully and correctly, the bigger picture will take care of itself. Greg had witnessed this first-hand, as did the many others that came after him.

Perhaps my most significant contribution to any negotiation is to take emotion out of the equation and to make sure that every move is made with a clear head. Emotions not only cloud your thinking, they also betray your cards to your opponent. Consequently, in the negotiation in which I now found myself with Sean and Adam, I had kept my feelings about UBS hidden from them.

In the fall of 2004, the market for mortgage personnel was red-hot. After a few perfunctory back-and-forths, HSBC made me an incredible offer. The amount of money was staggering — more than a hundred-fold higher than my starting salary at Honeywell — and yet, I felt ill at ease. Accepting the offer would mean going back to the sell side, where I had spent seven long and miserable years. At the same time, I felt that I had no choice but to abandon my comfortable life at UBS to ride out the coming storm.

Fortunately, I didn't have to go back to the dark side. Another door opened just in time.

In the spring of 2004, before I had fully realized to what extent UBS was built on a house of cards, a headhunter approached me on behalf of a newly formed British hedge fund, Brevan Howard. The hedge fund had been established by a group of former Credit Suisse traders and was named after its founders, Alan Howard and four others whose last names began with B, R, V, and N.

As I had done with every such invitation over the past five years, I turned the headhunter down without so much as a conversation. I was still happy at UBS at that point and saw no reason to look elsewhere. Over the next several months, I watched from the sidelines as the hedge fund interviewed more than fifteen candidates for the position, rejecting each and every one. When Brevan reached out again in November, this time using a Citigroup trader as an intermediary, I was ready to flee the sinking ship of UBS and had already reached a verbal agreement with HSBC. Nevertheless, I decided to fly to London as a challenge, to see if I could meet the high standards that this hedge fund had set for their first hire in America.

Brevan's offices were across the street from Christie's Auction House in the posh St. James district in central London. As I walked up the steps of Almack House on King Street, I couldn't help thinking about just how far I had come from the blackjack tables of Las Vegas. The game had truly changed my life.

All morning, the hedge fund's partners probed me about the mortgage market. Their questions took me back to the day, twelve years earlier, when the Lehman traders had grilled me on blackjack. Here, too, I made no effort to hide the fact that I knew a lot more about mortgages than anyone at Brevan. As the day wore on, I got the sense that the partners also approved of my brash attitude.

The first stumbling block came during lunch when one of them walked me to an upscale French brasserie nearby, W'Sens. The waiter had just placed a plate of penne with pesto in front of me when my interviewer posed a question that took me by surprise.

"I wanted to know what you think about a certain individual."

"Who?"

When he said the name, I was taken aback. The person he had asked me about was none other than the purveyor of the "buy IOs now or regret it for years" nonsense. I tried to remain calm even though my mind was racing.

What did any of this have to do with my job prospects at Brevan? The only logical answer was that the two knew each other. In that case, the Brevan partner must have asked him about me. What would he have said? The best that I could come up with was "Kamal is a smart guy but he hates me." So I figured that there was no point in being bashful now.

"I'm not a fan," I said.

"Why?"

The question was deeply unfair but I answered it anyway. I told him about my spat with the investment bank and the spectacular failure of the "buy IOs now or regret it for years" trade. I concluded the story with, "Given that he lost seven hundred million dollars during the 1998 Russian Crisis, I think he needs to be a little more humble."

The partner quickly jumped to the guy's defense. "He didn't lose seven hundred million, he only lost four hundred and fifty million dollars."

I was shocked that anyone would place an *only* in front of a loss of that magnitude and let him have it.

"Fine! Let me rephrase. Given that he lost four hundred and fifty million dollars, I think he needs to be more humble. I don't have anything against him personally; but professionally, I couldn't possibly disagree more."

That brought the conversation to a swift end. The way I saw it, if my views about a third person were going to be a problem for Brevan then so be it. I was in London only to prove something to myself. I didn't care whether I got the job or not. Also, the hedge fund had the option of hiring my nemesis, but had obviously chosen not to.

After lunch, I ran into another problem, albeit one of my own making. Another of Brevan's partners casually wandered into the conference room, sat down across from me, and asked me a simple question. Or so he thought.

"What was your biggest monthly loss?"

It wasn't his question that bothered me. I was annoyed by the fact that he had a copy of my résumé in his hand, the top line of which said *61 months of profit with zero months of loss*. For him to ask me this question, it meant that he hadn't even bothered to glance at the sheet of paper in front of him. In my book, interviewing a candidate without reading their résumé is a cardinal sin. Having nothing to lose at this point, I responded in kind.

"I don't understand the question," I said, shrugging.

"What's so difficult about the question? I just want to know what the most amount of money that you've lost in any given month is," he asked me again, his voice rising.

"I am not familiar with the concept," I said.

"What concept is that?" He appeared to be visibly annoyed now.

"Losing money in a month," I said, "what does that even mean?"

I could see the veins popping on the partner's forehead. He was getting angry and understandably so. He had posed a fairly straightforward question and I was unnecessarily being a smart-ass. From my point of view, it was inexcusable that he hadn't even looked at my résumé. Regardless, I thought that this little game of ours had gone far enough.

"Perhaps you should take a look at the paper in front of you," I said.

He immediately calmed down.

"Oh, I see. Fine. What was your biggest intra-month loss?"

This time I gave him a proper answer, without the accompanying attitude.

The rest of the afternoon went smoothly as I met the other partners as well as the firm's risk managers. Soon it was time for me to head to Heathrow to catch my return flight to New York. At the last minute, Alan pulled me aside and said, "We'll call you in a couple of days with our decision. I'm curious. If we do decide to move forward, what would it take to hire you?"

One of my strictest negotiating rules is *never* to answer that question. By telling a company what your price is, you immediately cede positional advantage. In Texas Hold'em, the player acting first is referred to as being *under the gun* because of the added pressure of having to act without any knowledge about the rest of the table's hands. The player who acts last makes the most informed decision. The same is true for a negotiation. By insisting that the other side act first, you force them to reveal information about their hand, which allows you to formulate a far more educated response. Better for them to be under the gun than you.

Another reason not to answer that question is that it's virtually impossible to get the answer right. Seeing dollar signs, most people succumb to the temptation of quoting too high a number when confronted with the "what would it take" question. That's a huge mistake. I have observed numerous instances of employers walking away from candidates who had made themselves too expensive. The most extreme example of this phenomenon occurred when I was trying to help place two mortgage traders at Deutsche Bank (DB). For some inexplicable reason, the geniuses quoted a truly astronomical figure when they were asked, "What would it take?"

"Twenty-two million dollars," they replied, causing the horrified DB managers to run away as fast as their feet would carry them. When I heard what they had done, I was furious.

"Twenty-two million dollars? Are you insane? Also, did I not warn you not to give out a number first?" I snapped at one of them.

The poor guy realized his mistake and begged me to try to bring the company back to the negotiating table. I pleaded with DB's head of mortgages, but the genie couldn't be put back into the bottle. The duo had revealed their true colors and the German bank had moved on, hiring the next candidate on their list for a paltry three million dollars. The sad thing was that if DB had been made to act first, they would have likely started around ten or twelve million for the two traders.

On the flip side, quoting a low number in response to "what would it take?" has its own drawbacks. In addition to immediately placing an upper limit on what you might get paid, the company might also wonder why you priced yourself so cheaply. Perhaps you are not as good as they thought you were. At the very least, it would betray that you were clueless about your own market value.

The objective in a negotiation is the same as in poker: play the game in a manner that induces an error from your opponent. By acting first, you remove all possibility of a company making a mistake and paying too much, something that occurs far more frequently than people realize.

Knowing this, there was zero chance of my giving Alan an answer to that offending question. Instead, I gave him the same scripted response that I had advised many individuals to deliver to their future bosses.

"I haven't thought about money. I came here to see if there was a fit. You guys hire people all the time. Just let me know what you are thinking and we can take it from there."

I flew back to New York and waited for the phone to ring. Two days later Brevan gave me their standard offer where they would pay me a fixed percentage of my profits. I quickly told Alan, "Sorry, that won't work." As expected, his follow-up question was "In that case, what do you want?" and my reply, a simple, "Not this."

It being a Friday afternoon, Alan asked me to think about it and to call him on Monday. I said I would, even though I had no intention of doing so. Oftentimes the best move in a negotiation is to do nothing and force your opponent to make another move. If Brevan wanted to hire me, they would have to call again. If and when they did, I would have gained the upper hand.

A full week passed before the hedge fund's co-CEO called, this time with a much-improved offer. I thought about it quickly and gave him my response. We went back and forth a couple of times and arrived at what I considered to be highly reasonable terms. It took all of five minutes.

With two vastly different job offers in front of me, I wasn't sure which one to accept. Kathleen, on the other hand, was.

"You cannot go to HSBC," she insisted. "You have to go to Brevan, if for no other reason than your arthritis. How on Earth will you manage the long hours at an investment bank, not to mention having to entertain clients in the evening? Also, you hated life on the sell side and were so much happier on the buy side."

"But HSBC is offering me so much money," I said.

She then said something that few Wall Street wives have ever said to their husbands.

"I don't care about that. We have plenty of money."

She was right, of course. The bet she had made in the spring of 1995, that I would figure something out, had paid off. Over the last ten years, I had earned more money than either one of us could ever have imagined. The lure of the lucrative HSBC contract was strong, but not strong enough to cause us to have our first ever disagreement about money.

I called Sean and Adam and gave them the bad news. They were crushed and asked if there was anything they could do to make me change my mind. Since I couldn't imagine them offering me anything other than more money, I said no.

The time had come for me to leave UBS.

In the first week of March 2005, I liquidated my position and walked over to my boss Ken's desk.

"Can we have a quick chat?"

"Don't fucking tell me you are quitting!" Ken shouted. He was no dummy.

"I think we should go into an office," I said softly.

I had barely closed the door of the small office on the edge of the trading floor when Ken erupted, "What the fuck is wrong with you? I thought you were happy here!" He was right. I had indeed been happy at UBS but that was before I had become aware of the hazards of CDOs and subprime mortgages. Since I couldn't tell him the real reason why I was leaving, I made up an excuse about getting paid more at a hedge fund, which only infuriated him further.

"Are you out of your mind? You are leaving UBS to go to a hedge fund? Do you know how many chances I've had to run a ten-billion-dollar hedge fund? I've turned them all down. You must be insane to choose a hedge fund over a Swiss bank," he shouted. I began to worry that he might pick up a chair and throw it at me.

With every fiber of my being, I wanted to scream at Ken that UBS was not a bank. It was a house of cards. I was leaving only because I didn't want to be around when the company blew up. But I kept my mouth shut and Ken calmed down. A few minutes later, I was able to escape from the office in one piece.

Everyone was shocked by what I had done, swapping a prestigious Swiss bank for an unknown British hedge fund that didn't even have an office in America. I, on the other hand, could not have been happier.

Three months after my departure, in June 2005, UBS announced that it was spinning PFG off as a standalone unit, renaming it Dillon Read Capital Management (DRCM). Even though the media portrayed the move as a windfall for my ex-colleagues, I knew it was the beginning of the end. I saw the spin-off for what it was: UBS pulling its capital from PFG and replacing it with funds from outside investors. I also knew that PFG's business would not stand up to scrutiny and that the plan was doomed to fail. I had gotten out just in time.

My fears were realized when UBS shuttered DRCM two years later, in May 2007. In the financial crisis of 2008, UBS would incur write-downs of over forty billion dollars, largely from its CDO and subprime mortgage exposure. The resulting losses would cause the Swiss bank's stock to drop in value by an astonishing one hundred billion dollars. Every senior manager at the firm would either quit or be fired. If not for the intervention of the U.S. Federal Reserve and the Swiss government, UBS would have ceased to exist.

It was a breathtaking reversal of fortune. The no-name hedge fund I had joined was on its way to becoming the largest in Europe, whereas the illustrious Swiss bank I had left was on the brink of death.

CHAPTER 30
The 2008 Financial Crisis

A t the 2005 Jackson Hole Symposium, the then chief economist of the International Monetary Fund (IMF) and my college classmate, Raghuram Rajan, presented a rather prescient paper, *Has Financial Development Made the World Riskier?* That year, the long-standing central banking conference had the added agenda of celebrating the career of the legendary Federal Reserve chairman, Alan Greenspan. As the world's leading economists patted each other on the back for a job well done, Raghu delivered a distinctly downbeat discourse.

In his presentation, Raghu correctly identified the prevailing trader option mentality on Wall Street as "there is typically less downside and more upside," and that this asymmetric personal risk/reward meant that "managers therefore have greater incentive to take risk." Raghu also asserted that "large institutions at the core of the financial sector will have to be supervised."

Raghu's claims flew directly in the face of the Greenspan Doctrine, which argued that financial markets were best left to "police themselves." In a 1997 speech, Greenspan had gone so far as to say that there should be competing federal regulators to avoid "overzealousness in regulation." This would allow banks to choose their own supervisor by changing their charter.

To the architects of the financial world, Raghu's remarks were nothing short of blasphemy. It fell upon Don Kohn, a lifelong member of the Federal Reserve and its future vice-chairman, to deliver a rebuttal. Kohn mounted a vigorous defense of the Greenspan Doctrine, drawing on recent history to assert that "actions of private parties to protect themselves — what Chairman Greenspan has called private regulation — are generally quite effective." While I found much to object to in Kohn's speech, one line in particular took my breath away. He could not have gotten it more wrong if he had tried.

While referring to mutual fund families and bank holding companies, Kohn said, "It is not in their interest to reach for short-run gains at the expense of longer-term risk" or to "endanger their reputations."

In fact, that focus on short-term profits was exactly what I had observed at UBS and why I had bolted from the company. Moreover, it wasn't just UBS. Most large financial institutions had done the same, a fact that I had become aware of during a spring 2005 meeting with Howard "Howie" Hubler, the head of Morgan Stanley's subprime effort.

I had first met Howie in 2001 at Palio, the elegant Tuscan restaurant located right next to UBS on Sixth Avenue. Over lunch, he expressed a growing frustration with his passthrough traders.

"I am not sure that we know what we are doing," he said.

I didn't have the heart to tell him that I was certain of that. Instead, I asked him why.

"Take coupon swaps for instance. How many variables do you take into account when trying to figure out what they're worth?" he asked.

"Somewhere between ten and fifteen," I replied.

"That many? We're lucky if we account for two or three. No wonder we are getting killed," he said glumly.

I shrugged and said nothing. Morgan Stanley's trading woes were not my problem. His next question, however, made me smile.

"I'm not trying to hire you, but I'm curious, what would it take?"

"Ten million dollars in small, unmarked bills," I replied half-jokingly.

That quickly banished any thoughts of recruiting me from Howie's head. Several years later, after the 2008 crisis, a Morgan Stanley salesperson would remark that the company would have been better off paying the ransom.

In the spring of 2005, I had gone to see Howie with the express purpose of asking him about a trade that he had executed with PFG. That trade, in which Howie had sold UBS a large amount of subprime risk, had jump-started Max's CDO program.

As soon as I sat down in Howie's cramped office on the edge of the Morgan Stanley trading floor, he said, "You know, Kamal, that trade with PFG allowed us to ramp up our subprime business by a factor of five!"

This came as a surprise to me. Until that morning, I had assumed that the transaction had allowed Howie to short subprime mortgages. I had expected him to tell me how overpriced the sector was and how he intended to profit from its collapse. Instead, I discovered that the trade had been Morgan Stanley's opening gambit into the subprime mortgage market. Far from being short, the investment bank's quintupling of its subprime footprint had likely made it long.

All these subprime mortgages had to have come from somewhere. It didn't take long to discover that they had been acquired from originators such as Countrywide, New Century, and Ameriquest. A few dealers went a step further and brought the lending business in house via outright purchases of subprime lenders. Deutsche Bank acquired MortgageIT Holdings for $429 million in July 2006, claiming, "This acquisition is expected to be earnings accretive in 2007." Merrill Lynch paid $1.3 billion for First Franklin Financial Corporation in December 2006 only to shutter its operations fifteen months later "because of the deterioration of the subprime lending market." Lehman Brothers went further than most and acquired five mortgage originators from 1997 to 2003, including a West Coast subprime lender, BNC Mortgage.

Wall Street had developed a voracious appetite for subprime mortgage bonds, driven partly by the CDO demand and partly by the need for high-yielding assets. In the aftermath of 9/11, the Federal Reserve had lowered interest rates to as low as one percent, making the excess yield offered by subprime bonds particularly attractive to banks and asset managers.

The demand proved irresistible to the subprime originators and they set about fulfilling it with gusto. The Wall Street bonus culture had trickled down to mortgage lenders as well. Countrywide, one of the largest originators in America, paid its sales representatives a larger commission for steering borrowers to high-risk subprime loans, even if they qualified for a lower interest rate prime mortgage. According to the *New York Times*, Countrywide's profit margin in 2004 on subprime loans was 3.64 percent as opposed to 0.93 percent for prime mortgages.

The steep margins led to the proliferation of a host of creative mortgage products. Alt-A loans occupied the no-man's-land between prime and subprime loans. No-doc and stated-income loans did not require any supporting documentation to verify the borrower's income. Interest only loans lowered monthly payments by postponing the payment of any principal, thereby allowing the borrower to pay a higher price for the house. A down payment became a relic of the past, with some originators going as far as issuing a $250,000 loan for a house worth $200,000. The pièce de résistance of all this mortgage "innovation" were NINJA loans. No income, no job, and no assets? No problem! True to their name, these ninja mortgages insidiously infiltrated bank balance sheets and almost brought down the global financial system.

The central assumption behind all of this madness was that home prices would always increase. For as long as anyone could remember, housing prices in America had gone up every year, at least on a nationwide basis. Downturns had all been regional in nature, like Texas in the 1980s or California in the early 1990s. A broad-based decline in home prices across the country had never been observed, making housing the surest bet there was.

Given that assumption, it almost didn't matter whether the borrower had a pulse. His ability to afford, and more importantly pay, the mortgage was deemed irrelevant. If the deadbeat were to fall behind on his monthly payments, the bank would simply repossess the house and sell it for a higher price to another unsuspecting sap. Investors around the world had bought into the fiction that an investment in housing would never lose money as long as it was spread across all fifty states.

I asked Howie the most obvious question: "What if housing prices were to fall everywhere in America?"

"Well, that would be a big problem," he said, laughing.

A housing crash was nowhere in sight, and yet I walked out of Howie's office with an uneasy feeling. The health of the global financial system rested on the flimsy belief that home prices would go up in perpetuity. I couldn't help but wonder if the entire world had gotten it wrong.

The following year, in 2006, Morgan Stanley placed Howie in charge of a newly created Global Proprietary Credit Group (GPCG). GPCG's profile was eerily similar to PFG and had the same objective. Gamble with the firm's capital in the hope of making a large amount of money.

To that end, Howie accumulated sixteen billion dollars' worth of exposure to AAA-rated CDOs to offset a two billion dollar short in subprime mortgages. Those supposedly bulletproof bonds became worthless during the financial crisis and GPCG lost an estimated nine billion dollars, the largest single trading loss in Wall Street history at the time.

In the five years leading up to the financial crisis, it appeared as if all of Wall Street had lost its mind. There was an explosion in the balance sheets of major financial institutions as they hunted for short-term profits, no matter the long-term cost. UBS's balance sheet had grown from 1.2 trillion Swiss francs in 2002 to 2.7 trillion in 2007, dwarfing Switzerland's GDP, which averaged half a trillion francs during the same period. Citigroup, the U.S. banking behemoth, doubled its asset base, from $1.1 trillion in 2002 to $2.2 trillion in 2007. In an interview with the *Financial Times*, the firm's CEO, Chuck Prince, famously summarized the prevailing atmosphere: "When the music stops, in terms of liquidity, things will be complicated. But as long as the music is playing, you've got to get up and dance. We're still dancing."

Deutsche Bank was late to the party. From 2002 to 2005, its balance sheet grew by a mere 230 billion euros, from 760 billion to 990 billion. After this period of relative sobriety, DB went on a drunken rampage, adding another trillion euros worth of assets in just two years. In the blink of an eye, the 130-year-old bank had doubled its balance sheet.

A trillion here, a trillion there, and pretty soon you're talking about real money.

Just three financial institutions — UBS, Citigroup, and Deutsche Bank — were responsible for injecting almost four trillion dollars into the global financial system. Goldman Sachs wasn't far behind, tripling its balance sheet from $355 billion in 2002 to $1.1 trillion in 2007. Morgan Stanley and Lehman Brothers also did their part, contributing about half a trillion each.

This lunacy wasn't limited to Wall Street. The government-sponsored enterprises (GSEs), Fannie Mae and Freddie Mac, also contributed. Despite having suffered an accounting scandal in 2004 and paying over $500 million in fines, these pillars of mortgage finance entered the crisis holding almost $1.5 trillion worth of mortgages. Even though dodgy mortgages such as Alt-A and subprime were a small fraction of their portfolio, it was enough to sink both entities.

In virtually every instance, this Brobdingnagian increase in the balance sheet was accompanied by a sharp rise in leverage ratio. In some cases, the incremental increase in leverage was almost 40 to 1, making LTCM's folly appear quaint in comparison. Merrill Lynch increased the assets on its balance sheet by $580 billion even though its total stockholder's equity rose by a meager $15 billion. In the meantime, the company's short- and long-term borrowings grew by a whopping $400 billion.

All in all, the total balance sheet explosion across the financial industry would approach the size of the U.S. economy, which stood at eleven trillion in 2002.

Helped along by mortgage originators of every ilk, a significant fraction of these trillions found its way into the U.S. housing market. Fueled by the run up in mortgage debt, home prices in America rose by a whopping eighty percent from 2000 to 2006 while median household income only grew by fifteen percent. In contrast, the previous six years (1994–2000) had seen housing and income move in lockstep with both increasing by thirty percent. The dislocation between housing prices and income during the early 2000s was a direct result of increased risk-taking on Wall Street.

None of this would have been possible without the complicity of the reputable credit rating agencies, Standard & Poor's, Moody's, and Fitch. They provided cover for the madness by doling out AAA ratings like candy. Even though only a handful of U.S. corporations had been considered worthy of the AAA rating, the agencies thought nothing of rating tens of thousands of private-label mortgage-backed securities and CDOs the same.

The rating agency models failed to anticipate a nationwide decline in housing prices. That allowed them to "honestly" rate dodgy mortgages and CDOs as AAA. How can you lose money in an asset whose value only goes up? Their standards had fallen so far that an astonishing seventy-three percent of mortgage-backed securities rated AAA by Moody's in 2006 would eventually be downgraded to junk status.

That AAA rating was the key to a wide range of investors adopting these securities. As far as they were concerned, they weren't buying a high-risk mortgage. They were buying an asset that had been judged to be ultra-safe by respected credit-rating agencies. The agencies had betrayed that faith by giving a subprime mortgage-backed CDO super-senior the same rating as Microsoft's debt.

The AAA rating was also instrumental in Wall Street's ability to borrow money. Money market funds happily made overnight loans to banks against these highly rated bonds. The banks also tapped the commercial paper market for short-term, unsecured loans. By indulging in such large-scale borrowing, these banks had prostituted reputations that had taken centuries to build. Citibank had gotten its start in 1812 whereas Barclays traced its ancestry all the way back to 1690.

In contrast to what Don Kohn had claimed in his response to Raghu, greedy CEOs had gambled away their firms' long-standing name and honor in search of short-term profits and larger bonuses. As Chuck Prince had astutely observed, virtually every Wall Street CEO ignored the looming iceberg and continued partying on the *Titanic*. When the ship sank, they walked away with tens, if not hundreds of millions of dollars each. Not one was held to account for conduct that caused banks to pay crisis-related fines of well over fifty billion dollars!

A triumvirate of rapacious investment banks, irresponsible originators, and reckless credit rating agencies had laid the groundwork for the perfect storm. It helped that homeowners willingly participated in the housing bubble, but in my opinion, they were more of a victim than a perpetrator. If not for the availability of cheap credit, the housing bubble would never have happened, nor the housing crash and the ensuing financial crisis.

The regulators had turned a blind eye to this insanity. As evidenced by Don Kohn's 2005 speech, this failure to regulate had been by design. The audience at Jackson Hole was made up of the leading financial minds of the era and they had crowned Kohn as the winner of the debate while casting Raghu as an outlier. No less a figure than Larry Summers, President Clinton's treasury secretary and the president of Harvard University, labeled Raghu a Luddite.

History, however, wouldn't be kind to Don Kohn, Larry Summers, and Alan Greenspan.

Post-crisis, there is little doubt in anyone's mind that Raghu was spot-on and Don Kohn's faith in self-regulation was, at best, misplaced. Even Alan Greenspan was forced to concede in a congressional hearing that he had "found a flaw" in his ideology and, as a result, he was in a state of "shocked disbelief." If Greenspan had only bothered to look at bank balance sheets in the years leading up to the crisis, his disbelief would have been replaced by shocked belief.

In the summer of 2009, I met Max for one last time. Over lunch at a midtown Indian restaurant, I asked him point blank, "How were you ever going to get out of these CDOs?"

Max looked me in the eye and said, "Kamal, you're the only one who thinks about an exit strategy," his voice not betraying the slightest hint of remorse.

I was stunned by the admission. All along, the idea had been to load up the firm's balance sheet without any regard for how it would end. It stands to reason that the plan at every other financial institution must have been the same. The only thing anyone — from line traders to the CEOs — had cared about was their year-end paycheck. Luckily for them, Wall Street bonuses were not refundable. Everyone walked away free and clear, without returning a dime of their ill-gotten gains.

Bernie Madoff would have been jealous.

CHAPTER 31

The 103-Month Streak

I had left UBS with an impeccable 63-0 track record to which I had added another forty months of no losses at Brevan Howard. After 103 consecutive months of positive returns, I finally had a losing month in September of 2008. My streak had lasted through nine years of extreme volatility in financial markets, the deadliest terror attack in American history, as well as my hip replacement surgery. The Lehman bankruptcy, however, proved to be a bridge too far.

The streak had started in December of 1999, during the waning days of the dot-com bubble. The technology-heavy Nasdaq index peaked in March 2000 and then proceeded to lose sixty percent of its value in the next twelve months.

In the fall of 2001, the tragic events of 9/11 led to sharp declines in global stock markets, causing gold and treasury bonds to spike upwards. A mini recession in 2001, followed by the Enron and WorldCom accounting scandals, caused the economic confidence of the 1990s to be replaced by a growing sense of uncertainty. A housing boom in the mid-2000s rescued the U.S. economy while also sowing the seeds of the 2008 financial crisis.

During the nine-year period from 1999 to 2008, the Federal Reserve first lowered interest rates from 6.5 percent to one percent and then raised them back up to 5.25 percent. The onset of the financial crisis caused the Fed to reverse course once more and they lowered rates to almost zero percent. U.S. stocks lost more than half of their value as fears of an economic depression loomed. Somehow, throughout all of this turbulence, my streak endured.

I had also managed to keep it alive during my 2005 hip replacement surgery. A quarter-century of arthritis had damaged my hip joints to the point where even the smallest of movements was excruciatingly painful. One evening, after taking the bus home from work, I found myself stranded in midtown Manhattan, unable to walk the last hundred yards to the entrance of my apartment building. With no taxis to be found, Kathleen had to pull the car out of the garage and drive one block to pick me up. That night we decided that the surgery I had been dreading for years could not be put off any longer.

While a hip replacement had become unavoidable, I had chosen not to have the neck surgery that Dr. John Jane had recommended years before. After a great deal of deliberation, I had decided that getting wires, plates, and screws put into my neck wasn't risk free either. Moreover, by doing nothing, I was giving my neck the chance to fuse naturally, making the complicated surgery unnecessary. The gamble turned out to be a good one. Ten years later, in 2004, another MRI showed no further movement in my neck vertebrae. Unbeknownst to everyone, my neck was already fused solid in 1994.

In preparation for my hip surgery, my parents flew in from India while my brother, Ami, flew in from Chicago. Everybody was nervous, especially Kathleen, who had seen her share of botched joint replacements. I, on the other hand, felt that there was no point in fretting beforehand. If something were to go wrong during the surgery, then I would deal with it afterwards.

The day of the surgery was one of the roughest of my life. I remember being wheeled into the operating room, where the anesthesiologist asked me to count to ten as he put me under. I lost consciousness at one. I woke up hours later, groggy and confused, to see my dad and Ami staring anxiously at my hospital bed. Also lurking in the background was Greg Andrews.

"How you doin', Goopy?" he said, cheerful as always.

"Never better," I mumbled.

I spent the rest of the afternoon in a daze, hoping desperately that the nausea would pass and that I would stop throwing up. Which is why I was shocked by just how good I felt the next morning. The pain in my right hip, which was now made of titanium, had vanished. The nine-inch incision on the side of my leg hurt like hell, but I knew that that pain was temporary and would go away in a few weeks.

Kathleen was incredulous when I said that I felt well enough to trade bonds from the hospital bed. When the famed surgeon Dr. Chitranjan Ranawat stopped by to check on his patient, Kathleen asked him about it.

"Kamal seems to think he can start working today," she said to the doctor.

"Let him," Dr. Ranawat said, to her surprise.

"What if he wants to go to the office?" she asked.

"He can go whenever he feels up to it," he replied, which made me laugh.

My initial euphoria notwithstanding, it was a couple of weeks before I was able to start work again. In the meantime, I had returned home and started walking with crutches. Our two boys, Jay, who was four, and Deven, who was a toddler, walked up and down the corridor alongside me, cheering me on. It took almost six months to make a complete recovery and for me to be able to walk normally. Miraculously, my streak had survived during those months as well.

I had also emerged unscathed from the March 2008 collapse of Bear Stearns, a traumatic event for the market in its own right, as well as the U.S. government's takeover of Fannie Mae and Freddie Mac. Amidst all this turmoil, I headed home on the evening of Friday, September 12, feeling good about how I had handled crisis after crisis, only to wake up on Monday morning to find my world turned upside down. Lehman Brothers had filed for the largest bankruptcy in American history on Sunday night and, for the first time in nine years, I had no idea what to do.

Markets had gone haywire that morning, but that was the least of my worries. A more pressing issue was the fact that Lehman was my prime broker and that all my bond holdings — over a billion dollars' worth — resided within the confines of the freshly bankrupt investment bank. I had lost access to my positions and was unable to determine which of my bonds still belonged to me, let alone buy or sell them. The employees of the 160-year-old company, distraught at having lost their nest eggs along with their jobs, were of little help. Even though Lehman's CEO had sold hundreds of millions of dollars' worth of stock in the years leading up to the financial crisis, the company's managers would frown upon any salesperson or trader who dared to do the same. That stock was now headed to zero.

Panic gripped the financial world, turning it into the equivalent of a smoke-filled turboprop. Over the next few weeks, fear ran rampant across the financial industry, causing the broader stock indices to lose an astonishing forty percent of their value. The mortgage market had all but ceased to function. Any hopes that the Mortgage-Backed Securities Clearing Corporation would step in and resolve counterparty exposures were quickly dashed. The agency left it up to the dealer community to deal with the matter, thereby leaving me at the mercy of a bankrupt institution. After a decade of carefully managing risk, I was confronted with a situation that I did not understand, nor had any control over. For four straight days I scrambled from morning to night, looking for a solution, making zero progress. On Thursday afternoon, I found myself in the same place where I had been on Monday morning: lost and confused.

Just as I was beginning to lose all hope, the clouds parted and a ray of sunshine peeked through. Peter, my Lehman salesman, delivered an extraordinary piece of good news.

"We can price out your exposure if you like," he said in a voice that was surprisingly calm, given the circumstances.

"You mean that I can get out of all my positions?" I asked Peter, just to make sure.

"Yes," he said.

I couldn't believe it. How was this possible? The only reason I could think of was that, in a stroke of luck, Lehman's European subsidiary had not filed for bankruptcy, at least not yet. At that moment, I was truly glad to be working for a British hedge fund. No matter the reason, I wasn't about to look a gift horse in the mouth. There was one question, though, that I did need answered.

"That would be great, Peter, but at what price?"

"I'll come back in a few minutes and give you the prices," he said and hung up.

It was a very long ten minutes before Peter called back. As he read out the prices, my heart sank. His numbers bore no resemblance to reality.

"These prices make no sense, Peter. You are bidding eighteen ticks for something that is trading in the open market at twenty-eight," I protested, knowing full well that the market price was of no significance in this situation. All my exposure was contained within Lehman and only Lehman could let me out of the trades. Even though the price in the market was considerably higher, I didn't have the option of transacting with any other dealer. Many hedge funds missed this fine point and suffered catastrophic losses by believing that they could offset their Lehman positions by trading with other investment banks. My only hope was to get a better price from Lehman. I tried, but failed.

"Kamal, I don't think you're in any position to negotiate here. You can either take it or leave it. Also, the window for us to do these trades is closing fast. We only have a few minutes," Peter said.

After four harrowing days, I wasn't willing to gamble any more. I knew that Peter's prices would cost me several million dollars and almost certainly cause me to have my first money-losing month. However, by accepting a guaranteed loss of a few million, I would avoid the possibility of losing tens of millions of dollars, if not more.

"Fine, I'll do it. Thank you," I said, breathing a quiet sigh of relief. In one fell swoop, my entire Lehman exposure had been neutralized and I could start with a clean slate.

Profits from the first half of September cushioned the blow from the liquidation and limited my loss for the month to a miniscule 0.09 percent. But a negative number was still a negative number, no matter how small. My 103-month streak was over. At the end of that fateful month, I was surprised to discover I felt a sense of relief. The end of the streak also meant an end to the pressure of keeping it going.

Even after accounting for the losses from my Lehman liquidation, 2007 and 2008 proved to be my best years yet, with annualized gains of 17.3 percent and 15.6 percent respectively (before fees). That performance stood in sharp contrast to the rest of the investors in the mortgage market, most of whom suffered devastating losses in the financial crisis. In addition to the absolute returns, what made my track record truly exceptional was my astronomically high nine-year Sharpe ratio of 5.4 (before fees). Even after accounting for the exorbitant fees charged by hedge funds, my Sharpe ratio remained a stratospheric 3.7.

Sharpe ratio is the most widely accepted measure of risk-adjusted performance in the financial industry. Developed by the Nobel Prize–winning economist William Sharpe, it is defined as the excess return of an investment strategy divided by its volatility. The higher the Sharpe ratio, the better the quality of earnings. A Sharpe Ratio of two is considered very good, three is believed to be excellent, and five is unheard of.

During my UBS interview, in the fall of 1999, I had told Hutch that I wanted to deliver the best risk-adjusted return in the market. Nine years later, I felt that I had done exactly that. It is difficult to know for sure, but it is possible that I had achieved one of the finest, if not the finest long-term track record produced by an individual in hedge fund history.

Unquestionably, my track record was a testimony to the robustness of my framework. I had designed it to be independent of macroeconomic conditions and it had performed exactly how I had hoped it would. My system had allowed me to consistently beat the market, regardless of whether the economy was on the upswing or in a downturn, interest rates went higher or lower, and whether the housing market was in a bubble or in a crash. My strategy of isolating the four major risk components of any mortgage construct — rates, curve, volatility, and prepayments — had paid rich dividends and kept me out of trouble in turbulent times.

While most market participants understood the first three risk factors, they had only a passing familiarity with prepayment risk. Instead of neutralizing those risks, as I had done, they relied upon complicated mathematical models to predict homeowner behavior for the next thirty years. Despite the repeated failures of those models, most hedge funds and money managers continued to place their trust in them. More than any other reason, this had led to the boom-bust cycle that the mortgage market had become famous for. My strategy on the other hand, was more like counting cards, where, given enough time, I fully expected to come out ahead.

When I showed up at Lehman without knowing what a tick was, I had no idea that casinos had been the perfect training ground for a career in high finance. Now, with the benefit of hindsight, I believe that virtually every skill that allowed me to succeed in this world had been honed by playing blackjack.

First and foremost among them was my single-minded focus on the game. During my gambling years, I had discovered that the key to happiness was playing the game well during the day and sleeping well at night. Money was merely the side effect of a game played well. Likewise, throughout my Wall Street years, I have been focused on playing the game to the best of my ability while making sure that my trades don't keep me up at night.

A game cannot be played well without an edge, at least not for any length of time. Blackjack is the only game where a player can gain an advantage over the house. Hence it was the only casino game that I ever played. Despite referring to myself as a professional gambler, I never believed that I was gambling in a casino. To me, card counting represented an investment strategy where a small edge was adequate to produce a high rate of return on capital. The same was true for how I had managed money over the past nine years. The only difference was that I had to create a system from scratch instead of learning it from *Million Dollar Blackjack*.

The time that I had spent in casinos allowed me to gain control over the twin emotions, fear and greed, that have led to the downfall of many on Wall Street. In Las Vegas, I learned to stay calm and focused regardless of whether I was winning or losing, an ability that has proven invaluable while battling volatile markets. Moreover, blackjack taught me to be disciplined and to trust my system, skills that turned out to be immensely useful in the world of finance.

The importance of patience in both games cannot be overstated. No matter how long it took, I made a large bet only when the count was high. Similarly, I have been willing to wait forever for a market opportunity to present itself and have never placed a trade out of frustration.

It is vital to play with a large bankroll or not play at all. Casinos love gamblers who walk in with a few hundred dollars, quickly lose it all and return home. Their worst nightmare is an informed bettor with deep pockets. Even the greatest of card counters will go broke without adequate protection against sustained losing streaks. Similarly, hedge fund after hedge fund blew up because they were overleveraged — a fancy word for bets that were too large for their bankroll. The partners of LTCM discovered this the hard way, as did the employees of Lehman Brothers. My bets have always been too small for my bankroll, in Las Vegas as well as in New York.

The game is not personal, and I never take it as such. The cards coming out of the shoe don't know who they are meant for and the market doesn't know that I exist. A bad turn of the cards or a string of trading losses is not because of a cheating dealer or a market conspiracy. The key to riding out short-term fluctuations is having a system, being disciplined, and operating with a large enough bankroll. Lose any one of those three things and disaster awaits.

Markets and blackjack are never-ending games. The longer the game goes on, the greater the likelihood that the true odds will be realized. The game will continue tomorrow from wherever it left off today. An advantage player is never in a rush.

Lastly, my experience with blackjack has taught me to remain equanimous in the face of ridicule and praise alike, a skill that has been crucial to my success on Wall Street. Over the years, I have been alternately referred to as the most hated man and the smartest guy in the mortgage market. I remained impervious to both titles as I charted my course in this industry.

This all leads me to an inescapable conclusion. The more I think about it, I don't believe it was luck that brought me to Wall Street.

It was destiny.

EPILOGUE

The Closer

I n the spring of 2018, Michael Gelband hired me for the fourth and final time. A quarter-century earlier, he had taken a chance on a blackjack player and given him a shot at a career in high finance. His bet had paid off, at least for me. By the time 2009 rolled around, a decade on the buy side had made me financially independent. I contemplated a variety of options for my future, ranging from an early retirement to starting my own hedge fund, before deciding to follow Michael to Millennium, the famed hedge fund founded by Israel "Izzy" Englander.

I left the hedge fund in 2012 to work on the stock market. Over the previous few years, I had been on the lookout for a new game and the eighteen-trillion-dollar stock market presented me with the perfect challenge. I was delighted to discover that stocks, despite being frequently irrational in the short-term, were also highly logical in the long-run. Otherwise, trying to develop any sort of a methodology would have been a waste of time. Over the next twelve months, I analyzed the financials of three hundred of the largest companies in the S&P 500 before settling on fifteen I found worthy of owning. I also managed to decipher a relationship between stock indices and the anticipated U.S. economic growth. The stock market, at its core, is a levered bet on corporate profits, which are predominantly a function of GDP. I became convinced that booms and busts in the stock market, apart from short-term perturbations, were the result of changing expectations of economic growth. This realization allowed me to deploy my long-standing belief — *short-term irrationality creates opportunities and long-term rationality creates profits* — in the stock market as well.

One year later, Michael asked me to return to Millennium, offering me an opportunity to manage money in equities along with mortgages. I didn't think it was possible to do both jobs simultaneously — that's why I had left in the first place — so I closed out my stock trades and went back to the mortgage market.

In 2017, I took another sabbatical from the hedge fund, this time to focus on Texas Hold'em. Despite having spent a great deal of time in casinos, I had never dabbled in poker, mostly because I had no interest in winning money from other players. I had only ever wanted to beat the house, and the house, by virtue of taking a cut from every pot, always wins in poker. It had taken another twenty-five years for me to become fascinated with the intellectual challenge of no-limit Hold'em. I began to fantasize about playing in the World Series of Poker (WSOP), quickly discovering that it would be impossible for me to do so. Not only was I too old — the average age of the WSOP main event winner from 2010 to 2018 was a mere 27 years — but four decades of arthritis had made it impossible for me to sit at a table for the long hours that the tournament required. The following year, in 2018, I gave up on my WSOP dream and agreed to join Michael once again.

The fourth time around was different. After thirty-five years in the business, Michael was starting his own hedge fund, ExodusPoint Capital. I decided to come on board even though the company had only a handful of employees, and no office space or investors.

The first task for any startup hedge fund is to raise capital. I was surprised when Michael asked me to help because, despite having spent two decades on the buy side, I had no experience in marketing. Most large hedge funds keep their two functions — raising money and investing it — separate.

Over the next two months, on a dozen or so occasions, I sat across from entities that collectively managed trillions of dollars and set about persuading them to invest in the newly formed company the only way I knew how. I told them my story. After all, what was marketing if not the telling of a good story?

Investors sat transfixed as I recounted how I came to America, played blackjack, and ended up on Wall Street. They were intrigued by my gambling past, but reserved most of their questions for the mortgage market. They probed me endlessly about my methodology as well as my trading strategy. By the end of each hour-long meeting, I had convinced them of two things. One, my method was different from any other hedge fund, and two, it worked. One large investor went so far as to say, "You're the most interesting portfolio manager that we have ever met." The encounters proved to be so successful that ExodusPoint's marketing head dubbed me "the Closer" and started scheduling me as the last meeting of the day, just before the money men (and women) headed out to make a decision about their investment.

In three short months, Michael went from trying to raise capital to turning it down. I wasn't the least surprised when, in June 2018, ExodusPoint Capital became the largest hedge fund launch in history with a whopping eight billion dollars under management.

This experience opened my eyes to the power of a good story and set me on an irrevocable path towards launching my own startup. This book.

ACKNOWLEDGMENTS

As someone who has played a variety of games in his life, I can attest that the most satisfying has been writing a memoir and having it published. That's not to say that it was easy. I had never written anything before and putting a book together often felt like a Sisyphean task. If not for the help and support of many around me, I could never have done it.

The person I need to thank first and foremost is my friend and colleague for the past twenty-five years, Jessica Wan. She plowed through the first draft of every chapter — half of which didn't even make it into this book — while meticulously fact checking every story against her own recollections. Christopher Babu was a constant source of inspiration, encouragement, and guidance, especially when the going got rough. Sharad Chaudhary was the first to figure out that I was a storyteller and he has accompanied me on every step of this journey. Thanks to Alex Zirakzadeh for being a great friend throughout my Wall Street years and for rescuing me in September 2008.

I also owe a huge thank you to my beta readers — Aditi Gupta, Raj Hathiramani, Edward Xiao, and Michael Phillips — all of whom devoted a considerable amount of their time to this project.

I cannot say enough about my agent extraordinaire, Sam Hiyate, and his team at The Rights Factory. From the very outset, Sam had a clear vision for the book even if I couldn't see it at the time. Tamanna Bhasin did a terrific job of tightening up the narrative in the early version of the manuscript. I am also immensely grateful to Mita Kapur of Siyahi who did a wonderful job of marketing the book in India.

Thanks to Jack David and Jennifer Smith of ECW Press and to Prerna Vohra of Bloomsbury Publishing India for giving an unknown a chance. To Karen Milner of Milner & Associates for turning the dreaded prospect of substantive editing into an absolute pleasure. To Jen Knoch, Pia Singhal, Jessica Albert, Samantha Chin, Caroline Suzuki, and Claire Pokorchak of ECW Press for guiding me through the publishing process. To Maura Wogan of Frankfurt Kurnit for the legal read and to Ryan Fox of Lyons and Salky for the contract review. And to Kristi Hughes and Corinne Moulder of Smith Publicity for getting the book out there.

None of this would have been possible without my parents, Amar and Saras, who deserve a great deal of credit for putting up with my unyielding nature for all these years. I owe my brother, Amitabh, for many things, including being the only person to believe in me when I decided to play blackjack.

I would not have survived on Wall Street, let alone made it this far, without the love and support of my wife, Kathleen. She has been the biggest champion of *Play It Right* as well as its toughest critic. Her painstaking (and merciless) edits turned *Play It Right* into a far better book than it would have been otherwise. Thanks also to our two sons, Jay and Deven, who have also cheered me on throughout. I love you both.

And finally, I would like to express my gratitude to everyone I encountered during my journey, even those who made life difficult for me. Otherwise, I would have had nothing to write about.

ENVIRONMENTAL BENEFITS STATEMENT

ECW Press Ltd saved the following resources by printing the pages of this book on chlorine free paper made with 100% post-consumer waste.

TREES	WATER	ENERGY	SOLID WASTE	GREENHOUSE GASES
58	4,600	24	200	25,000
FULLY GROWN	GALLONS	MILLION BTUs	POUNDS	POUNDS

Environmental impact estimates were made using the Environmental Paper Network Paper Calculator 4.0. For more information visit www.papercalculator.org